Exam Ref MS-100
Microsoft 365
Identity and Services

Orin Thomas

Exam Ref MS-100 Microsoft 365 Identity and Services

Published with the authorization of Microsoft Corporation by:
Pearson Education, Inc.

ISBN 978-0-13-556573-5
ISBN 0-13-556573-1

Library of Congress Control Number: 2019937251

1 2019

Trademarks

Microsoft and the trademarks listed at *https://www.microsoft.com* on the "Trademarks" webpage are trademarks of the Microsoft group of companies. All other marks are property of their respective owners.

Warning and Disclaimer

Every effort has been made to make this book as complete and as accurate as possible, but no warranty or fitness is implied. The information provided is on an "as is" basis. The authors, the publisher, and Microsoft Corporation shall have neither liability nor responsibility to any person or entity with respect to any loss or damages arising from the information contained in this book or programs accompanying it.

Special Sales

For information about buying this title in bulk quantities, or for special sales opportunities (which may include electronic versions; custom cover designs; and content particular to your business, training goals, marketing focus, or branding interests), please contact our corporate sales department at corpsales@pearsoned.com or (800) 382-3419.

For government sales inquiries, please contact governmentsales@pearsoned.com.

For questions about sales outside the U.S., please contact intlcs@pearson.com.

Editor-in-Chief	Brett Bartow
Executive Editor	Loretta Yates
Sponsoring Editor	Charvi Arora
Development Editor	Troy Mott
Managing Editor	Sandra Schroeder
Senior Project Editor	Tracey Croom
Editorial Production	Backstop Media
Copy Editor	Liv Bainbridge
Indexer	MAP Systems
Proofreader	Jana Gardner
Technical Editor	Andrew Bettany
Cover Designer	Twist Creative, Seattle

Contents at a glance

Contents

Chapter 2   Manage user identity and roles   91

Chapter 3   Manage access and authentication   157

Chapter 4   Plan Office 365 workloads and applications   209

Acknowledgments

Orin Thomas Putting a book together, even if you've done a lot of them, isn't an easy task. Although there is usually only one name on the cover, without the support of countless individuals, none of my books would have made it past being a blank new document in Microsoft Word.

Orin would love to thank Troy Mott, Andrew Bettany, Loretta Yates, Rooslan Thomas, Oksana Thomas, Andrew McMurray, Rick Claus, Sonia Cuff, Michael Bender, Anthony Bartolo, Pierre Roman, Thomas Maurer, Neil Peterson, Phoummala Schmitt, Mick Both & Mischka the Cat for all the ways that they contributed, both directly, and indirectly to the process.

About the Author

ORIN THOMAS is a Principal Cloud Operations Advocate at Microsoft and has written more than 3 dozen books for Microsoft Press on topics including Windows Server, Windows Client, Azure, Office 365, System Center, Exchange Server, Security, and SQL Server. He has authored Azure Architecture courses at Pluralsight, has authored multiple Microsoft Official Curriculum and EdX courses on a variety of IT Pro topics, and is completing a Doctorate of Information Technology on cloud computing security and compliance at Charles Sturt University. You can follow him on Twitter at *http://twitter.com/orinthomas*.

Introduction

The MS 100 exam deals with advanced topics that require candidates to have an excellent working knowledge of Microsoft 365 identity and services functionality. Some of the exam comprises topics that even experienced Microsoft 365 administrators may rarely encounter unless they are consultants who deploy new Microsoft 365 tenancies on a regular basis. To be successful in taking this exam, candidates not only need to understand how to manage Microsoft 365 identity and services, they need to understand how to integrate Microsoft 365 with an on-premises Active Directory environment. They also need to keep up to date with new developments with Microsoft 365, including new features and changes to the interface.

Candidates for this exam are Information Technology (IT) professionals who want to validate their advanced Microsoft 365 identity and services management skills, configuration skills, and knowledge. To pass this exam, candidates require a strong understanding of how to design and implement Microsoft 365 services, manage user identity and roles, manage access and authentication and understand the steps involved in planning Office 365 workloads and applications. To pass, candidates require a thorough theoretical understanding as well as meaningful practical experience implementing the technologies involved.

This edition of this book covers Microsoft 365 and the MS 100 exam objectives circa mid-2019. As the Microsoft 365 suite evolves, so do the Microsoft 365 exam objectives, so you should check carefully if any changes have occurred since this edition of the book was authored and study accordingly.

This book covers every major topic area found on the exam, but it does not cover every exam question. Only the Microsoft exam team has access to the exam questions, and Microsoft regularly adds new questions to the exam, making it impossible to cover specific questions. You should consider this book a supplement to your relevant real-world experience and other study materials. If you encounter a topic in this book that you do not feel completely comfortable with, use the "Need more review?" links you'll find in the text to find more information and take the time to research and study the topic. Great information is available on *docs.microsoft.com* and in blogs and forums.

Organization of this book

This book is organized by the "Skills measured" list published for the exam. The "Skills measured" list is available for each exam on the Microsoft Learning website: *http://aka.ms/examlist*. Each chapter in this book corresponds to a major topic area in the list, and the technical tasks in each topic area determine a chapter's organization. If an exam covers six major topic areas, for example, the book will contain six chapters.

Microsoft certifications

Microsoft certifications distinguish you by proving your command of a broad set of skills and experience with current Microsoft products and technologies. The exams and corresponding certifications are developed to validate your mastery of critical competencies as you design and develop, or implement and support, solutions with Microsoft products and technologies both on-premises and in the cloud. Certification brings a variety of benefits to the individual and to employers and organizations.

> **MORE INFO** **ALL MICROSOFT CERTIFICATIONS**
>
> For information about Microsoft certifications, including a full list of available certifications, go to *https://www.microsoft.com/learn*.

Check back often to see what is new!

Quick access to online references

Throughout this book are addresses to webpages that the author has recommended you visit for more information. Some of these addresses (also known as URLs) can be painstaking to type into a web browser, so we've compiled all of them into a single list that readers of the print edition can refer to while they read.

Download the list at *MicrosoftPressStore.com/ExamRefMS100/downloads*

The URLs are organized by chapter and heading. Every time you come across a URL in the book, find the hyperlink in the list to go directly to the webpage.

Errata, updates, & book support

We've made every effort to ensure the accuracy of this book and its companion content. You can access updates to this book—in the form of a list of submitted errata and their related corrections—at:

MicrosoftPressStore.com/ExamRefMS100/errata

If you discover an error that is not already listed, please submit it to us at the same page.

For additional book support and information, please visit:
https://MicrosoftPressStore.com/Support.

Please note that product support for Microsoft software and hardware is not offered through the previous addresses. For help with Microsoft software or hardware, go to https://support.microsoft.com.

Stay in touch

Let's keep the conversation going! We're on Twitter: *http://twitter.com/MicrosoftPress*.

Important: How to use this book to study for the exam

Certification exams validate your on-the-job experience and product knowledge. To gauge your readiness to take an exam, use this Exam Ref to help you check your understanding of the skills tested by the exam. Determine the topics you know well and the areas in which you need more experience. To help you refresh your skills in specific areas, we have also provided "Need more review?" pointers, which direct you to more in-depth information outside the book.

The Exam Ref is not a substitute for hands-on experience. This book is *not* designed to teach you new skills.

We recommend that you round out your exam preparation by using a combination of available study materials and courses. Learn more about available classroom training and find free online courses and live events at *http://microsoft.com/learn*. Microsoft Official Practice Tests are available for many exams at *http://aka.ms/practicetests*.

This book is organized by the "Skills measured" list published for the exam. The "Skills measured" list for each exam is available on the Microsoft Learn website: *http://aka.ms/examlist*.

Note that this Exam Ref is based on this publicly available information and the author's experience. To safeguard the integrity of the exam, authors do not have access to the exam questions.

CHAPTER 1

Design and implement Microsoft 365 services

Although it's possible to simply start deploying Microsoft 365 once your organization has made the decision to adopt the technology, your organization will get more out of its Microsoft 365 deployment if some planning and design work has occurred before any Microsoft 365 services are configured. In this chapter you will learn about managing the Microsoft 365 domain namespace, how to plan a Microsoft 365 implementation, how to setup a Microsoft 365 tenancy and subscription, how to manage that subscription and tenancy's health, and the steps that you'll need to take to plan the migration and users from a traditional on-premises environment to a Microsoft 365 environment.

> **IMPORTANT**
>
> **Have you read page xvii?**
>
> It contains valuable information regarding the skills you need to pass the exam.

Skills in this chapter:

- Manage domains
- Plan a Microsoft 365 implementation
- Setup Microsoft 365 tenancy and subscription
- Manage Microsoft 365 subscription and tenant health
- Plan migration of users and data

Skill 1.1: Manage domains

This section deals with managing domain name configurations for a Microsoft 365 tenancy. To master this skill you'll need to understand how to configure a Microsoft 365 tenancy to use a DNS name managed by your organization. You'll also need to know how to configure that domain name to work with a variety of Microsoft 365 services, as well as configure user names and email addresses to leverage the new domain name.

> **This section covers the following topics:**
> - Add and configure additional domains
> - Verify custom domain
> - Configure user identities for new domain name
> - Configure workloads for new domain name
> - Design domain name configuration
> - Set primary domain name

Add and configure additional domains

When you create a Microsoft 365 subscription, the subscription tenancy is automatically assigned a custom onmicrosoft.com domain. The tenant name is in the format name.onmicrosoft.com, where name is the name you want to assign to your organization's tenancy. This name has to be unique, and no two organizations can share the same tenant name. When you initially create the tenancy, a check is performed against your proposed tenancy name. If a tenant already exists with that name, you'll be alerted and required to select an alternative. While you're unlikely to actually use the onmicrosoft.com domain name once you have fully configured your organization's tenancy, it's important to note that the tenant name cannot be changed after you configure your Microsoft 365 subscription. The tenant name chosen at setup remains with the subscription over the course of the subscription's existence, and cannot be removed. Resist the temptation to assign an amusing name, because your organization will be stuck with it even if it isn't the primary domain name used.

You can assign a domain name that you own to the tenant so that you don't have to use the tenant name on a regular basis. For example, you might sign up to a Microsoft 365 subscription with the tenant name contoso.onmicrosoft.com. Any accounts you create will use the contoso.onmicrosoft.com email suffix for their Office 365 Exchange mailboxes. Once you've set up Microsoft 365, however, you can assign a custom domain name and have the custom domain name used as the primary email suffix. For example, assuming that you owned the domain name contoso.com, you could configure your tenancy to use the custom domain name contoso.com with the contoso.onmicrosoft.com tenancy.

Microsoft 365 supports the addition of up to 900 domains to a single subscription. You can use separate domain names with a subscription, such as contoso.com, or tailwindtraders.com. You can also associate subdomains of a domain name such as partners.tailwindtraders.com or australia.contoso.com.

Acquiring a domain name

If your organization wants to use a new domain name with its Microsoft 365 tenancy, it can procure one with a registrar. When you do this, you can choose to have the registrar host the name server records for the domain, or select your own name server records. The vast majority of organizations will have already procured a domain name and have it hosted either with a specific domain registrar, their ISP, or even on their own DNS servers. To use a domain with Microsoft 365, the DNS servers used as name servers for the domain need to support the following record types:

- **CNAME records**   To fully support Skype for Business online, the name server DNS servers need to be able to support multiple CNAME records in a DNS zone.
- **SPF/TXT records**   These records allow you to configure sender protection framework records, which can be used to combat unsolicited commercial email. TXT records are also one method of verifying domain ownership.
- **SRV records**   SRV records are used for Skype for Business Online IM and presence integration using the Outlook Web App as well as federation with Skype for Business Online users in different organizations including public Internet connectivity with Microsoft accounts.
- **MX records**   These records are used to route mail to Exchange Online mail servers.

Purchasing a domain through Microsoft 365

In some regions, you're able to purchase a custom domain name from within Microsoft 365. When you do this, you're limited to the following top level domains:

- .biz
- .com
- .info
- .me
- .mobi
- .net
- .org
- .tv
- .co.uk
- .org.uk

Purchasing a domain through Microsoft 365 has the advantage of meaning that the vast majority of DNS related operations will be performed automatically for you. You shouldn't choose this option if your organization will continue to use email services outside Microsoft 365 because you won't be able to modify the appropriate MX records.

Configuring a custom domain name

To configure Microsoft 365 to use a custom domain name, you need to add the name of the custom domain name to Microsoft 365. The account used to perform this action must be an Global Administrator of a business or enterprise plan.

To add a custom domain to Microsoft 365, perform the following steps:

1. In the Microsoft 365 Admin Center, click **Domains** under **Setup** as shown in Figure 1-1.

FIGURE 1-1 Domains node

2. If your organization already has a domain, click **Add A Domain**. The alternative is that the console provides the option to buy a domain through Office 365 and GoDaddy. The advantage of buying through GoDaddy is that you can have the entire process of assigning a custom domain to Microsoft 365 occur automatically. If your organization's domain is already hosted elsewhere, you'll instead have to confirm ownership of that domain by configuring special TXT or MX records that can be checked by the setup process.

3. When you click **Add A Domain**, you are presented with the New Domain page. Enter the name of the existing domain you want to configure as shown in Figure 1-2 and click **Next**.

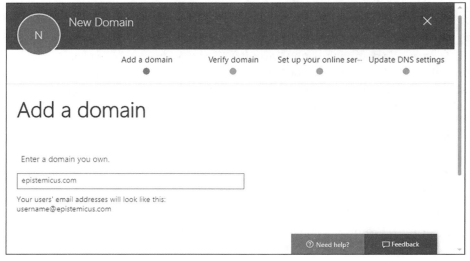

FIGURE 1-2 Add a new domain in Microsoft 365

4. This will begin the process of adding the domain, but you'll need to confirm ownership before you can use the domain.

Verify custom domain

You can only use a custom domain name with Microsoft 365 if your organization owns the domain name. Microsoft requires that you perform a series of DNS configuration changes to the domain name that will prove that your organization controls and has ownership of the domain.

To confirm ownership of your organization's domain, perform the following steps:

1. Once you've specified the domain you want to add, verify the domain on the Verify Domain page. This involves adding a TXT or MX record with the properties listed on the Verify Domain page show in Figure 1-3 to the DNS zone. You do this by configuring the DNS zone with the DNS provider.

FIGURE 1-3 Verify Domain

2. Figure 1-4 shows the TXT record configured as part of the DNS zone, epistemicus.com, hosted in DNS on Microsoft Azure.

FIGURE 1-4 TXT record in Azure DNS

3. Once you have added the record, click **Verify**. Microsoft 365 will then attempt to confirm the presence of the record. Depending on how DNS is configured, it may take up to 15 minutes before the verification process will successfully complete.

> **MORE INFO   ADDING A DOMAIN TO MICROSOFT 365**
>
> You can learn more about topic at: *https://docs.microsoft.com/office365/admin/setup/add-domain?view=o365-worldwide*.

Configure workloads for new domain name

By configuring a custom domain's purpose, you can choose how it will be used with a variety of Microsoft 365 services. For example, you might want to use one custom domain as an email suffix, and another custom domain for use with Exchange and Mobile Device Management for Office 365. You can only configure a domain purpose once you've verified the DNS zone. Microsoft 365 allows you to configure separate domains for the Exchange, Skype for Business, and Mobile Device Management for Office 365 workloads.

To configure domain purpose, continue the wizard after verifying the DNS zone and select which services you wish the zone to support. Once you have added the records to the DNS zone, you can verify that the records have been entered correctly by clicking **Verify** as shown in Figure 1-5.

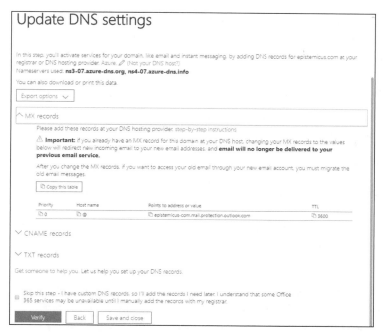

FIGURE 1-5 TXT record in Azure DNS

Exchange Online related DNS records

When you provision Microsoft 365 for your organization, Microsoft takes care of ensuring that the DNS records for your organization's tenant domain, which is the onmicrosoft.com domain, are configured properly so that email addresses that use the tenant domain as an email domain suffix have mail routed properly.

For example, if you provision a Microsoft 365 tenant, and the tenant domain is contoso. onmicrosoft.com, then email sent to users at this email domain, such as an email sent to *don. funk@contoso.onmicrosoft.com*, will arrive at the correct location because Microsoft 365 will provision the appropriate DNS records automatically when the tenancy is provisioned.

When you add a custom domain to Microsoft 365, you need to configure an appropriate set of DNS records to ensure that mail flows properly to Exchange Online mailboxes that use the custom domain. For example, if your custom domain is tailspintoys.com, you need to configure DNS so that email will function properly for Exchange Online mailboxes that are configured to use the tailspintoys.com email domain. When properly configured, the user associated with the Exchange Online mailbox don.funk@tailspintoys.com will receive email sent from other hosts on the Internet.

If your custom DNS zone is hosted by GoDaddy, Microsoft 365 can configure the appropriate DNS records for you automatically. If your custom DNS zone is hosted by another DNS hosting provider, you'll have to manually configure DNS records.

You need to configure the following DNS records:

- Autodiscover CNAME record for Autodiscover service

- MX record for mail routing
- SPF (Sender Policy Framework) record to verify identity of mail server
- TXT record for Exchange federation
- CNAME record for Exchange federation

These records are listed in Table 1-1. The specifics of records will be provided for you by the Microsoft DNS setup wizard. The MX record takes the form <customdnsname>.mail.protection.outlook.com, and will vary depending on the custom domain name being registered.

TABLE 1-1 Microsoft 365 Exchange DNS records

Type	Priority	Host name	Value	TTL
MX	0	@	*<customdnsname>*.mail.protection.outlook.com	1 HR
TXT	-	@	v=spf1 include:spf.protection.outlook.com -all	1 HR
CNAME	-	autodiscover	autodiscover.outlook.com	1 HR

MX RECORD

You need to configure an MX record in your custom domain to point to an Office 365 target mail server. The address of this target mail server will depend on the name of the custom domain and is described in the documentation as being in the form <mx token>.mail.protection.outlook.com. You can determine the value for MX token by performing the following steps:

1. In the Microsoft 365 Admin Center, navigate to the **Domains** node under **Settings**.
2. Select the Custom Domain; this will open the Domain Properties page.
3. Locate the MX record as shown in Figure 1-6.

FIGURE 1-6 TXT record in Azure DNS

To ensure that mail routes properly, you need to configure the MX priority for the record to be a lower value than any other MX records configured for the custom domain. When mail is being routed, a check is performed to determine which MX record has the lowest value for the priority field. For example, an MX record with a priority of 10 will be chosen as a destination for mail routing over an MX record with a priority of 20.

Figure 1-7 shows the MX record for the epistemicus.com domain configuration when the DNS zone is hosted in Azure DNS.

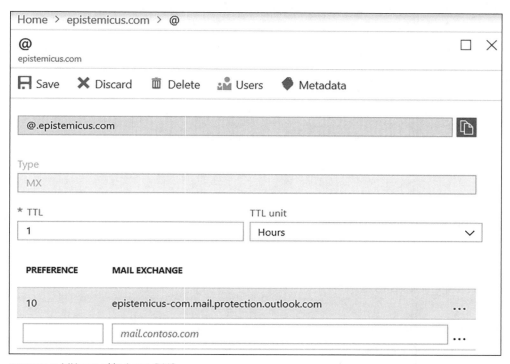

FIGURE 1-7 MX record in Azure DNS

SPF RECORD

The Sender Protection Framework (SPF) record is a special TXT record that reduces the possibility of malicious third parties using the custom domain to send spam or malicious email. An SPF record is used to validate which email servers are authorized to send messages on behalf of the custom domain. The SPF record must be a TXT record where the TXT value must include **v=spf1 include:spf.protection.outlook.com –all**. The record should also be set with a TTL value of **3600**. Only one TXT record for SPF should exist within a specific zone. If an SPF record is already present, append the Microsoft 365 values to the existing record rather than creating a new one. Figure 1-8 shows an SPF record for Exchange Online hosted in Azure DNS for the epistemicus.com domain.

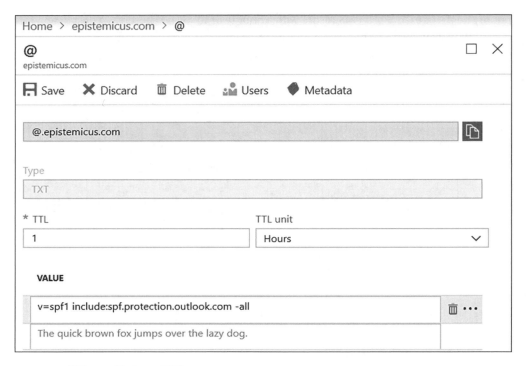

FIGURE 1-8 SPF record in Azure DNS

AUTODISCOVER CNAME RECORD

You need to create a CNAME record that uses the Autodiscover alias to point to the hostname Autodiscover.outlook.com, so that Outlook clients have their settings automatically provisioned for Exchange Online. For example, if the custom domain you assigned to Microsoft 365 was tailspintoys.com, you would need to create the CNAME record Autodiscover. tailspintoys.com and have it point to Autodiscover.outlook.com. Figure 1-9 shows this type of record configured for the epistemicus.com domain using Azure DNS.

FIGURE 1-9 Autodiscover record in Azure DNS

EXCHANGE FEDERATION TXT RECORDS

If you are configuring federation between an on-premises Exchange deployment and Exchange Online, you need to create two special TXT records that will include a custom-generated domain-proof hash text.

The first record will include the custom domain name and the hash text, such as tailspintoys.com and Y96nu89138789315669824, respectively. The second record will include the name exchangedelegation, with the custom domain name and then the custom generated domain-proof hash text like exchangedelegation.tailspintoys.com and Y3259071352452626169.

EXCHANGE FEDERATION CNAME RECORD

If you are configuring federation, you need an additional CNAME record to support federation with Office 365. This CNAME record will need the alias autodiscover.service, and should also point to autodiscover.outlook.com.

> **MORE INFO EXCHANGE ONLINE DNS RECORDS**
>
> You can learn more about DNS records for Exchange Online at: *https://docs.microsoft.com / office365/enterprise/external-domain-name-system-records#external-dns-records-required-for-office-365-core-services.*

Skype for Business related DNS records

Skype for Business requires you to configure two types of DNS records if you have a custom domain. You need to configure two SRV records and two CNAME records to get Skype for Business working properly with a custom domain, as shown for the epistemicus.com domain in Figure 1-10.

FIGURE 1-10 Skype for Business related DNS records

SKYPE FOR BUSINESS ONLINE CNAME RECORDS

If you want to use Skype for Business with a custom domain, you also need to create two separate CNAME records. The first CNAME record uses the alias sip, and points to sipdir.online. lync.com. This CNAME record allows the client to find the Skype for Business service and assists in the process of signing in. The second CNAME record assists the Skype for Business mobile device client to find the Skype for Business service and also assists with sign-in. The alias for this record is lyncdiscover, and the record target is webdir.online.lync.com. These records are listed in Table 1-2.

TABLE 1-2 Microsoft 365 Skype for Business CNAME DNS records

Type	Host name	Value	TTL
CNAME	sip	sipdir.online.lync.com	1 HR
CNAME	lyncdiscover	webdir.online.lync.com	1 HR

SKYPE FOR BUSINESS ONLINE SRV RECORDS

Skype for Business Online requires two SRV records. The first record is used to coordinate the flow of data between Skype for Business clients. This record should have the following properties:

- Service **_sip**
- Protocol **_TCP**
- Priority **100**
- Weight **1**
- Port **443**
- Target **sipdir.online.lync.com**

The second record is used by Skype for Business to share instant messaging features with clients other than Lync for Business by allowing SIP federation. This record should have the following properties:

- Service **_sipfederationtls**
- Protocol **_TCP**
- Priority **100**
- Weight **1**
- Port **5061**
- Target **sipfed.online.lync.com**

These records are also listed in Table 1-3.

TABLE 1-3 Microsoft 365 Skype for Business SRV DNS records

Service	Protocol	port	target	name	TTL
_sip	_tls	443	sipdir.online.lync.com	@	1 HR
_sipfederationtls	_tcp	5061	sipfed.online.lync.com	@	1 HR

> **MORE INFO SKYPE FOR BUSINESS DNS RECORDS**
>
> You can learn more about DNS records for Skype for Business Online at: *https://docs.microsoft.com/office365/enterprise/external-domain-name-system-records#external-dns-records-required-for-skype-for-business-online.*

Mobile Device Management for Microsoft 365 DNS records

If you are using Mobile Device Management for Microsoft 365, you need to create two CNAME records, also known as Alias, so that devices can find the appropriate location to register with. These two records are listed in Table 1-4.

TABLE 1-4 Microsoft 365 Mobile Device Management DNS records

Type	Host name	Value	TTL
CNAME	enterpriseregistration	enterpriseregistration.windows.net	1 HR
CNAME	enterpriseenrollment	enterpriseenrollment.manage.microsoft.com	1 HR

Verifying DNS settings

You can check DNS settings at any time by selecting the domain in the Microsoft 365 Admin Center, and clicking **Check DNS**, as shown in Figure 1-11. When you do this, Microsoft 365 will perform a query against the records required for the services you have chosen and validate that the results returned by the query match those that are required by Microsoft 365.

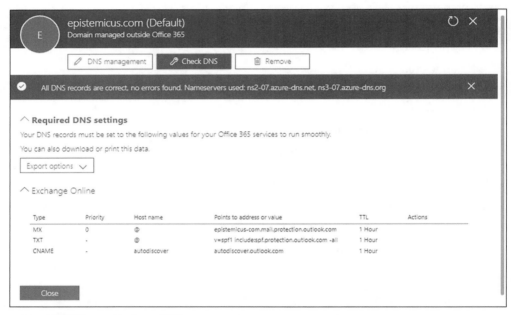

FIGURE 1-11 TXT record in Azure DNS

> **MORE INFO MICROSOFT 365 DOMAINS FAQ**
>
> You can learn more about configuring domains for Microsoft 365 at: *https://docs.microsoft. com/office365/admin/setup/domains-faq?view=o365-worldwide*.

Set default domain

Setting the default domain configures which domain suffix will automatically be used with Microsoft 365 user accounts. You can only select a default domain if you have configured Microsoft 365 with at least one custom domain.

To configure the default domain:

1. Sign into the Microsoft 365 Admin Center as a Global Admin.

2. Under Setup, click **Domains** and then click on the domain that you wish to configure as the default domain.

3. On the domain's page, shown in Figure 1-12, click **Set As Default**.

FIGURE 1-12 TXT record in Azure DNS

Set primary domain name

You can also set the primary domain name in Exchange Online. This works in a similar way to the default domain for Microsoft 365, although it is possible to have a primary domain name for Exchange Online that is different from the default domain for Microsoft 365. When you do this, the email address that a user has will default to the primary domain name, but the sign-in name for Microsoft 365 will use the default domain. To avoid confusion, it is simpler to set the default domain and primary domain to the same value.

To configure the primary domain type for Exchange Online, perform the following steps:

1. Sign into the Microsoft 365 admin center as a Global Admin.
2. Under Admin Centers, click **Exchange**. This will open the Exchange Admin Center.
3. Under Mail Flow, shown in Figure 1-13, click **Accepted Domains**.

FIGURE 1-13 Accepted domains in Exchange admin center

4. Set the domain that you wish to have become the primary domain and click the Pencil (Edit) icon.
5. On the Accepted Domain page, ensure that the domain is configured as Authoritative and that the domain is set to be the default domain as shown in Figure 1-14.

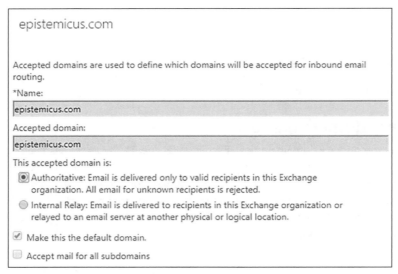

FIGURE 1-14 Configuring Default Domain

Configure user identities for new domain name

When your Microsoft 365 organization adopts a new custom domain name, it will also be necessary to decide what steps you should take in terms of allowing users to leverage that domain name. For example, should all newly created user accounts be assigned that domain name for email and the UPN sign in? Should existing user accounts be modified so that they use the new domain name for email and UPN sign in? Should the new domain name simply be added as an alternative domain suffix to the existing organizational email address? In this section you'll learn what steps you can take to modify the primary address so that it uses a new domain name.

Manage email address

The default address, also known as the primary address and as the reply-to address, is the address that users use to sign in to Microsoft 365 resources, including Office 365, and which recipients reply to when they receive an email message from a user. You can view the primary email address for a user in the Microsoft 365 Admin Center on the user's properties page, as shown in Figure 1-15.

FIGURE 1-15 Primary Email Address

It's possible to change the primary email address once you have added an additional email address to an Office 365 user. It is important to note that changing the primary email address also changes the user name. For example, the warning in Figure 1-16 indicates that by changing the primary email address associated with the Adele Vance user account, the user name will also be changed. The email suffix for the primary address must be configured as an accepted domain for the Office 365 tenancy.

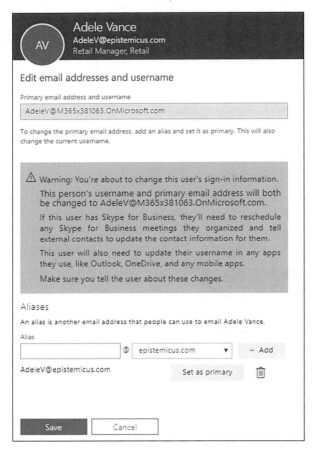

FIGURE 1-16 Change Primary Email Address

You can perform a bulk email address update using PowerShell. You might choose to do this in the event that the organization renames itself. This step should be taken with extreme care because supporting a small number of users through a transition to a new email and logon address is relatively simple, whereas supporting every user in the organization through a transition to a new email and logon address is what might politely be termed "logistically complex."

To update the email and logon domains of multiple users, perform the following steps:

1. In the Active Users node of the Microsoft 365 Admin Center, select all of the users whose email and logon domains you want to update, as shown in Figure 1-17.

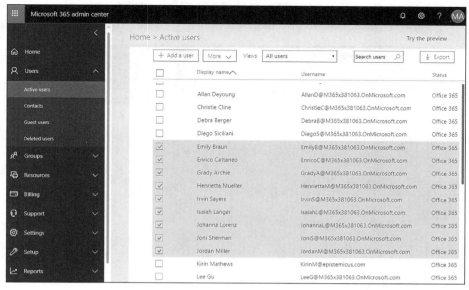

FIGURE 1-17 Select multiple users

2. Once the users are selected, on the **More** drop down menu, click **Edit Domains**.

3. On the **Edit Domains** drop down, select one of the domains that has been added to Microsoft 365, as shown in Figure 1-18, and click Save. You will be presented with a warning that email addresses and usernames in apps associated with Microsoft 365 will need to be updated.

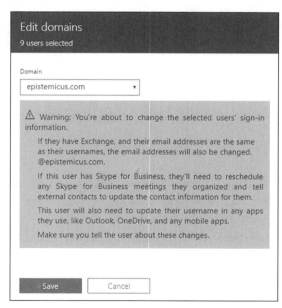

FIGURE 1-18 Select multiple users

4. When the operation is complete, a confirmation dialog will be displayed as shown in Figure 1-19. Click **Close** to dismiss the dialog.

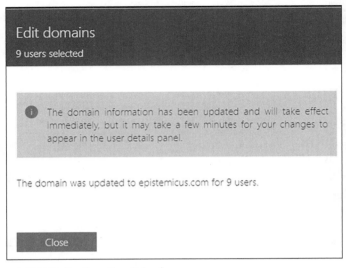

FIGURE 1-19 Confirmation dialog box

Additional email addresses

Additional email addresses allow mailboxes to receive messages from more than a single address. Also known as proxy or secondary addresses, they can take any format and can use any domain name associated with the organization's Microsoft 365 tenancy. For example, Adele Vance's user account could have the primary username and address as AdeleV@contoso. com, but could also have the following addresses also associated with the same Exchange mailbox:

- adele.vance@contoso.com
- adele.vance@tailwindtraders.com
- adeleV@fabrikam.com
- feedback@contoso.com
- suggestions@contoso.com

You can add additional email addresses to an Office 365 account's Exchange Online mailbox using a variety of methods. To add an additional email address to an Exchange Online mailbox using Exchange Admin Center, perform the following steps:

1. Sign in to the Microsoft 365 Admin Center with a user account that has Tenant Administrator permissions.
2. In the Microsoft 365 Admin Center, click **Exchange** under Admin Centers, as shown in Figure 1-20.

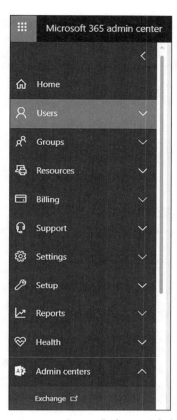

FIGURE 1-20 Locate Exchange Admin Center

3. In Exchange Admin Center, click **Recipients** and then click **Mailboxes**. Select the recipient to which you wish to add an additional email address. Figure 1-21 shows the Adele Vance mailbox selected.

FIGURE 1-21 Recipients

4. Click the Edit (Pencil) icon.

5. On the User Mailbox properties page, click **Email Address**, as shown in Figure 1-22.

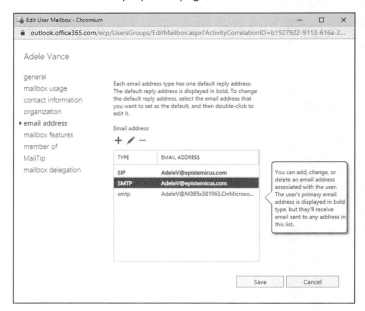

FIGURE 1-22 Email addresses

6. Click the Plus (**+**) icon.

7. On the New Email Address page, ensure that SMTP is selected, as shown in Figure 1-23, and then enter the new email address. You can also specify the new email address as the default reply-to address.

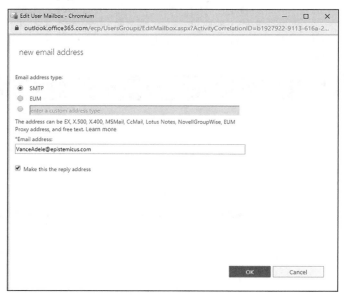

FIGURE 1-23 New Email Address

8. Click OK to save changes

To add an additional email address to an Exchange Online mailbox using the Microsoft 365 Admin Center, perform the following steps:

1. In the Office Admin Center, select **Active Users** under Users.

2. Select the user for which you want to configure the primary email address. Figure 1-24 shows Debra Berger selected.

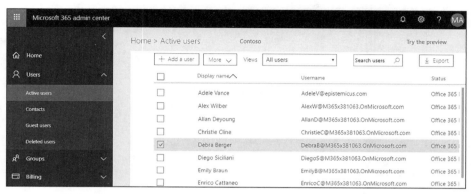

FIGURE 1-24 Debra Berger user account

3. On the **More** menu, click **Edit Email Addresses And Username**.

4. In the Alias box, shown in Figure 1-25, type the new email address and click **Add**.

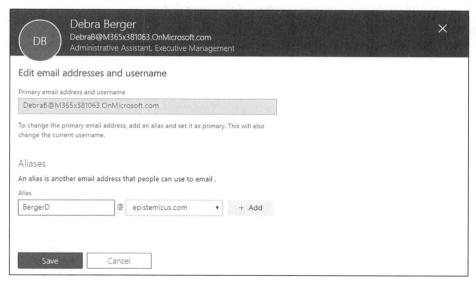

FIGURE 1-25 Edit Email Address

5. To set the new email address as the new primary email address, as shown in Figure 1-26, click **Set As Primary**.

FIGURE 1-26 Other Email Addresses

You can use the Set-Mailbox cmdlet to add additional email addresses. For example, to add the email address berger.debra@epistemicus.com to Debra Berger's Exchange Online mailbox, issue the following command using PowerShell as a global admin:

```
Set-Mailbox "Debra Berger" -EmailAddresses @{Add=berger.debra@epistemicus.com}
```

> **MORE INFO** **SECONDARY EMAIL ADDRESS**
>
> You can learn more about adding an email address to a mailbox at: *https://docs.microsoft. com/Exchange/recipients/user-mailboxes/email-addresses.*

Design domain name configuration

As you learned earlier in this chapter, you can configure a Microsoft 365 subscription with up to 900 domain names, which can be completely different domain names and subdomains of a given domain name. Being able to associate up to 900 domain names with a single subscription gives your organization a substantial number of options when it comes to implementing a domain name design. For example, you can configure each of the services that are associated with a Microsoft 365 subscription with a different domain name. For example, you might choose to have the following configuration if your organization owned the contoso.com domain:

- **Contoso.com** Domain name associated with Exchange Online. Each user signs into Microsoft 365 using an account with a contoso.com UPN suffix.
- **Skype.contoso.com** Subdomain name associated with the Skype for Business services.

- **Mdm.contoso.com** Subdomain name associated with mobile device management functionality for Microsoft 365.

You might also choose to configure separate subdomains and provide them as alternate email domains used with secondary addresses for Exchange Online mailboxes. For example, you might have adele.vance@contoso.com as the primary email address for a mailbox, but configure adele.vance@tailwindtraders.com as a proxy address, allowing the Adele Vance mailbox to receive email addressed to multiple addresses in the same mailbox.

Skill 1.2: Plan a Microsoft 365 implementation

This section deals with the steps that your organization needs to take to plan a Microsoft 365 deployment. This includes understanding what you'll need to do to prepare the infrastructure for a brand-new deployment for a new organization, as well as what steps to take to integrate Microsoft 365 into an organization that already has an on-premises Active Directory and network infrastructure present. To master this skill, you'll need to understand the types of planning steps that you'll need to undertake to prepare your organization for Microsoft 365, and understand what the most appropriate identity and authentication solution is for your organization.

> **This section covers the following topics:**
> - Plan for Microsoft 365 on-premises infrastructure
> - Plan identity and authentication solution

Plan for Microsoft 365 on-premises infrastructure

When planning a migration to Microsoft 365, or starting from scratch, "green-field," or a brand-new deployment, you'll have to make sure certain on-premises infrastructure prerequisites have been met. These on-premises infrastructure requirements relate to networking configuration, identity dependencies, client operating systems, deployment of Office 365 pro plus, as well as choices on strategy for mobile device management and information protection.

Networking

Traditional networks have provided users with access to data and applications hosted on datacenters owned and operated by the organization, and protected by strong perimeter defenses such as firewalls. In this traditional model, users primarily access resources from protected internal networks, over WAN links from branch locations, or remotely via VPN connections.

The M365 and O365 model shifts some, if not all, applications and data from locations on protected internal networks to locations hosted beyond the network perimeter in the public cloud. When moving from an environment where all resources are hosted on-premises, to where a substantial amount of infrastructure is hosted in the cloud, it is necessary to ensure that the on-premises networking environment is configured in such a way that M365 can function effectively and efficiently. Unless steps are taken to optimize the flow of traffic between users and M365 and O365 services, this traffic will be subject to increased latency caused by packet inspection, network hairpins, and possible inadvertent connections to geographically distant M365 and O365 service endpoints.

Understanding the networking requirements for M365 also allows you to make an assessment as to whether M365 is appropriate for a particular organization. For example, there are challenges around deploying M365 effectively at a scientific base in Antarctica where there is limited low bandwidth connectivity to the Internet.

INTERNET CONNECTIVITY FOR CLIENTS

To use Office 365, clients need to establish unauthenticated connections over port 80 and port 443 to the Microsoft 365 and Office 365 servers on the Internet. On some networks, especially those configured for small businesses, you may run into the following network connectivity problems:

- **Clients configured with APIPA addresses**   If clients are configured with IP addresses in the APIPA range (169.254.0.0 /16), they most likely cannot make a connection to the Internet. This means they can't interact with M365 and O365 resources. Clients configured with an APIPA address should be configured with IP addresses in the private range with an appropriate default gateway configured to connect either directly or indirectly to the Internet.

- **No default gateway**   Clients need to be configured with a default gateway address of a device that can route traffic to the Internet. The default gateway device doesn't need to be directly connected to the Internet, but it needs to be able to route traffic to a device that eventually does connect to the Internet. Clients without a default gateway configured will not be able to connect to M365 and O365 resources.

- **Firewall configuration**   Clients require access to certain endpoints used by M365 and O365. The details of these endpoints will be outlined later in this chapter.

- **Proxy server authentication**   M365 and O365 will not function if an intervening proxy server requires authentication for connections. You'll have to configure an authentication bypass for M365 and O365 endpoints, or disable proxy server authentication to Microsoft 365 and Office 365 endpoints on the Internet.

MANAGING OFFICE 365 ENDPOINTS

A Microsoft 365 or Office 365 endpoint is a URL or IP address that hosts a specific Microsoft 365 or Office 365 service, such as the addresses used when connecting an Outlook client to Exchange Online or a mobile device to an enrollment point. Organizations that have one or more office locations need to ensure that their network is configured to allow access to these endpoints.

Microsoft recommends that organizations optimize traffic for M365 and O365 endpoints by routing all traffic directly through the perimeter firewall and having that traffic be made exempt from packet level inspection or processing. Taking these steps will reduce latency to M365 and O365 resource endpoints. This configuration will also reduce the impact on those perimeter devices, which will ignore this traffic to known trusted locations.

Microsoft places each M365 and O365 endpoint into one of three categories. These categories allow you to deal with traffic to M365 and O365 endpoints in the most appropriate manner. The category endpoints that Microsoft uses are: Optimize, Allow, and Default. These endpoint categories have the following properties:

- **Optimize**   Endpoints with this classification are required for connectivity for every M365 and O365 service. Optimize classified endpoints will account for approximately 75% of bandwidth, volume of data, and individual connections. Endpoints with the Optimize classification cause the most problems when there are disruptions to network performance, latency, and availability.

- **Allow**   Endpoints with this classification are also required for connectivity for every M365 and O365 service, but differ from Optimize classified endpoints in that they are less problematic when there are disruptions to network performance, latency, and availability.

- **Default**   Endpoints with this classification don't require any specific optimization and can be treated the same as other traffic bound for locations on the Internet.

Microsoft provides recommendations for how to configure traffic flow to endpoints. These recommendations are listed in Table 1-5.

TABLE 1-5 Endpoint optimization methods

Endpoint Type	Recommendation
Optimize, Allow	Bypass or whitelist endpoints on network devices and services that perform TLS decryption, traffic interception, content filtering, and deep packet inspection.
Optimize	Bypass on-premises and cloud based proxy devices or services used for general Internet browsing.
Optimize, Allow	Treat these endpoints as fully trusted by network infrastructure and perimeter systems.
Optimize, Allow	Reduce or eliminate WAN backhauling. Facilitate direct distributed internet egress for endpoints from branch office locations.
Optimize	Configure split tunneling for VPN users to allow direct connectivity to these endpoints.
Optimize, Allow	Configure prioritization for endpoints when configuring SD-WAN to minimize latency and routing.
Optimize, Allow	Ensure DNS name resolution matches routing egress path for endpoints.

In the past, Microsoft provided alternate guidance categories to the ones listed earlier. The prior guidance categories were Required and Optional, rather than the current categories of Optimize, Allow, and Default. Some documentation still refers to these earlier endpoint categories.

OUTBOUND FIREWALL PORTS

Clients, such as computers running Windows 10, need to be able to make connections to the M365 and O365 endpoints on the Internet using specific protocols and ports. If certain ports and protocols are blocked by a perimeter network firewall, clients will be unable to use specific M365 and O365 services. Table 1-6 lists the protocols and ports that need to be open for clients on an internal network to hosts on the Internet.

TABLE 1-6 Office 365 Outbound Port requirements

Protocol	Port	Used by
TCP	443	■ Office 365 portal ■ Outlook ■ Outlook Web App ■ SharePoint Online ■ Skype for Business client ■ ADFS Federation ■ ADFS Proxy
TCP	25	Mail routing
TCP	587	SMTP relay
TCP	143/993	IMAP Simple Migration Tool
TCP	80/443	■ Microsoft Azure Active Directory Connect tool ■ Exchange Management Console ■ Exchange Management Shell
TCP	995	POP3 secure
PSOM/TLS	443	Skype for Business Online: Outbound data sharing
STUN/TCP	443	Skype for Business Online: Outbound audio, video, and application sharing sessions
STUN/UDP	3478	Skype for Business Online: Outbound audio and video sessions
TCP	5223	Skype for Business mobile client push notifications
UDP	20000-45000	Skype for Business Online outbound phone
RTC/UDP	50000-59000	Skype for Business Online: Outbound audio and video sessions.

The number of IP addresses and URLs that you need to configure for exclusion is substantial and a complete list is beyond the scope of this book. The URLs and IP address ranges that are associated with Microsoft and Office 365 are always changing, and it is possible to subscribe to a REST based web service that provides the list of endpoints, the current version of the list, and changes made to the list for use in configuring network perimeter devices including firewalls and proxy servers.

> **MORE INFO MANAGING OFFICE 365 ENDPOINTS**
>
> You can learn more about Office 365 URLS and IP addresses at: *https://docs.microsoft.com/office365/enterprise/urls-and-ip-address-ranges.*

EGRESS NETWORK CONNECTIONS LOCALLY

A method of reducing connection latency is to ensure that you configure branch office networks for local DNS and Internet egress, rather than forcing all DNS and Internet egress traffic to be routed over a WAN link to a head office before being routed to the Internet. Routing Internet bound branch office traffic across a WAN before allowing it to egress is also termed "WAN Backhauling," and should be avoided when it comes specifically to M365 and O365 traffic that has the Optimize categorization.

M365 and O365 services run on the Microsoft Global Network. This network is configured with servers around the world. This means that there is likely to be a front end server in proximity to each branch office location and that routing traffic across a WAN rather than letting it egress directly from the branch office will introduce unnecessary latency. DNS traffic to M365 and O365 endpoints should also egress at the branch office, as this will ensure that DNS servers respond with the closest local frond end server. If DNS queries are relayed across WAN links and only egress through a single head office location, clients will be directed to front end servers closest to the head office location, rather than the branch office where the DNS query originated.

AVOIDING NETWORK HAIRPINS

Network hairpins occur when VPN or WAN traffic destined for a specific endpoint must first pass through an intermediate location, such as a security appliance, cloud-based web gateway, or cloud access broker, which may introduce a redirection to a geographically distant location. For example, if Tailwind Traders has an Australian branch office, but all traffic to M365 and O365 endpoints need to go through a cloud-based security device located in a Canadian cloud provider datacenter, then it's likely that unnecessary latencies will be introduced. Even if branch office traffic is egressed locally, there will be a deleterious impact on performance if it is routed through a geographically distant intermediate location.

There are several methods that minimize the chance of network hairpins, including:

- Ensure that the ISP that provides Internet egress for the branch office has a direct peering relationship with the Microsoft Global Network in proximity to that location.

- Configure egress routing to send trusted M365 and O365 traffic directly to M365 and O365 endpoints rather than having them processed by intermediate services and devices.

DEPLOY SD-WAN DEVICES

Software Defined Wide Area Network (SD-WAN) devices are networking devices that can be configured automatically so that traffic is most efficiently routed to M365 and O365 Optimize and Allow endpoints. When configured, other network traffic, including traffic to on-premises workloads, general Internet traffic, and traffic to M365 and O365 default endpoints can be forwarded to appropriate locations including network security devices. Microsoft has a partner program for SD-WAN providers to enable automatic configuration of devices.

> *MORE INFO* **M365 NETWORK CONNECTIVITY PRINCIPLES**
>
> You can learn more about M365 network infrastructure requirements at: *https://docs. microsoft.com/office365/enterprise/office-365-network-connectivity-principles*.

RECOMMEND BANDWIDTH

There are many factors that influence the amount of bandwidth that an organization will require to successfully use Office 365. These factors include:

- The specific Office 365 services to which the organization has subscribed.
- The number of client devices connecting to Office 365 from a site at any point in time.
- The type of interaction the client is having with Office 365.
- The performance of the Internet browser software on each client computer.
- The capacity of the network connection available to each client computer.
- Your organization's network topology.

Microsoft provides a number of tools that can be used to estimate the bandwidth requirements of an Office 365 deployment. These include:

- **Exchange client network bandwidth calculator**   This tool allows you to estimate the bandwidth required for Outlook, Outlook Web App, and mobile device users.
- **Skype for Business Online bandwidth calculator**   This tool allows you to estimate the amount of bandwidth you will require based on the number of Skype for Business users and the specific features those users will be leveraging.
- **OneDrive for Business synchronization calculator**   This tool provides network bandwidth estimates based on how users use OneDrive for Business.

> *MORE INFO* **BANDWIDTH PLANNING**
>
> You can learn more about bandwidth planning for Office 365 at: *https://docs.microsoft.com/ office365/enterprise/network-and-migration-planning*.

Windows 10 Enterprise

A Microsoft 365 Enterprise license includes a license for the Windows 10 Enterprise edition operating system. Part of the process of adopting M365 will involve ensuring that all Windows client computers are running this edition of the Windows 10 operating system.

Organizations that have an existing Windows 7 or Windows 8.1 deployment should perform an in-place upgrade using System Center Configuration Manager or Microsoft Deployment Toolkit. System Center Configuration Manger (Current Branch) provides organizations with the most automated method of upgrading and migrating existing computers from previous versions of the Windows client operating system to Windows 10.

Organizations that are deploying new computers that have Windows 10 Enterprise edition version 1703 or later can use Windows Autopilot to trigger the deployment and configuration process by signing in using their school or work credentials. Organizations running the Pro edition can also have those computers automatically updated to the Enterprise edition through Windows Autopilot.

> **MORE INFO M365 AND WINDOWS 10 ENTERPRISE**
>
> You can learn more about the relationship between M365 and Windows 10 Enterprise edition at: *https://docs.microsoft.com/microsoft-365/enterprise/windows10-infrastructure.*

Information protection

When planning your organization's M365 information protection strategy, the first and perhaps most important step is to liaise with the organization's legal and compliance teams to determine which compliance standards, such as the General Data Protection Regulation (GDPR) or Health Insurance Portability and Accountability Act (HIPAA) that the organization is subject to. Once you've determined the specific compliance standards, or regulation to which your organization must adhere, you will need to make determinations for the following questions:

- What are the appropriate security and information protection levels for our organization?
- What is an appropriate document classification schema for our organization?
- What steps must be taken to ensure the appropriate security level is configured within M365 and O365?
- Is it necessary to configure privileged access management for M365 and O365?

SECURITY AND INFORMATION PROTECTION LEVELS

M365 allows organizations to develop their own security and protection levels. While it's possible to create a bewildering number of information protection security levels, doing so increases complexity both for end users attempting to understand which level is appropriate, and for compliance staff who have to make a determination as to whether the appropriate level has been selected.

Microsoft recommends that organizations plan to use at least three separate information protection security levels. As information protection security levels increase, data becomes more protected, but it also becomes more cumbersome for users to interact with that data. Only accessing the most sensitive data should require a user to go through a multi-factor authentication process each time they open a document. Microsoft suggests the following levels:

- **Baseline** Organizations should have a minimum standard for the protection of data, identities, and the devices used to interact with organizational data.

- **Sensitive** This intermediate standard is appropriate for data that is considered sensitive, but for which the most stringent security controls are not appropriate.

- **Highly regulated** This standard requires the most stringent security controls, and is likely to be appropriate only for a small amount of the organization's data. For example, you may require that data only be accessed from a managed device for a limited amount of time after a user has performed multi-factor authentication.

CLASSIFICATION SCHEMAS

Classification schemas allow you to assign an information protection level to specific information such as a document or email message. Microsoft 365 includes the following three classification schemas:

- **Sensitive information types for Office 365** Office 365 automatically recognizes specific information types, such as credit card or passport numbers. You can leverage Office 365 sensitive information types to automatically apply data loss prevention rules and policies so that this data has the appropriate level of protection.

- **Office 365 retention labels** Office 365 retention labels allow you to determine how long specific data should be stored in Exchange, SharePoint Online, and OneDrive for Business. Office 365 retention labels can use the security and information protection levels outlined earlier: baseline, sensitive, highly regulated, or the custom information protection levels determined by the organization.

- **Azure Information Protection (AIP) labels and protection** AIP provides another set of options for the classification and protection of documents and email messages. An advantage of AIP is that it can be used with documents stored beyond Office 365 locations such as Exchange Online, SharePoint Online, and OneDrive for Business. AIP labels of protection can be applied automatically based on rules and conditions defined by an administrator, manually by users, or in conjunction with automatic recommendations displayed to users.

IMPROVING SECURITY LEVELS

When planning your M365 information protection strategy, you'll need to go beyond information classification, retention policies, and information protection. You'll also need to enable additional M365 security technologies. These technologies include:

- **Threat management policies** You can configure threat management policies in the Security & Compliance Center. Policies include ATP (Advanced Threat Protection) anti-phishing, anti-malware, ATP Safe Attachments, ATP Safe Links, Anti-Spam (Mail Filtering) and Email Authentication.

- **Exchange Online tenant wide settings** You can improve security by implementing appropriate Mail Flow, also known as Transport Rules, and enabling modern authentication, which allows you to then use multi-factor authentication (MFA).

- **SharePoint tenant wide settings** Security can be strengthened by configuring external sharing settings. Options include limiting sharing to authenticated external users, allowing anonymous access links, configuring anonymous access link expiration, and default link types.

- **Azure Active Directory settings** You can enhance security by configuring named locations, which is part of conditional access, and to also block apps that don't support modern authentication.

- **Cloud App Security** Cloud App Security allows organizations to improve their security posture by providing evaluations of risk, and alerts against suspicious activity and automatic remediation actions. Cloud App Security requires an M365, O365 or EMS E5 plan.

PRIVILEGED ACCESS MANAGEMENT

The effectiveness of an information protection strategy depends on how secure the administrative accounts used to manage that strategy are. If the accounts that can be used to configure and manage an information protection strategy aren't properly secured, then the information protection strategy itself can be easily compromised.

Privileged access management allows you to configure policies that apply just-in-time administrative principles to sensitive administrative roles. For example, if someone needs access to configure an information protection policy, they would need to go through an approval process to temporarily gain access to that set of rights as opposed to having an Azure AD account that had permanently been assigned those rights.

> **MORE INFO INFORMATION PROTECTION INFRASTRUCTURE**
>
> You can learn more about M365 information protection infrastructure at: *https://docs.microsoft.com/microsoft-365/enterprise/infoprotect-infrastructure*.

Plan identity and authentication solution

Identity providers are the primary source of authority and host user and group accounts. When you select a primary source of identity, that location is where authoritative changes to an account or group are made. For example, if you perform a password change, the password change isn't understood to apply unless it applies at the primary source of identity. For example, in a hybrid scenario it's possible to change the password of an account that is replicated from an on-premises directory to a cloud based Azure Active Directory. You might change the password of the account in the cloud, but that change may be overwritten the next time synchronization occurs from the primary identity source.

M365 and O365 use Azure Active Directory (Azure AD) as the user and group identity and authentication service. This means that Azure AD stores user, group, and device account objects and is also responsible for performing M365 and O365 authentication. When deploying M365 and O365 you can choose whether identity management is cloud only or whether a relationship exists between an on-premises identity provider such as Active Directory Domain Services (AD DS) and Azure AD.

Cloud authentication

When you select cloud authentication, authentication occurs against Azure Active Directory. How you implement cloud authentication depends on whether or not your organization has an existing on-premises Active Directory Domain Services deployment and what your plans are for that deployment in the future.

CLOUD-ONLY

The cloud-only authentication model addresses management of user and group accounts that exist only from within M365. You can create and manage users in the M365 admin center shown in Figure 1-27, in the Azure Active Directory portal or blade, or by using the appropriate PowerShell cmdlets.

FIGURE 1-27 Create and manage M365 users

A cloud only identity and authentication solution is appropriate if:

- Your organization has not deployed an on-premises Active Directory Domain Services environment.

- Your organization has a very complex on-premises directory solution and wants to avoid attempting to integrate it.

- Your organization has an on-premises Active Directory Domain Services environment, but wants to run a pilot or trial of M365 and will worry about integrating with the existing environment if the pilot or trial proves successful.

PASSWORD HASH SYNC WITH SINGLE SIGN-ON

When planning an identity and authentication solution using password hash synchronization, your organization will synchronize on-premises AD DS user accounts with the Azure AD service used by M365 and O365. When you adopt this strategy, cryptographic hashes of on-premises user passwords are synchronized to Azure AD.

The cryptographic hashing operation is one way. This means that it's not possible to run a reverse cryptographic operation on the hash to derive the password it was generated from, although there are techniques that iterate possible passwords to see if they match a cryptographic hash should one manage to be captured. The use of cryptographic hashes means that the user passwords aren't stored in Azure AD. When authentication occurs, the password the user enters has the same cryptographic operation performed on it, and the hash of that password is then compared to the one stored in Azure AD. If the hashes match, the user is authenticated. If the hashes do not match, the user is not authenticated. If a password is changed in the on-premises account database, a new password hash is calculated and the new cryptographic hash is synchronized to and stored in Azure AD.

Choose this method when you want to have on-premises Active Directory Domain Services remain the authoritative source for user accounts and the regulations that your organization is subject to allow for cryptographic hashes of passwords to be stored in the cloud. This solution requires Azure Active Directory Connect, which you'll learn about in Chapter 2, "Manage User Identity and Roles".

PASS-THROUGH AUTHENTICATION WITH SINGLE SIGN-ON

When you implement pass-through authentication with single sign-on, you install a software agent on one or more on-premises Active Directory Domain Services (AD DS) domain controllers. When a user authenticates against Azure Active Directory, the request is passed through to the on-premises Active Directory instance through the agent to determine whether the authentication request is valid.

This solution is appropriate when your organization is constrained from allowing any form of password synchronization to the cloud. This may include being restricted from allowing cryptographic hashes of passwords to be stored in the cloud. In this scenario, you would choose pass through authentication with single sign-on as an appropriate solution. It is also appropriate where on-premises account states, password policies, and logon hours must be enforced. You'll learn more about configuring pass-through authentication with single sign-on in Chapter 2, "Manage User Identity and Roles".

Federated authentication

Federated authentication is an alternative to cloud authentication, although it's often substantially more complicated to configure and maintain. Most organizations use Azure AD Connect to synchronize identity information between on-premises Active Directory Domain Services and Azure AD. Organizations that want to allow additional authentication options, such as smart-card based authentication, or third-party multi-factor authentication such as an RSA token device.

FEDERATED IDENTITY WITH ACTIVE DIRECTORY FEDERATION SERVICES

When you use federated identity with Active Directory Federation Services (AD FS), you deploy servers hosting the AD FS role on your organization's on-premises network and perimeter network. You then will need to configure federation between your on-premises AD FS instance and Azure AD. When you implement this identity and authentication technology, users use the same authentication options to access M365 and O365 resources as they do on-premises resources. This authentication method is generally chosen by organizations that have authentication requirements that are not natively supported by Azure AD.

THIRD-PARTY AUTHENTICATION AND IDENTITY PROVIDERS

Organizations that use a non-active Directory on-premises identity provider can integrate that identity provider with Azure AD through federation as long as that third party identity provider's federation solution is compatible with Azure AD. When this solution is implemented, users are able to access M365 and O365 resources using their on-premises identity provider username and password.

> *MORE INFO* **UNDERSTANDING M365 AND O365 IDENTITY**
>
> You can learn more about understand identity at: *https://docs.microsoft.com/office365/ enterprise/about-office-365-identity*.

EXAM TIP

Remember, the difference between password hash sync with single sign-on and pass-through authentication with single sign-on.

Skill 1.3: Setup Microsoft 365 tenancy and subscription

This section deals with configuring Microsoft 365 tenancy and subscription settings. To master this skill you'll need to understand which specific roles are appropriate for certain M365 workloads. You'll also need to be able to evaluate the appropriateness of M365 for an organization, to plan and create a tenancy, and to upgrade existing subscriptions to M365.

> **This section covers the following topics:**
> - Configure subscription and tenant roles and workload settings
> - Evaluate Microsoft 365 for organization
> - Plan and create tenant
> - Upgrade existing subscriptions to Microsoft 365
> - Monitor license allocations

Configure subscription and tenant roles and workload settings

The principle of least privilege suggests that organizations will be more secure if privileged users are assigned the minimum amount of administrative rights required to accomplish their roles. For example, rather than giving every IT support technician the M365 Global Administrator role, users that were responsible only for changing passwords would be assigned the Helpdesk Administrator (Password Administrator) role and IT support technicians that are responsible for assigning licenses should be assigned the License Administrator role. In this section you'll learn about the M365 administrative roles and how they can be used to manage specific workload settings.

Global administrator

Global administrators have the most permissions over a Microsoft 365 tenancy. A global administrator has the following permissions:

- View organization and user information
- Manage support tickets
- Reset user passwords
- Perform billing and purchasing operations
- Create and manage user views
- Create, edit, and delete users
- Create, edit, and delete groups
- Manage user licenses
- Manage domains
- Manage organization information
- Delegate administrative roles to others
- User directory synchronization

Users that have the global administrator role in the Microsoft 365 tenancy have the following roles in Exchange Online:

- Exchange Online admin
- Company admin
- SharePoint Online admin
- Skype for Business Online admin

Billing administrator

Members of the billing administrator role are responsible for making purchases, managing Microsoft 365 subscriptions, managing support tickets, and monitoring the health of Office 365 services. Members of the billing administrator role have the following permissions:

- View organization and user information

- Manage support tickets
- Perform billing and purchasing operations

Members of this role do not have any equivalent roles in Exchange Online, SharePoint Online, or Skype for Business Online.

Dynamics 365 service administrator

Users that hold the Dynamics 365 service administrator role can manage Dynamics 365 instances, including performing backup and recovery operations. Users that hold this role can also perform Dynamics 365 copy and reset actions. They can open support tickets with Microsoft and are able to view the service dashboard and message center.

Customer Lockbox access approver

Members of the Customer Lockbox access approver role manage customer lockbox requests for the tenancy. They will receive email notifications for Customer Lockbox requests. Users that hold this role can approve or deny requests using the Microsoft 365 Admin center. Users that hold this role are also able to enable and disable the Customer Lockbox feature. Only users that hold the Global Administrator role are able to reset the password of users that hold the Customer Lockbox access approver role.

Exchange administrator

The Exchange administrator role is also known as the Exchange Online Administrator role. Users who have delegated the Exchange Online administrator role are able to manage mailboxes and anti-spam policies for their tenancy. This includes being able to:

- Recover deleted items from mailboxes
- Configure how long deleted items will be retained before permanent deletion
- Configure mailbox sharing policies
- Configure Send As and Send on Behalf of delegates for a mailbox
- Configure anti-spam and malware filters
- Create shared mailboxes

> **MORE INFO** **EXCHANGE ONLINE ADMINISTRATOR**
>
> You can learn more about Exchange Online administrator role at: *https://docs.microsoft.com/office365/admin/add-users/about-exchange-online-admin-role.*

Helpdesk (Password) administrator

Members of the Helpdesk (password) administrator role are responsible for resetting passwords for non-privileged users and other members of the password administrator role. Members of this role are also able to manage service requests and monitor service health. Members of this role have the following permissions:

- View organization and user information.
- Manage support tickets.
- Reset non-privileged user passwords as well as passwords of other password administrators. Cannot reset passwords of global administrators, user management administrators, or billing administrators.
- Manage the Exchange Online Help Desk admin role.
- Manage the Skype for Business Online admin role.

License administrator

Users assigned the License administrator role are able to add, remove, and update license assignments for users. They can also manage group based licensing, as well as configure the usage location for users. Users assigned this role are unable to purchase or manage subscriptions, create or manage groups, or modify users beyond configuring usage location.

Skype for Business administrator

Users delegated the Skype for Business administrator role are able to perform the following tasks:

- Set up dial-in conferencing
- Set up PSTN calling
- Transfer phone numbers to Skype for Business Online
- Enable Skype Meeting Broadcast
- Allow users to contact external Skype for Business users
- Allow users to add external contacts from Skype
- Determine who is able to view online presence
- Enable and disable mobile notifications
- Create customized meeting invitations
- View Skype for Business Online online activity reports

Message center reader

Users assigned the message center reader role are able to view all posts made to the Microsoft 365 message center. Users assigned this role are also able to share these message with other users by forwarding those messages through email. Users assigned this role also have read access to a subset of admin center resources including users, groups, domains, and subscriptions.

Power BI service administrator

Users assigned the Power BI admin role have access to Microsoft 365 and Office 365 Power BI usage metrics. Users assigned this role are able to manage the organization's usage of PowerBI.

Reports reader

Users that hold the reports reader role are able to view all Microsoft 365 activity reports, as well as any reports that are published through the reporting APIs.

Service administrator

Members of the service administrator role are able to manage service requests and monitor the health of services. Before a global administrator can assign the service administrator role to a user, the user must be assigned administrative permissions to one of the Office 365 services, such as SharePoint Online or Exchange Online. Service administrators have the following permissions over the assigned service:

- View organization and user information
- Manage support tickets

SharePoint administrator

Also known as the SharePoint Online administrator. Users delegated the SharePoint Online administrator role are able to use the SharePoint Online admin center. They are able to perform the following tasks:

- Create and manage site collections
- Manage site collections and global settings
- Designate site collection administrators
- Manage site collection storage limits
- Manage SharePoint online user profiles

> **MORE INFO** **SHAREPOINT ONLINE ADMINISTRATOR**
>
> You can learn more about the SharePoint Online administrator role at: *https://support. office.com/article/About-the-SharePoint-Online-admin-role-f08144d5-9d50-4922-8e77-4e1a27b40705*.

Teams Communications administrator

Users that hold this role are able to manage the calling and meeting features of Teams. This includes the assignment of phone numbers as well as meeting policies. Users that hold this role are also able to use call analytics tools and troubleshooting tools.

Teams Communications support engineer

Users that hold this role are able to troubleshoot communications issues in Teams. They can access call analytics tools as well as view call record information for all call participants.

Teams Communications support specialist

Users that hold this role are able to troubleshoot communications issues in Teams. This role differs from the support engineer role in that the specialist can only view call record information for a specific user rather than all call participants.

Teams service administrator

Users that hold this role are able to administer all aspects of Microsoft Teams, except the assignment of licenses. Users that hold this role are able to:

- Manage calling policies
- Manage messaging policies
- Manage meetings policies
- Use call analytics tools
- Manage users and their telephone settings
- Manage M365 groups

User management administrator

Members of the user management administrator role are able to reset some user passwords, monitor service health, manage some user accounts and groups, and service requests. Members of this role have the following permissions:

- View organization and user information
- Manage support tickets
- Reset the passwords of all user accounts except those assigned the global administrator, billing administrator, or service administrator roles
- Create and manage user views
- Can create, edit, and delete users and groups except users that are assigned global administrator privileges
- Can manage user licenses
- Have the Skype for Business Online admin role

Delegated administrator

Delegated administrators are people outside the organization that perform administrative duties within the Office 365 tenancy. Administrators of the tenancy control who is delegated administrator permissions. You can only assign delegated administrator permissions to users that have Office 365 accounts in their own tenancy.

When you configure delegated administration, you can choose one of the following permission levels:

- **Full administration**   When you assign the full administration role to a delegated administrator, that administrator has the same privileges as a member of the global admin role.

- **Limited administration** When you assign the limited administration role to a delegated administrator, that administrator has the same privileges as a member of the password admin role.

> **MORE INFO DELEGATED ADMINISTRATORS**
>
> You can learn more about delegated administrators at: *https://support.office.microsoft.com/ article/Partners-Offer-delegated-administration-26530dc0-ebba-415b-86b1-b55bc06b073e.*

Manage role membership

You can assign an administrative role on the Edit user roles page of a Microsoft 365 user's properties as shown in Figure 1-28. When you assign an administrative role, you specify the role that you want to assign, and an alternate email address. This allows you to perform password recovery if necessary. You can only add Microsoft 365 users to a role. You cannot add a Microsoft 365 group to a role.

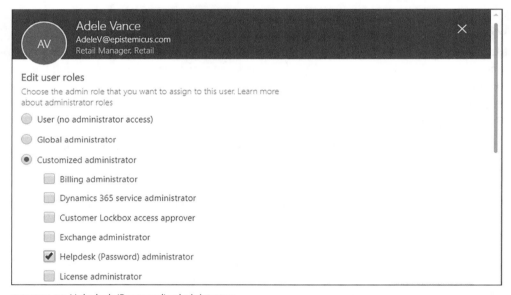

FIGURE 1-28 Helpdesk (Password) administrator

You can use this page of a user's account to remove an assigned role. To do this, deselect the role that you want to remove and select the **No Option** and then click **Save**. You can view a list of users assigned a particular role by using the Active Users node in the M365 Admin Center and selecting the role whose membership you wish to view. Figure 1-29 shows the members of the Password Admins role.

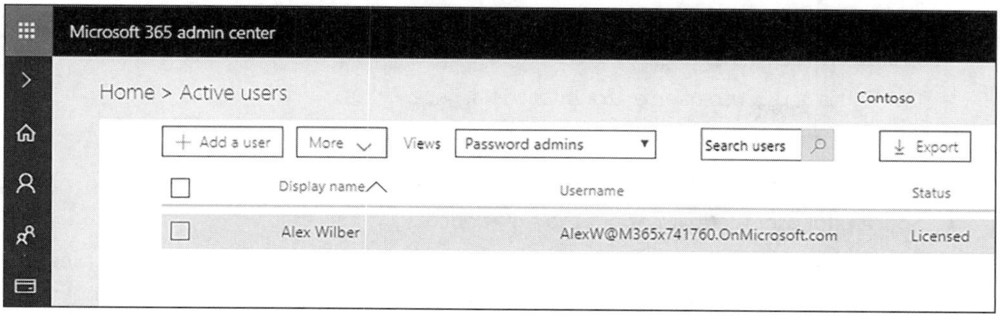

FIGURE 1-29 List of password administrators

Evaluate Microsoft 365 for organization

Organizations that are considering adopting Microsoft 365 can create a trial subscription which is available to existing O365 subscribers. A trial subscription allows the organization to create and use a Microsoft 365 tenancy as well as the associated Microsoft 365 services for a 30 day evaluation period. The trial period provides 25 licenses and the trial can be converted to a traditional Microsoft 365 subscription after the trial period is completed.

Prior to initiating the trial, an organization should perform some planning so that they will be able to use the 30 day evaluation period for maximum benefit. While the organization should approach the trial as a pilot that will eventually transfer into an ongoing subscription, certain actions, such as integrating the on-premises directory with Azure AD, should not be taken until the organization is satisfied that Microsoft 365 is appropriate and an ongoing subscription will be obtained.

You should ensure that you have done the following before initiating a Microsoft 365 trial:

- Ensure that you have 25 users ready to participate in the trial. These users should be representative of how Microsoft 365 are used in your organization.

- Provide the users with separate computers with trial versions of Windows 10 Enterprise edition installed. If your organization has no plans to migrate to Windows 10 in the near future, then Microsoft 365 might be less appropriate than separately adopting Office 365 and EMS. It is important to remember that Windows 7 falls out of support in January 2020 and that Windows 8.1 falls out of extended support in January 2023, so organizations cannot hold off adopting Windows 10 indefinitely. Microsoft 365 may be a less appropriate solution for an organization where all client computers run MacOS.

- Ensure that meaningful workloads are run during the trial. It is important that a determination be made as to whether M365 is appropriate for your organization during the trial and that any potential hurdles are identified in the trial period rather than once full adoption of M365 has occurred.

Creating a test plan or use case involves developing a formal process to describe how the pilot will proceed and how the results of the pilot will be assessed. The test plan should involve the following general phases.

- Deploying the Microsoft 365 tenancy that will be used for the pilot
- Create user accounts for pilot users
- Configure active use of email for pilot users
- Deploy Office 365 ProPlus software
- Enable pilot user access to Microsoft 365 services
- Solicit pilot user feedback about the experience

Each organization's plans will be slightly different. You need to ensure that pilot user feedback is recorded so that you can use it when evaluating how decisions made in the planning phase stack up against real-world outcomes, allowing you to make adjustments to the deployment phase.

It is possible to migrate the email accounts of a small number of users from your on-premises environment to Microsoft 365 while keeping the majority of your existing mailboxes in the on-premises mail solution. The method for doing this is termed Simple domain sharing for SMTP email addresses.

For example:

- Your organization has provisioned the contoso.microsoftonline.com Office 365 tenancy.
- Your organization has its own on-premises mail solution. It uses the contoso.com email suffix.
- Your organization hosts its own DNS records on servers dns1.contoso.com and dns2. contoso.com.
- An MX record in the contoso.com zone points to the host mailserver.adatum.com with a priority of 10.
- An SPF record on in the contoso.com DNS zone the value v=spf1 mx include:contoso. com -all.

To configure Office 365 so that some pilot users are able to receive email through Microsoft 365, while others still use the on-premises solution, take the following steps:

- Update the SPF record to "v=spf1 mx include:contoso.com include:spf.protection.outlook.com -all.
- Confirm ownership within Microsoft 365 of the contoso.com DNS zone by configuring the appropriate TXT record.
- Mark the domain as shared in Exchange Online. This is done from the mail flow node of Exchange Admin Center. Exchange Admin Center is available from the Microsoft 365 Admin Center by clicking the Exchange node under the ADMIN node.
- You set the domain as an Internal Relay domain.
- Configure the on-premises mail solution to configure mail forwarding of each pilot user account to the contoso.microsoftonline.com mail domain. For example, the on-premises mailbox for the don.funk@contoso.com email account should forward all incoming email to don.funk@contoso.microsoftonline.com.

- Configure each pilot user's account in Microsoft 365 to use the on-premises DNS zone mail domain. For example, Don Funk's Microsoft 365 user account should be configured with a reply-to address of don.funk@contoso.com.

- You can migrate the contents of pilot users' on-premises mailboxes using Exchange Admin Center.

> **MORE INFO** **TRIAL MICROSOFT 365**
>
> You can learn more about trialing Microsoft 365 if you have an existing O365 subscription at: *https://docs.microsoft.com/office365/admin/try-or-buy-microsoft-365*.

Plan and create tenant

The most important initial decisions that you make about your Microsoft 365 tenancy are the tenant name and the tenant region. You learned about tenant names and how the onmicrosoft.com domain you choose when creating the tenancy can never be removed, even if you add a custom DNS domain earlier in this chapter.

Tenant region determines which Microsoft 365 services will be available to the subscription, the taxes that will be applied as a part of the subscription charges, the billing currency for the subscription, and the Microsoft datacenter that will host the resources allocated to the subscription. For example, selecting United States for a region will mean that your organization's Microsoft 365 tenancy is allocated resources in a United States datacenter. Selecting New Zealand currently means that your organization's Microsoft 365 tenancy will be allocated resources in a datacenter in Australia because this is currently the closest Microsoft datacenter to New Zealand.

Unlike other Microsoft 365 settings, you cannot change the tenant region once you have selected it. The only way to alter a tenant region is to cancel your existing subscription and to create a new subscription. Selecting the correct tenant is very important from a compliance perspective and there are many stories of consultants in countries outside the US setting up US tenancies, only to find out later that they need to recreate the tenancy because customer data is stored outside the associated organization's national borders.

> **MORE INFO** **WHERE TENANCY DATA IS STORED**
>
> You can learn more about where tenancy data is stored at: *https://products.office.com/where-is-your-data-located*.

Upgrade existing subscriptions to Microsoft 365

Microsoft 365 is a combination of the following existing Microsoft products:

- Office 365
- Enterprise Mobility + Security (EMS)
- Windows 10

An organization that already has Office 365 subscriptions for its users can upgrade those subscriptions to Microsoft 365, just as an organization that has Office 365 and EMS subscriptions can upgrade to Microsoft 365 licenses. You can purchase additional services in the Purchase Services node under Billing in the Microsoft 365 Admin Center, as shown in Figure 1-30. Once the appropriate licenses have been purchased, they can be assigned to users. If organizations need assistance, they can take advantage of Microsoft's FastTrack for Microsoft 365 service, which provides information and advice on upgrading an existing deployment or performing a new deployment.

FIGURE 1-30 Subscriptions node

Monitor license allocations

You can manage Microsoft 365 tenant subscriptions from the Subscriptions node, which is under the Billing node, and is shown in Figure 1-31.

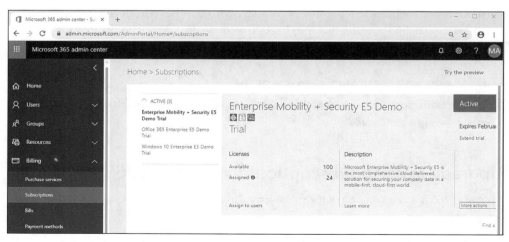

FIGURE 1-31 Subscriptions node

Assigning licenses

Microsoft 365 users require licenses to use Outlook, SharePoint Online, Skype for Business, and other services. Users who have been assigned the global administrator or user management administrator roles can assign licenses to users when creating new Microsoft 365 user accounts or can assign licenses to accounts that are created through directory synchronization or federation.

When a license is assigned to a user, the following occurs:

- An Exchange Online mailbox is created for the user.
- Edit permissions for the default SharePoint Online team site are assigned to the user.
- The user will have access to Skype for Business features associated with the license.
- For Office 365 ProPlus, the user will be able to download and install Microsoft Office on up to five computers running Windows or macOS.

You can view the number of valid licenses and the number of those licenses that have been assigned on the Licenses node, which is underneath the Billing node in the Microsoft 365 Admin Center.

> **MORE INFO ASSIGN LICENSES**
>
> You can learn more about topic at: *https://docs.microsoft.com/office365/admin/ subscriptions-and-billing/assign-licenses-to-users.*

EXAM TIP

Remember that an Exchange Online mailbox is created for a user when an M365 license is assigned to that user.

Skill 1.4: Manage Microsoft 365 subscription and tenant health

This skill section deals with managing subscription and tenant health for an M365 deployment. To master this skill you'll need to understand options when it comes to managing service health, how to create and manage service requests, how to create a health response plan, how to monitor service health, create and review reports, schedule and review security and compliance reports and schedule and review usage metrics.

This section covers the following topics:

- Manage service health alerts
- Create and manage service requests
- Create internal service health response plan
- Monitor service health
- Configure and review reports, including BI, OMS, and Microsoft 365 reporting
- Schedule and review security and compliance reports
- Schedule and review usage metrics

Manage service health alerts

The Service Health dashboard allows you to view the health of all of the services related to your organization's Microsoft 365 subscription. For example, the screenshot of the Service Health dashboard shown in Figure 1-32 shows that all services are in a healthy state.

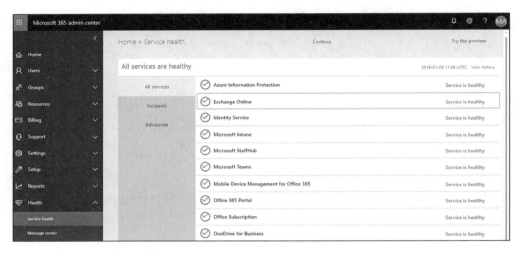

FIGURE 1-32 Service health dashboard

Services have the status definitions listed in Table 1-7.

TABLE 1-7 M365 Service Status Definitions

Status	Definition
Investigating	Microsoft is aware of the issue and is conducting an investigation as to the cause and scope of impact.
Service degradation	Microsoft has confirmed that an issue is present in a specific M365 service or feature. This status is often assigned when a service is performing in a slower than normal state or when intermittent interruptions are occurring.
Service interruption	Microsoft is aware that significant disruption is occurring with the listed system.
Restoring service	Microsoft has determined the cause of the issue and is in the process of restoring full functionality.
Extended Recovery	Microsoft has restored full functionality for most users, but some users may require more time before the fix reaches them.
Investigation suspended	Microsoft has requested additional information from customers to determine the cause of a disruption.
Service restored	Microsoft has confirmed that remediation actions have resolved the problem and that the service is in a healthy state. View service issues to learn details of the disruption.
Post-incident report published	Microsoft has published a detailed post-incident report that includes root cause information and steps that have been taken to ensure that the issue does not arise again.

> **MORE INFO MICROSOFT 365 SERVICE HEALTH**
>
> You can learn more about checking Microsoft 365 service health at: *https://docs.microsoft.com/office365/enterprise/view-service-health.*

History

Service health history displays the status history of services over the past 30 days. Figure 1-33 shows history over the last 7 days. This may allow you to diagnose issues that may have occurred previously that you were not aware of, such as if you needed to provide an explanation to a user as to why they were unable to access specific functionality over the weekend. Clicking on each item provides further details.

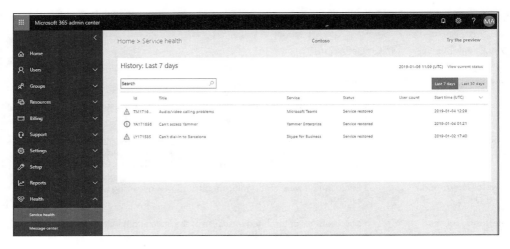

FIGURE 1-33 Service health history

Create and manage service requests

Service requests allow tenant administrators to contact Microsoft to resolve problems. You can create a service request online through the Microsoft 365 Admin Center, or by telephone. To create a service request online, perform the following steps:

1. Sign into the Microsoft 365 Admin Center with an account that has tenant administrator privileges.
2. In the left pane, click **Support**. Under **Support** click **New Service Request**.
3. On the Need Help page, shown in Figure 1-34, provide information about what you require help with and click **Get Help**.

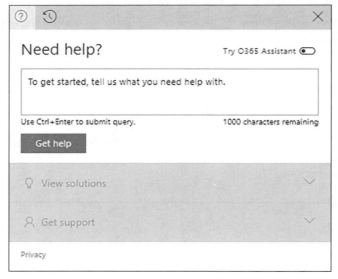

FIGURE 1-34 Get Help

4. You'll be provided with the results of a search query that may or may not actually help you resolve your problem. Under the query results, click **New Service Request By Phone**.

5. On the New Service Request By Phone Page, shown in Figure 1-35, verify your contact details. You will be provided with an estimated time before a M365 support representative will call you to address the service request. You can add attachments related to the support request. Click **Call Me** to enter the M365 telephone support call back queue.

FIGURE 1-35 Ask Microsoft to call you

MORE INFO SERVICE REQUESTS

You can learn more about topic at: *https://docs.microsoft.com/office365/admin/contact-support-for-business-products*.

Create internal service health response plan

Microsoft provides a variety of methods for your organization to become aware that there is some form of service disruption beyond end users ringing the service desk to complain that they can't get "the thing to work." You can monitor these service communication channels so that you are aware of potential issues and take steps to notify users before they notice the impact of these events. Service communication channels include the following:

- **The Office 365 Admin App**   This app will provide M365 and O365 administrators with the ability to monitor service status from a mobile device. Tenant administrators are able to use the app to view service health information and maintenance status updates.

- **Office 365 Management Pack for System Center Operations Manager** Organizations that use System Center Operations Manager to monitor their environment can install the O365 Management Pack so that alerts are visible within the Operations Manager console. The Management pack includes sections on Subscription Health, Service Status, Active Incidents, Resolved Incidents and Message Center. Figure 1-36 shows the Office 365 Monitoring Dashboard.

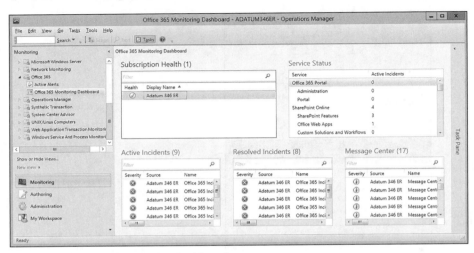

FIGURE 1-36 Office 365 Monitoring Dashboard

- **Office 365 Service Communications API** The O365 service communications API allows you to interact with O365 service communications in a manner that suits your organization. This API provides you with a method of connecting existing monitoring tools to O365 service communications. The API allows you to monitor real-time service health, message center communications, and planned maintenance notifications.

> **MORE INFO SERVICE HEALTH RESPONSE**
>
> You can learn more about service health response at: *https://docs.microsoft.com/office365/ servicedescriptions/office-365-platform-service-description/service-health-and-continuity.*

Monitor service health

M365 provides administrators with information about upcoming maintenance events through planned maintenance notifications. You can view planned maintenance events by navigating to the message center and setting the view to **Plan For Change**, as shown in Figure 1-37.

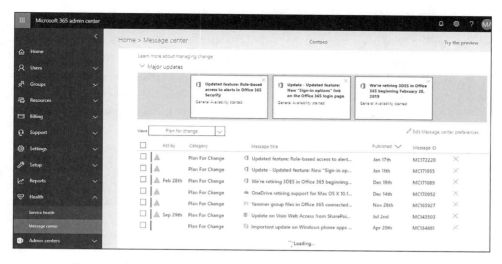

FIGURE 1-37 Planned maintenance

MORE INFO SERVICE HEALTH DASHBOARD

You can learn more about the Service Health dashboard at: *https://docs.microsoft.com/office365/enterprise/view-service-health.*

Schedule and review security and compliance reports

Microsoft 365 security and compliance reports, shown in Figure 1-38, are split across four categories. These reports allow you to view how security and compliance rules and technologies are being used across your Microsoft 365 organization.

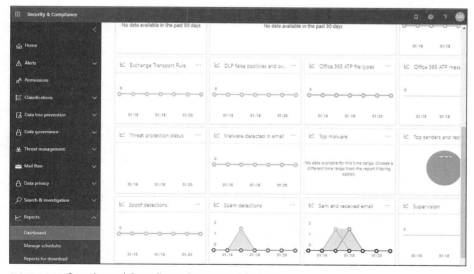

FIGURE 1-38 Security and Compliance Report Dashboard

You need the following permissions to view reports in the Security and Compliance center:

- You need to have been assigned the Security Reader Role in Exchange. This role is assigned by default to the Organization Management and Security Reader role groups.
- You will need to have been assigned the DLP Compliance Management Role in Security & Compliance Center to view DLP reports and policies. This role is assigned by default to the Compliance Administrator, Organization Management, and Security Administrator role groups.

> **MORE INFO SECURITY AND COMPLIANCE REPORTS**
>
> You can learn more about the Office 365 security and compliance reports at: *https://docs. microsoft.com/office365/securitycompliance/reports-in-security-and-compliance*.

Auditing reports

The following security and compliance reports are available through the Security and Compliance Center:

- **Office 365 Audit Log report** View user and admin activity for the M365 organization including viewing changes made to administrator role groups.
- **Azure AD reports** This option allows you to view Azure Active Directory reports including reports for unusual or suspicious sign-in activity. It requires a paid Azure Active Directory subscription.
- **Exchange Audit reports** Use this report to search for mailboxes accessed by people other than their owners. Requires mailbox audit logging to be enabled.

Data Loss Prevention reports

The following Data Loss Prevention (DLP) reports are available through the Office 365 Admin Center:

- **Top DLP policy matches for mail** Allows you to view the top DLP policy matches for sent and received email.
- **Top DLP rule matches for mail** Allows you to view the top DLP rule matches for sent and received email.
- **DLP policy matches by severity for mail** Allows you to track DLP policy matches by severity.
- **DLP policy matches, overrides, and false positives for mail** Allows you to view DLP matches, overrides, and false positives for incoming and outgoing messages.

Protection reports

The following protection reports are available through the Office 365 Admin Center:

- **Top senders and recipients**   This report allows you to view the top mail senders, the top mail recipients, the top spam recipients, and the top malware recipients across the Office 365 subscription.

- **Top malware for mail**   This report shows the amount of malware received through e-mail for the reporting period.

- **Malware detections**   This report shows the amount of malware sent and received through the Office 365 subscription for the reporting period.

- **Spam detections**   This report shows the amount of spam on the basis of the content being filtered or the original sending host being blocked.

- **Sent and received mail**   This report shows the amount of sent and received mail categorized by good mail, malware, spam, and messages dealt with by rules.

Rules reports

The following rules reports are available through the Office 365 Admin Center:

- **Top rule matches for mail**   This report allows you to view the number of messages based on sent and received transport rule matches.

- **Rule matches for mail**   This report shows all rule matches for received and sent email.

Schedule and review usage metrics

Activity Reports, shown in Figure 1-39, allow you to view how users in your organization are using Microsoft 365 services. You can review reports over periods of 7 days, 30 days, 90 days and 180 days. Reports are not generated immediately, but become available after 48 hours.

FIGURE 1-39 Usage Reports

Reports can be viewed by users who hold the following roles:

- Office 365 global administrator

- Exchange administrator

- SharePoint administrator

- Skype for Business administrator

- Report reader

- Teams Service Administrator

- Teams Communications Administrator

Email Activity

The Email Activity report, shown in Figure 1-40, shows the number of send, receive, and read actions across the organization, with a per user breakdown. You can use this report to get high level information about email traffic at your organization, including the last activity date, the number of send actions, receive actions, and read actions. You can use this report to view email activity over the last 7 days, 30 days, 90 days and 180 days.

FIGURE 1-40 Email Activity report

> **MORE INFO EMAIL ACTIVITY REPORT**
>
> You can learn more about the email activity report at: *https://docs.microsoft.com/ office365/ admin/activity-reports/email-activity.*

Mailbox Usage

The Mailbox Usage report, shown in Figure 1-41, shows the total number of mailboxes, the total number of active user mailboxes, the amount of storage used across all mailboxes, and the mailboxes by quota status (good, warning issued, send prohibited, and send/receive prohibited). You can also view the number of deleted items, the last activity date, and the number of items in each user's mailbox. The report allows you to view data from the last 7 days, 30 days, 90 days and 180 days.

FIGURE 1-41 Mailbox Usage

> **MORE INFO MAILBOX USAGE REPORT**
>
> You can learn more about the mailbox usage report at: *https://docs.microsoft.com / office365/admin/activity-reports/mailbox-usage.*

Office Activations

The Office Activation report provides data on the users who have activated their Office 365 subscription on one or more devices. You can use it to determine activations for Office 365 ProPlus, Project, and Visio Pro for Office 365. You can also view activation information including whether the product was activated on a computer running Windows, macOS, or devices running the iOS or Android mobile operating systems. This report is displayed in Figure 1-42.

FIGURE 1-42 Activations reports

> **MORE INFO OFFICE ACTIVATIONS REPORT**
>
> You can learn more about the Activations report at: *https://docs.microsoft.com/office365/ admin/activity-reports/microsoft-office-activations?view=o365-worldwide.*

Active Users

The Active Users report, shown in Figure 1-43, provides information on the number of licenses that are being used across your organization. It also provides you with information about the products licensed by specific users. You can use this report to determine which products are not fully being used.

FIGURE 1-43 Active Users report

Email App Usage

The Email App Usage report provides information on the email app used by each user to access Exchange Online. Each app used to interact with Exchange Online is tracked, so you can determine the app usage profile of each user. This report tracks usage through Outlook on Windows, Outlook on Mac OSX, Outlook on the web, as well as mobile clients.

OneDrive for Business User Activity

The OneDrive Activity report, also known as the OneDrive for Business Activity Report, allows you to view the activity of all Office 365 OneDrive for Business users. This report, shown in Figure 1-44, provides information on the following:

- Last OneDrive for Business Activity
- Files viewed or edited
- Files synced
- Files shared internally
- Files shared externally

FIGURE 1-44 OneDrive for Business Activity Report

OneDrive for Business usage

The OneDrive for Business usage report, provides a high-level overview of how files are used in your organization's OneDrive for Business subscription. The report, shown in Figure 1-45, provides details of the following:

- **URL**   This is the file's location within OneDrive for Business
- **Owner**   Office 365 account associated with the file
- **Last activity date (UTC)**   Last date that the file was accessed
- **Files**   Number of files associated with the user
- **Active files**   Number of user's files being actively used
- **Storage used (MB)**   Storage consumed by the user's files

FIGURE 1-45 OneDrive Usage Report

SharePoint Activity

The SharePoint Activity report allows you to track how Microsoft 365 users in your organization interact with SharePoint Online. This report provides the following information on a per-user basis:

- **Last activity date**   The last time the user interacted with SharePoint Online.
- **Files viewed or edited**   This is the number of files that the user interacted with that were hosted on the organization's SharePoint Online instance.
- **Files synced**   This is the number of files that have synchronized between the devices used by the user and SharePoint Online.
- **Files shared internally**   The number of files shared with other Office 365 users through SharePoint Online.
- **Files shared externally**   The number of files shared through Office 365 with external users.

> **MORE INFO   SHAREPOINT ACTIVITY REPORT**
>
> You can learn more about the SharePoint Activity report at: *https://docs.microsoft.com/office365/admin/activity-reports/sharepoint-activity*.

SharePoint Site Usage

The SharePoint Site Usage report, shown in Figure 1-46, provides information on how SharePoint sites in your organization's SharePoint Online deployment, are used. This report provides you with the following information:

- **Site URL**   The address of the site within your SharePoint deployment
- **Site owner**   Microsoft 365 user assigned ownership of the site
- **Last Activity date**   Last time activity was recorded against the site
- **Files**   Number of files stored on the SharePoint online site
- **Files viewed or edited**   Files that have recently been viewed or modified
- **Storage used**   The amount of storage consumed by files on the site

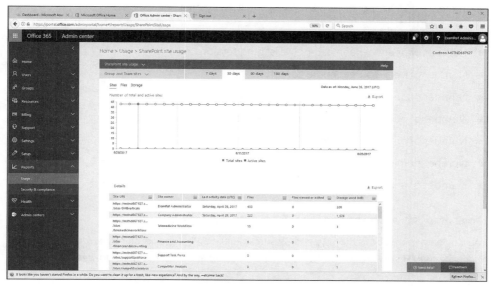

FIGURE 1-46 SharePoint Site Usage Report

MORE INFO **SHAREPOINT SITE USAGE REPORT**

You can learn more about the SharePoint Site Usage report at: *https://docs.microsoft.com/office365/admin/activity-reports/sharepoint-site-usage*.

Skype for Business Activity

The Skype for Business Activity report provides you with information on Skype for Business activity on a per-user basis across your Office 365 organization. This includes information on the following:

- Last activity date
- Peer-to-peer
- Organized conferences
- Participated in conferences

MORE INFO **SKYPE FOR BUSINESS ONLINE ACTIVITY REPORT**

You can learn more about the Skype for Business Online Activity report at: *https://docs.microsoft.com/SkypeForBusiness/skype-for-business-online-reporting/activity-report*.

Skype for Business Peer-To-Peer Activity

The Skype for Business Online Peer-To-Peer Activity report provides information about communication that occurs between individual Skype for Business users outside of Skype for Business conferences. This report tracks the following activity on a per-user basis:

- Last activity date
- Number of peer-to-peer Instant Messaging sessions
- Number of peer-to-peer audio conferences
- Number of peer-to-peer video conferences
- Number of peer-to-peer application sharing sessions
- Number of peer-to-peer file transfers
- Number of minutes spent in peer-to-peer audio conferences
- Number of minutes spent in peer-to-peer video conferences

MORE INFO **SKYPE FOR BUSINESS PEER-TO-PEER ACTIVITY REPORT**

You can learn more about the Skype for Business Peer-to-Peer report at: *https://docs.microsoft.com/SkypeForBusiness/skype-for-business-online-reporting/peer-to-peer-activity-report*.

Skype for Business Conference Organizer Activity

The Skype for Business Conference Organizer Activity Report provides information about conferences initiated by your organization's Skype for Business users. This report presents the following information over a 7 day, 30 day, 90 day, and 180 day time frame by username:

- Last activity
- IM sessions organized
- Audio and Video sessions organized
- Application sharing conferences organized
- Web conferences organized
- Dial-in/out – 3rd party conferences organized
- Total audio/video minutes of conferences organized by this user
- Total number of minutes where Microsoft functioned as the dial-in audio conferencing provider
- Total number of minutes where Microsoft functioned as the dial-out audio conferencing provider

> **MORE INFO** **SKYPE FOR BUSINESS CONFERENCE ORGANIZER ACTIVITY REPORT**
>
> You can learn more about the Skype for Business Conference Organizer Activity report at: *https://docs.microsoft.com/SkypeForBusiness/skype-for-business-online-reporting/conference-organizer-activity-report*.

Skype for Business Conference Participant Activity

The Skype for Business Conference Participant Activity report provides information about Skype for Business from a participant, rather than an organizer perspective. This report includes the following information on a per-user basis:

- Last activity date
- Number of IM conferences the user participated in
- Number of audio and video conferences the user participated in
- Number of application sharing conferences that the user participated in
- Number of web conferences that the user participated in
- Number of Dial-in/out – 3rd party conferences that the user participated in using a 3rd party audio conferencing provider where Skype for Business was used for audio
- Total audio and video minutes

> **MORE INFO** **SKYPE FOR BUSINESS CONFERENCE PARTICIPANT ACTIVITY REPORT**
>
> You can learn more about the Skype for Business Conference Participant Activity report at: *https://docs.microsoft.com/SkypeForBusiness/skype-for-business-online-reporting/conference-participant-activity-report*.

Yammer Activity

The Yammer Activity report provides information about how much users in your organization are interacting with Yammer. It provides information about the number of unique users posting to Yammer, how many read a specific message, how many like a specific message and the general level of interaction across the organization.

> **MORE INFO YAMMER ACTIVITY REPORT**
>
> You can learn more about the Yammer Activity report at: *https://docs.microsoft.com/office365/admin/activity-reports/yammer-activity-report.*

Yammer Device Usage

The Yammer Device Usage report provides you with data about the specific types of devices that are used to interact with the organization's Yammer instance. The report provides information on:

- Number of daily users by device type
- Number of users by device type
- Per user device usage

> **MORE INFO YAMMER DEVICE USAGE REPORT**
>
> You can learn more about the Yammer Device Usage report at: *https://docs.microsoft.com/office365/admin/activity-reports/yammer-device-usage-report.*

Yammer groups activity report

The Yammer Groups activity report provides information about how users in your organization interact with Yammer groups. The report will provide you with information on the number and identity of groups that are created as well as how much utilization those groups are receiving. Activity tracked includes:

- Group name
- Group administrator
- Group type
- Connection to Office 365
- Last Activity Date
- Members
- Messages posted
- Messages read
- Messages liked

Microsoft Teams User Activity

The Microsoft Teams User Activity report provides you with information about how users in your organization interact with the tenancy's Microsoft Teams instance. Activities that are tracked by the report include:

- Channel messages
- Chat messages
- Calls
- Meetings
- Other activities

Microsoft Teams Device Usage

The Microsoft Teams Device Usage report provides information about the specific devices that M365 users are using to interact with the tenancy's Microsoft Teams instance. The report will track the following operating systems and devices:

- Windows
- Mac
- Web
- iOS
- Android Phone
- Windows Phone

Schedule Reports

You can use the Security & Compliance center to regularly generate reports according to a schedule. To complete this task, perform the following steps:

1. In the M365 Security & Compliance center, navigate to **Dashboard** under **Reports**.
2. Select the report that you wish to schedule.

3. Click the **Create Schedule** button. Figure 1-47 shows this button on the Sent and Received email report.

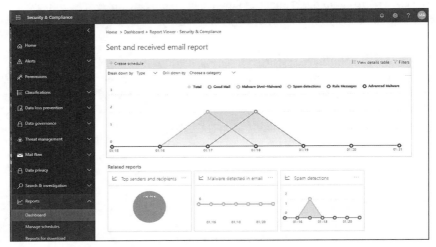

FIGURE 1-47 Sent and received email report

4. On the **Create Schedule** page, shown in Figure 1-48, you can configure the report to be generated according to the default frequency by clicking **Create Schedule**. You can also click **Customize Schedule** to create a customized schedule for the report.

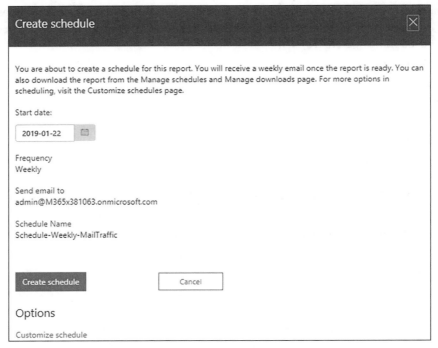

FIGURE 1-48 Create Schedule

EXAM TIP

The best way to learn about the reports available in Microsoft 365 is to access them through your organization's subscription or to create your own trial subscription and to investigate them there.

Skill 1.5: Plan migration of user and data

This section deals with migrating data from an existing on-premises deployment to Microsoft 365 and Office 365. To master this skill you'll need to understand how to identify data that needs to be migrated, how to identify mailboxes to migrate, how to migrate them, how to migrate users and groups, and how to import PST files.

> **This section covers the following topics:**
> - Identify data to be migrated and method
> - Identify users and mailboxes to be migrated and method
> - Plan migration of on-prem users and groups
> - Import PST files

Identify data to be migrated and method

Each organization will have a different set of challenges when it comes to identifying which data should be migrated from their on-premises environment to Microsoft 365. This is because each organization's data is unique and the data that is critical to one organization might be seen as trivial to another. When assessing which data needs to be migrated to Microsoft 365, consider the following questions:

- What on-premises data is critical to the organization? Planning a migration to Microsoft 365 gives an organization a chance to assess whether all of the data that it retains actually needs to be retained.

- What data needs to be moved from the on-premises environment to Microsoft 365? Not every file and folder needs to be migrated to Microsoft 365. For example, do files stored on file servers that haven't been accessed for the last two years need to be migrated to Microsoft 365?

- What data will remain on-premises? Moving to M365 doesn't mean that all data must be removed from on-premises locations. There may be compliance reasons, especially in countries that do not have Microsoft datacenters, that dictate that certain types of data must remain within specific geographic boundaries that cannot be stored in Microsoft's cloud.

- Where is the data currently located? For example, does your organization use file shares? Do you want to move all file share data across to SharePoint Online or will you implement a solution such as Azure File Sync? Is the data located on end-user computers?

Once you've determined which data needs to be migrated to Microsoft 365, you can determine the appropriate method to perform that migration. You'll learn about migration methods later in this chapter.

Moving Data to SharePoint Online

There are a variety of methods that you can use to migrate data from an on-premises environment to SharePoint Online. These methods are listed in Table 1-8.

TABLE 1-8 Data migration methods

Method	Description
SharePoint Migration Tool	This tool allows you to migrate files from on-premises SharePoint document libraries, lists and regular file shares to SharePoint Online
OneDrive sync client	Allows you to drag and drop files on a client computer and have those files sync either with OneDrive for Business or SharePoint Online
Manual upload	Manually upload files one at a time to the SharePoint Online tenant

> **MORE INFO** **MIGRATING DATA TO SHAREPOINT ONLINE**
>
> You can learn more about migrating SharePoint data to SharePoint Online at: *https://docs. microsoft.com/sharepointmigration/migrate-to-sharepoint-online*.

Migrating known local folders to OneDrive for Business

Many organizations have known folders such as the Documents folders directed to an on-premises file share. As part of a migration strategy to move these files to Office 365, you can redirect these folders from an on-premises file share to OneDrive for Business. This can be done through group policy for organizations where computers are members of Active Directory domains. In organizations where computers aren't members of a domain, you will have to instead use more manual and intensive methods of moving files into folders used by OneDrive for Business. This process is manual because in non-domain environments where users have more freedom to configure computers as they see fit, rather than being subject to domain policy, users are more likely to store their files in idiosyncratic locations.

When redirection of known folders to OneDrive for Business is implemented, users continue to use folders such as the Documents folder in the normal manner. In the background, the contents of these known folders will automatically be synced with OneDrive for Business. When using this method, Group Policy will determine if the OneDrive for Business folder has been configured on the target computer. If the folder doesn't exist, known folders, such as the Documents folder, will not be redirected. once the OneDrive for Business folder is present, because the sync client has been deployed.

When you have redirected known folders, shortcuts to those folders will point to the new location linked with OneDrive for Business. The existing folder structure will still be in place, and the contents of those folders will remain in the original location. Similarly, if known folders are currently redirected to network shares, you will need to migrate data from that location to OneDrive for Business after you redirect the known folders to OneDrive for Business. Microsoft recommends scripts that use XCopy or Robocopy to perform this task.

You can only use this strategy if OneDrive files are being stored in the default location, which is %userprofile%\OneDrive - <TenantName>. If OneDrive for Business files are being stored in another location, you can't use the known folder redirection strategy.

As mentioned earlier, the known folder redirection strategy requires that computers be members of an Active Directory Domain Services Domain. The other step to take is to download and install the OneDrive for Business Group Policy objects onto a Domain Controller. The ADML and ADMX files are located in the OneDrive installation directory, %localappdata%\Microsoft\OneDrive\BuildNumber\adm\, of a computer with the OneDrive client installed. Redirecting known folders to OneDrive involves the following steps:

1. Open the Group Policy Management Editor and edit the policy that will apply to users whose folders you will redirect to OneDrive for Business.

2. Edit the User Configuration\Policies\Administrative Templates\OneDrive\Prevent users from changing the location of their OneDrive policy, and set it to enabled. This will block users from moving their OneDrive for Business folder.

3. Create a new environment variable using the User Configuration\Preferences\Windows Settings edit the Environment item and create a new Environment Variable named OneDriveSync that has the value %userprofile%\<SyncFolder>, where <SyncFolder> is the name of your default folder. An example is OneDrive – Adatum, as shown in Figure 1-49.

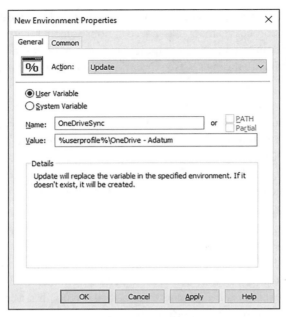

FIGURE 1-49 New environment setting

4. On the Common tab of the New Environment Properties dialog box, select Item-level targeting, click **Targeting**, click **New Item**, and then click **File Match**. Choose the Folder that exists from the Match type drop down, and in the Path box type **%userprofile%\<SyncFolder>**, where <SyncFolder> is the name of your OneDrive folder, as shown in Figure 1-50.

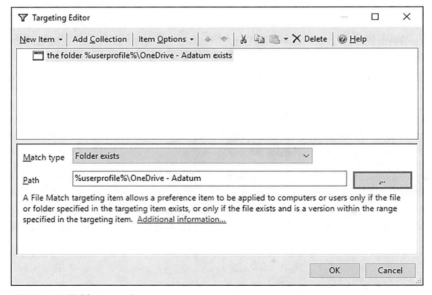

FIGURE 1-50 Folder targeting

5. Click **OK** twice to close the Targeting Editor dialog box and the New Environment Properties dialog box.

6. Edit the properties of the User Configuration\Policies\Windows Settings\Folder Redirection\Documents node, and choose Basic – Redirect Everyone's Folder To The Same Location. Under Target Folder Location, choose Redirect To The Following Location. In the Root Path box, type **%OneDriveSync%\Documents** option, as shown in Figure 1-51.

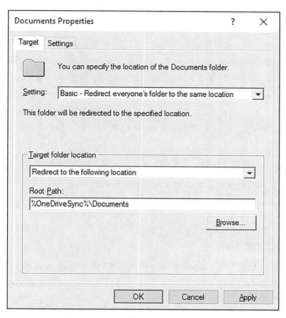

FIGURE 1-51 Document redirection policy

7. In the Settings tab, clear the Move The Contents Of Documents To The New Location check box. The reason you do this is that if there are files in both locations with the same name, you may lose data. If there are no files in the new location, you can leave this setting enabled and files will be migrated without the need for scripts.

8. Use this same process to redirect other known folders such as Pictures, Music, Videos, Downloads, and others.

MORE INFO **REDIRECTING FOLDERS**

You can learn more about Redirecting known folders to OneDrive for Business at:
https://docs.microsoft.com/onedrive/redirect-known-folders.

MORE INFO **MIGRATING ORGANIZATIONAL DATA TO OFFICE 365 ENTERPRISE**

You can learn more about migrating organizational data to Office 365 Enterprise:
https://docs.microsoft.com/office365/enterprise/migrate-data-to-office-365

Identify users and mailboxes to be migrated and method

Adopting Microsoft 365 and Office 365 provides organizations with the ability to determine whether all of the users and mailboxes that exist in the on-premises environment will be required in the cloud hosted environment. As is the case with the migration of data, there may also be regulatory and compliance reasons why certain mailboxes in a hybrid deployment must be kept on on-premises Exchange Servers, since the data that they host may need to be kept within specific national boundaries. This is, something that can be a challenge when deploying Microsoft 365 in countries that do not have Microsoft datacenters. Which users and mailboxes can be migrated will depend on the organization and its needs. Organizations must also keep in mind that user mailboxes in an Office 365 Enterprise E1 subscription cannot exceed 50 GB in size and that user mailboxes in an Office 365 Enterprise E3 and E5 subscription cannot exceed 100 GB in size. The Office 365 Enterprise E3 and E5 subscriptions allow archive mailboxes of unlimited size. Organizations that have users whose mailboxes exceed 100 GB in size may have to migrate some data to online archive mailboxes as they migrate those users to Exchange Online.

> **MORE INFO MIGRATING MAIL ACCOUNTS TO OFFICE 365**
>
> You can learn more about migrating email accounts to Office 365 Enterprise:
> *https://docs.microsoft.com/Exchange/mailbox-migration/mailbox-migration*

Remote move migration method

You use a remote move migration when you have an Exchange hybrid deployment. A hybrid deployment is where you have coexistence between an on-premises Exchange deployment and an Exchange Online deployment. You have to use a hybrid deployment and use the remote move migration method when you need to migrate more than 2,000 Exchange Server 2010, Exchange Server 2013, or Exchange Server 2016 mailboxes to Exchange Online.

With a hybrid deployment, you get the following advantages:

- User accounts are managed through your on-premises tools.
- Directory synchronization connects your on-premises Exchange organization with Exchange Online.
- Users are able to use single-sign on to access their mailbox whether the mailbox is hosted in the on-premises Exchange organization or Exchange Online.
- Email is routed securely between the on-premises Exchange deployment and Exchange Online.
- Free/busy calendar sharing between users with mailboxes hosted in the on-premises Exchange organization and mailboxes hosted in Exchange Online.

Prior to performing a remote move migration you need to ensure the following prerequisites are met:

- A hybrid deployment has already been configured between your on-premises Exchange organization and Exchange Online.

- You need to have been assigned the appropriate permissions. For mailbox moves in a hybrid deployment, this means that you need to have an account that is a member of the Organization Management, or the Recipient Management role groups.
- You need to have deployed the Mailbox Replication Proxy Service (MRSProxy) on all on-premises Exchange 2013 or Exchange 2016 Client Access servers.

Once these prerequisites have been met, you can move mailboxes from your on-premises Exchange deployment to Exchange Online by performing the following steps:

1. **Create migration endpoint**   Migration endpoints host connection settings for an on-premises Exchange server running the MRSProxy service.
2. **Enable MRSProxy service**   The MRSProxy service is hosted on on-premises Client Access servers. This service can be enabled using the Exchange Administration Console by selecting the Client Access server, editing the properties of the EWS virtual directory, and ensuring that the MRSProxy Enabled check box is selected.
3. **Move mailboxes**   You can move mailboxes using the Office 365 tab in EAC on the on-premises Exchange server by creating a new migration batch in Exchange Admin Console, or by using Windows PowerShell. When moving mailboxes, you move some, not all mailboxes, at a time in groups that are termed batches.
4. **Remove completed migration batches**   Once the migration of a batch is complete, remove the migration batch using Exchange Administration Center, or Windows PowerShell.
5. **Re-enable offline access for Outlook on the Web**   If users have been migrated from on-premises Exchange Server to Office 365, it is necessary to reset the offline access setting in their browser.

> *MORE INFO* **REMOTE MOVE MIGRATION**
>
> You can learn more about remote move migrations at:
> *https://docs.microsoft.com/exchange/hybrid-deployment/move-mailboxes.*

Staged migration method

In a staged migration, you migrate mailboxes from your on-premises Exchange organization to Office 365 in groups, termed batches. You select a staged migration in the following circumstances:

- Your organization has more than 2,000 on-premises mailboxes hosted in Exchange 2007. You can't use a staged migration to migrate Exchange 2010 or later mailboxes. It is also important to remember that Exchange 2007 is no longer publicly supported by Microsoft as of mid-2017, and requires a specific support agreement.
- Your organization intends to completely move its messaging infrastructure to Office 365.
- Your available migration period is in the timeframe of several weeks to several months.
- After migration completes, you still manage user accounts using on-premises management tools and have account synchronization performed with Azure Active Directory.
- The primary domain name used for your on-premises Exchange organization must be configured as a domain associated with the tenancy in Office 365.

Staged migration involves the following general steps:

1. You create a CSV file that includes a row for every user who has an on-premises mailbox that you want to migrate. This is not every user in the organization, just those who you will migrate in a particular batch.

2. Create a staged migration batch using Exchange Admin Center, or using Windows PowerShell.

3. Trigger the migration batch. Once the migration batch is triggered, Exchange Online performs the following steps:

   - Verify that directory synchronization is enabled and functioning. Directory synchronization migrates distribution groups, contacts, and mail enabled users.

   - Verify that a mail-enabled user exists in Office 365 for every user listed in the batch CSV file.

   - Convert the Office 365 mail-enabled user to an Exchange Online mailbox for each user in the migration batch.

   - Configure mail forwarding for the on-premises mailbox.

4. Once these steps have been completed, Exchange Online sends you a status report informing you of which mailboxes have migrated successfully and which mailboxes have not migrated successfully. Successfully migrated users can start using Exchange Online mailboxes.

5. Once migration is successful, you convert the mailboxes of successfully migrated on-premises users to mail-enabled users in the on-premises Exchange deployment.

6. You configure a new batch of users to migrate and delete the current migration batch.

7. Once all users have been migrated, the administrator assigns licenses to Office 365 users, configures MX records to point to Exchange Online, and creates an Autodiscover record that points to Office 365.

8. Decommission the on-premises Exchange deployment.

> **MORE INFO STAGED MIGRATION METHOD**
>
> You can learn more about staged migrations at: *https://docs.microsoft.com/exchange/mailbox-migration/what-to-know-about-a-staged-migration.*

Cutover migration method

In a cutover migration, all mailboxes in an on-premises Exchange deployment are migrated to Office 365 in a single migration batch. Cutover migrations migrate global mail contacts as well as distribution groups. Cutover migrations are suitable when:

- You intend all mailboxes to be hosted in Office 365 when the migration completes.
- You intend to manage user accounts using Office 365 tools.
- You want to perform the migration period in less than a week.
- Your organization has less than 2,000 mailboxes.

- Your on-premises messaging solution is Exchange Server 2010 or later.
- The primary domain name used for your on-premises Exchange organization must be configured as domain associated with the tenancy in Office 365.

You can perform a cutover migration using the Exchange Admin Center or by using Windows PowerShell.

The cutover migration method involves the following general steps:

1. An administrator creates empty mail-enabled security groups in Office 365.

2. An administrator connects Office 365 to the on-premises Exchange deployment. This is also termed creating a migration endpoint.

3. An administrator creates and starts a cutover migration batch using Exchange Admin Center or Windows PowerShell.

4. Once the migration batch is triggered, Exchange Online performs the following steps:
   - The address book of the on-premises Exchange deployment is queried to identify mailboxes, distribution groups, and contacts.
   - New Exchange Online mailboxes are provisioned.
   - Distribution groups and contacts are created within Exchange Online.
   - Mailbox data, including email messages, contacts, and calendar items, are migrated from each on-premises mailbox to the corresponding Exchange Online mailbox.

5. Exchange Online forwards the administrator a report providing statistics including the number of successful and failed migrations. The migration report includes automatically generated passwords for each new Exchange Online mailbox. Users are forced to change passwords the first time they sign in to Office 365.

6. Incremental synchronization occurs every 24 hours, updating Exchange Online with any new items created in the on-premises mailboxes.

7. Once migration issues have been resolved, the administrator changes the MX records to point to Exchange Online.

8. Once mail flow to Exchange Online has been successfully established, the administrator deletes the cutover migration batch. This terminates synchronization between the on-premises mailboxes and Office 365.

9. Administrator performs post migration tasks, including assigning Office 365 licenses, creating an Autodiscover DNS record, and decommissioning on-premises Exchange servers.

> **MORE INFO CUTOVER MIGRATION**
>
> You can learn more about cutover migrations at:
> *https://docs.microsoft.com/exchange/mailbox-migration/cutover-migration-to-office-365.*

Minimal Hybrid or Express Migration

Minimal hybrid or express migration is appropriate for organizations that are running Exchange 2010 or later, have a migration timetable that is shorter than a few weeks, and where your organization does not intend to have an ongoing directory service configuration. For example, this method is appropriate, where your organization intends to retire its on-premises Active Directory Domain Services infrastructure after migration is complete.

Performing a minimal hybrid migration involves performing the following steps:

1. In the Microsoft 365 console, add the domain that you use for your on-premises Exchange organization by configuring a TXT record (or by signing into GoDaddy if your organization uses that registrar) and verify that the TXT record is properly configured.

2. Sign into the Microsoft 365 account using global admin credentials and start the Exchange Hybrid Configuration Wizard from the Data Migration page under Setup in the Microsoft 365 admin console and connect to the on-premises Exchange Server organization. Choose the Minimal Hybrid Configuration.

3. Select the option to synchronize users and passwords one at a time. You will be prompted to install Azure AD Connect with the default options. Synchronization will occur once and then be turned off.

4. Configure Office 365 licenses for migrated users and then begin migrating user mailbox data.

5. Update DNS MX records to point away from the on-premises Exchange deployment to Exchange Online.

> **MORE INFO** **MINIMAL HYBRID MIGRATION**
>
> You can learn more about minimal hybrid migrations at: *https://docs.microsoft.com/exchange/mailbox-migration/use-minimal-hybrid-to-quickly-migrate*.

IMAP migration

IMAP migrations use the IMAP protocol to move the contents of on-premises user mailboxes to Exchange Online. IMAP migrations are suitable where the on-premises mail server is not running Exchange Server, but is instead running an alternate mail server solution.

IMAP migration is supported for the following on-premises messaging solutions:

- Courier-IMAP
- Cyrus
- Dovecot
- UW-IMAP

IMAP migrations involve the following general steps:

1. A tenant administrator creates Office 365 user accounts and assigns them Exchange Online user licenses. This provisions the user accounts with Exchange Online mailboxes.

2. The tenant administrator creates a CSV file. This CSV file includes a row for each on-premises user who will be migrated to Exchange Online using IMAP. This CSV file needs to include the passwords used by each on-premises IMAP mailbox user. It is recommended that you reset user passwords for on-premises IMAP mailbox users to simplify this process.

3. The administrator creates and then triggers an IMAP migration batch. This can be done using the Migration dashboard, available in the Data Migration blade under setup and shown in Figure 1-52, or through Windows PowerShell.

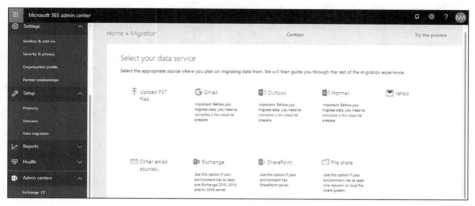

FIGURE 1-52 Select data service

4. Once the migration batch is initiated, the following occurs:
   - Exchange Online creates a migration request for each user in the CSV file.
   - Each migration request includes the credentials for the user in the on-premises IMAP messaging system.
   - Messages from each user's IMAP mailbox are copied to the corresponding Exchange Online mailbox until all data is migrated.

5. Exchange Online provides a status email to the administrator informing them of the status of the migration. This email contains statistics about the number of mailboxes successfully migrated, how many could not be migrated, and any error reports.

6. Exchange Online and the IMAP messaging system are synchronized every 24 hours to move any new messages from the on-premises environment to Exchange Online.

7. Once all migration issues have been resolved, the administrator updates MX records to point to Exchange Online. Once mail is flowing to Exchange Online, the administrator deletes the migration batches.

MORE INFO **IMAP MIGRATIONS TO EXCHANGE ONLINE**

You can learn more about IMAP migrations to Exchange Online at: *https://docs.microsoft.com/exchange/mailbox-migration/migrating-imap-mailboxes/migrating-imap-mailboxes.*

Migration comparison

Table 1-9 lists the difference between the different methods you can use to migrate from an on-premises messaging environment to Exchange Online.

TABLE 1-9 Migration type comparison

On-premises messaging environment	Number of mailboxes	Will user accounts be managed on-premises	Migration method
Exchange 2010 to Exchange 2019	Less than 2,000	No	Cutover migration
Exchange 2010	Less than 2,000	No	Staged migration
Exchange 2010	More than 2,000	Yes	Staged migration or remote move migration in hybrid deployment
Exchange 2010 or Exchange 2019	More than 2,000	Yes	Remote move migration in hybrid deployment
Non-Exchange on-premises messaging system	No maximum	Yes	IMAP migration

> **MORE INFO MAILBOX MIGRATION**
>
> You can learn more about mailbox migration at:
>
> *https://docs.microsoft.com/exchange/mailbox-migration/decide-on-a-migration-path*.

Plan migration of on-prem users and groups

Most organizations already have an on-premises identity solution that hosts user and groups accounts. These user and group accounts are stored in on-premises Active Directory Domain Services. When planning the migration of on-premises users and groups, you need to come to a determination about the following:

- Understanding user categories
- Understanding groups
- When bulk import is appropriate

It's also important to recognize that migration is different to hybrid coexistence. In a hybrid coexistence scenario your organization retains its on-premises Active Directory environment. In a migration scenario, your organization is moving from an on-premises Active Directory environment to having Azure AD host accounts, with the on-premises Active Directory environment decommissioned. While it is possible to use Azure AD Connect to synchronize accounts to Azure AD and then decommission your on-premises environment, that technique will be covered in Chapter 2 where you'll also learn more about Azure AD Connect and hybrid coexistence.

Understanding user categories

Not every user account in your organization's on-premises Active Directory instance is the same. While the vast majority of on-premises user accounts are used to sign on to workstations and access resources, a small number of accounts are used for different purposes, the most straightforward example being service accounts. Prior to performing a migration of accounts you should make the following determination:

- Is the user account still active? Unless your organization has an effective user deprovisioning strategy, it is likely that there will be accounts in Active Directory that are associated with people that are no longer employed by your organization. There is no reason to migrate inactive user accounts from an on-premises Active Directory environment to Microsoft 365.

- Should the account be migrated to Microsoft 365? Some user accounts exist for specific purposes, such as being used as service accounts or as administrative accounts for specific services or workloads that will not be migrated to Microsoft 365. Service accounts and accounts used for specific on-premises workloads are unlikely to be required once your organization migrates to Microsoft 365.

Using the bulk import process

If your organization is planning to completely migrate to Azure AD as the primary identity provider and to decommission Active Directory, you might choose to perform a bulk import of user accounts rather than attempt manual creation. If the organization that you are migrating only has a small number of users, it may be simpler to manually create those users using the Microsoft 365 administration tools. If you need to migrate a larger number where the manual creation process is both laborious and tedious, you may instead choose to perform a bulk import.

The bulk import process allows you to import a list of users from a specially formatted CSV file into Microsoft 365. This CSV file must have the following fields in the first row:

- User Name
- First Name
- Last Name
- Display Name
- Job Title
- Department
- Office Number
- Office Phone
- Mobile Phone
- Fax

- Address
- City
- State or Province
- ZIP or Postal Code
- Country or Region

Each of these fields must be on the first line and each must be separated by a comma. Both a sample and a blank CSV file can be downloaded from the Bulk Add Users page. Once you have populated the CSV file with the account information you want to import, complete this operation by performing the following steps:

1. In the Microsoft 365 Admin Center, click **On The Active Users** node under the **Users** node.

2. Click **More** and then click **Import Multiple Users**.

3. On the Select a CSV file page, shown in Figure 1-53, select the specially formatted file that has the user account information and click **Next**.

FIGURE 1-53 Select a CSV file

4. On the Import Multiple Users page, specify whether the users are allowed to sign in and access services. You will also need to specify the user location on this page. Choose which licenses are assigned, as shown in Figure 1-54.

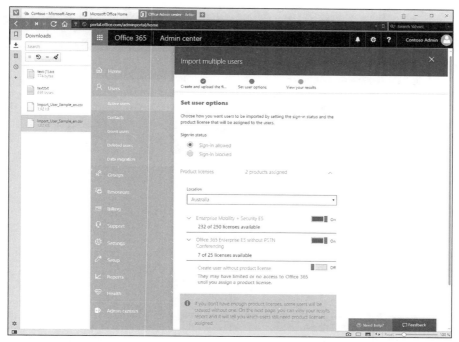

FIGURE 1-54 Import multiple users

5. On the Results page, you will see a list of users created and a list of temporary passwords assigned.

Using soft delete

Some accounts that you migrate to Microsoft 365 may not be necessary. Similarly, there may be user accounts created during the trial or pilot Microsoft 365 deployment that are no longer appropriate once existing user accounts are migrated to Office 365. There are several methods that you can use to delete Microsoft 365 user accounts. Whether the user account is permanently deleted, termed a "hard delete," or is moved to the Azure Active Directory Recycle Bin, termed a "soft delete," depends on the method used to delete the account.

You can use the following methods to delete a Microsoft 365 user account:

- Delete the user account from the Microsoft 365 admin portal. This involves navigating to the **Users** node, selecting the **Active Users** node, selecting the user that you want to delete, and selecting **Delete User** from the list of tasks associated with the user, as shown in Figure 1-55.

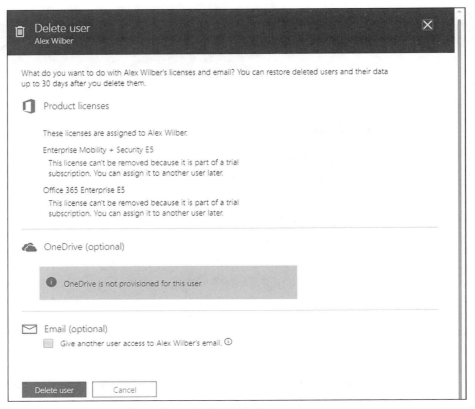

FIGURE 1-55 Delete a user from Microsoft 365 Admin Center

- Delete using the Remove-MsolUser cmdlet, located in the Azure Active Directory module for Windows PowerShell.
- User accounts can be deleted through the Exchange Admin Center in Exchange Online.
- If directory synchronization is configured, users can be deleted when removed from the on-premises Active Directory Directory Services instance.

You can view a list of soft deleted users in the Deleted Users section, under the Users area of the Microsoft 365 Admin Center as shown in Figure 1-56. Soft-deleted users remain visible for for 30 days and can be recovered during this period. After this period expires, the user account is deleted and is unrecoverable.

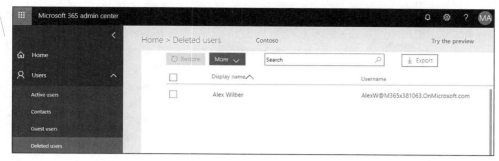

FIGURE 1-56 List of deleted Microsoft 365 users

To recover a soft deleted user, select the user account in the Deleted Users node of Microsoft 365 admin console and click **Restore**. When you restore an account, you'll be asked whether to auto-generate a new password for the user, assign a password yourself, and whether you want to have the user change their password when they sign on as shown in Figure 1-57.

FIGURE 1-57 Deleted user properties

> **MORE INFO DELETING USER ACCOUNTS IN MICROSOFT 365**
>
> You can learn more about deleting Microsoft 365 user accounts at: *https://docs.microsoft.com/azure/active-directory/active-directory-users-delete-user-azure-portal*.

Migrating Groups to Microsoft 365

On-premises groups come in a variety of types and scopes. For the purposes of migrating to Microsoft 365, group scope, which can include domain local, domain global, and universal, isn't relevant. This is because if you've chosen to migrate users to Azure Active Directory and decommission your organization's on-premises directory, you're unlikely to be concerned whether a group is visible in other domains in an Active Directory forest, simply because you are intending to retire that particular security construct.

Office 365 groups allow you to set up a collection of resources that a set of users can share. Resources might include a shared calendar, SharePoint Online document library, or a shared Exchange Online mailbox. Groups can be configured as public or private. Content in a public group is visible to anyone who has an account in the tenancy. Content in a private group is only visible to members of that group.

There are three methods through which Office 365 groups can be provisioned. These are as follows:

- **Open** The default method of provisioning O365 groups. Allows M365 users to create their own groups as needed.
- **IT-led** Users are able to request a group from IT.
- **Controlled** Group creation is limited to users that have been delegated the group creation role.

Each group can have one or more owners. Group owners have the ability to add or remove members as well as to perform basic group curation tasks. O365 groups have the following limits:

- A group can have up to 100 owners.
- A user can create up to 250 groups.
- A tenancy can have up to 500,000 groups.
- 1000 users can access a group conversation concurrently, though it is possible for a group to have more members.
- A user can be a member of 1000 groups.
- A group can store up to 1 terabyte of data with an additional 10 GB per subscribed users. It is possible to purchase additional storage for a group.
- A group mailbox has a size limit of 50 GB.

> **MORE INFO** **UNDERSTANDING OFFICE 365 GROUPS**
>
> You can learn more about Office 365 groups at: *https://support.office.com/article/learn-about-office-365-groups-b565caa1-5c40-40ef-9915-60fdb2d97fa2.*

Import PST files

Importing PST files to Office 365 mailboxes provides a method of moving an organization's existing email messages so that they are hosted in Exchange Online. The intelligent import feature allows you to filter which items stored in PST files will be imported into Exchange Online. Importing PST files also allows you to ensure that your organization is able to meet compliance obligations as organizational messages will be available for Discovery searches, something that is more challenging when email is stored on each person's individual computer in a separate

PST file. Importing PST files also ensures that a user has access to their existing messages no matter which device they use to interact with Exchange. If messages are stored in an offline PST file, and the user doesn't have access to the computer that hosts that PST file, they will not have access to those messages. PST files from Outlook 2007 and later can be imported to Exchange Online.

Network upload allows you to import PST files into Office 365. This can be done either by directly uploading the files or by shipping encrypted hard drives to Microsoft and having them import data directly. When you ship an encrypted hard drive to Microsoft, Microsoft will upload the data to Azure within 10 days of receiving the hard drive before returning the physical device to you.

To import PST files, perform the following steps:

1. Ensure that the Organization Management group is assigned the Mailbox Import Export role in Exchange Online.

2. In the **Data Governance** section of the **Security & Compliance** center, use the **Import** section, shown in Figure 1-58, to create a Shared Access Signature (SAS) key, also known as the SAS URL. This key provides the necessary permission and location to upload PST files to an Azure storage location. This location in Azure will be in the same region as your Microsoft 365 organization.

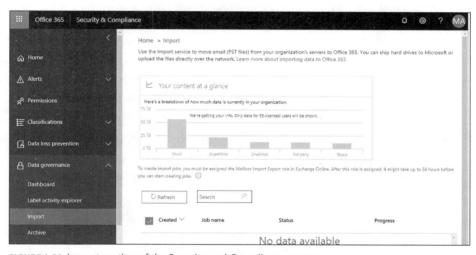

FIGURE 1-58 Import section of the Security and Compliance center

3. Download and install the PST import tools. One of these tools is the Azure AzCopy tool. Use AzCopy with the SAS URL to upload one or more PST files to Azure.

4. Once uploaded, review the list of PST files that have been successfully transferred to Office 365. You can do this with Azure Storage Explorer.

5. Create a mapping file that maps uploaded PST files to Office 365 mailboxes. This file must be in CSV format.

6. Create a PST import job from the Import page of the Security & Compliance center. You specify the mapping file when creating this job. You will be provided with an opportunity to configure a filter to control, which data is actually imported into mailboxes.

7. Run the job to import the data into the appropriate Office 365 mailboxes.

The user account that will create the import jobs in the Office 365 import service must be assigned the Mailbox Import Export role in Exchange Online. This role can be added to the Organization Management role group or it's possible to create a new role group and assign this role and then add user accounts to this group. In addition to having this role, the account used to perform this task must be assigned the Mail Recipients role in Exchange Online, available to the Organization Management and Recipient Management role groups, or be a global administrator for the Microsoft 365 organization.

PST files uploaded using the network upload method will be stored in an Azure blob container that is assigned the name ingestiondata. The PST files will remain in this blob storage for 30 days after the most recent import job has been created in the Security & Compliance Center. If you upload PST files using the network upload method, but do not create an import job within 30 days, the PST files will be deleted.

PST Import has the following additional caveats and characteristics:

- PST import occurs at approximately 24 GB per day, but jobs run in parallel. For example, importing 5 24 GB PST files will take approximately the same amount of time as importing 20 24 GB PST files.

- Multiple PST files can be imported to the same mailbox simultaneously.

- If a PST file stores any mailbox items that exceed 150 megabytes in size, those individual large items will not be imported into the Office 365 mailbox. Items smaller than 150 megabytes in size will still be imported, even though the larger items are skipped.

- Original message metadata isn't modified during the import process.

- Import is not supported where a PST files has more than 300 levels of nested folders.

- PST files can be imported into online archive mailboxes.

- PST files cannot be imported into Exchange Online public folders.

> **MORE INFO IMPORTING PST FILES**
>
> You can learn more about importing PST files into Office 365 mailboxes at:
> *https://docs.microsoft.com/office365/securitycompliance/importing-pst-files-to-office-365*

EXAM TIP

Remember the process that is used to import PST files into Exchange Online mailboxes

Thought experiment

In this thought experiment, demonstrate your skills and knowledge of the topics covered in this chapter. You can find answers to this thought experiment in the next section.

You have been asked to provide some advice to Fabrikam, a small manufacturing business that migrated to Microsoft 365. Fabrikam needs your advice because the person responsible for Fabrikam's IT recently left the company. During the process, they handed over the credentials of all their Microsoft 365 accounts to the CEO.

The CEO also reports to you that there have been license problems. The company initially purchased a 50-license subscription. Since then, 10 new users have been employed to replace 10 people who left the company over the last few months. The employees who departed still have Microsoft 365 accounts.

Fabrikam has signed up for a Microsoft 365 subscription and is currently using the tenant name Fabrikam.onmicrosoft.com. Fabrikam wants to assign their custom domain, Fabrikam.com, to Microsoft 365 and to have Microsoft DNS servers host this zone. With this information in mind, answer the following questions:

1. What kind of DNS record must be added to confirm ownership of the Fabrikam.com DNS zone?

2. Which DNS records must be modified to have Microsoft DNS servers host the Fabrikam.com DNS zone?

3. Describe the nature of at least one user account that will have global administrator rights for Fabrikam's Office 365 subscription.

4. What methods can be used to resolve the license conflicts?

Thought experiment answers

This section contains the solution to the thought experiment. Each answer explains why the answer choice is correct.

1. A TXT record must be added to confirm ownership of the Fabrikam.com DNS zone.

2. The NS records for the zone must be modified to allow Microsoft to host the Fabrikam.com DNS zone.

3. The first user account created for a subscription will be assigned global administrator privileges. This will be the user account of the IT staff member who recently left and who set up Microsoft 365.

4. The license conflict can be resolved by either manually removing licenses from the 10 users who have left the organization, or by deleting their user accounts.

Chapter summary

- When you create a Microsoft 365 subscription, the subscription tenancy is automatically assigned a custom onmicrosoft.com domain.

- No two organizations can share the same tenant name.

- The tenant name chosen at setup remains with the subscription over the course of the subscription's existence.

- You can assign a domain name that you own to the tenant so that you don't have to use the onmicrosoft.com tenant name.

- To use a domain with Microsoft 365, the DNS servers used as name servers for the domain need to support CNAME, SPF/TXT, SRV and MX Records.

- You can confirm ownership of a domain by configuring special TXT or MX records.

- Setting the default domain configures which domain suffix will automatically be used with Microsoft 365 user accounts.

- Changing the primary email address also changes the user name.

- You can perform a bulk email address update using PowerShell.

- Additional email addresses allow mailboxes to receive messages from more than a single address and can use any domain name associated with the organization's Microsoft 365 tenancy.

- A Microsoft 365 endpoint is an URL or IP address that hosts a specific Microsoft 365 or Office 365 service.

- Microsoft places each M365 and O365 endpoint into one of three categories: Optimize, Allow, and Default. Optimize requires minimum disruptions caused by latency and availability. Allow endpoints are less problematic, and Default endpoints do not require optimization.

- Privileged access management allows you to configure policies that apply just-in-time administrative principles to sensitive administrative roles.

- Cloud authentication occurs against Azure Active Directory. Use it with a password hash with a single sign-on and pass-through authentication with single sign-on.

- Federated authentication can occur using AD FS or a third party authentication provider.

- Mail reports allow you to view how Office 365 mailboxes are used.

- Usage reports allow you to view information about browsers, operating systems, and license consumption.

- Skype for Business reports allow you to see how Skype for Business is being used in the organization.

- SharePoint reports allow you to see how SharePoint is being used with the Office 365 subscription.

- Auditing reports allow you to view information about auditing of mailboxes, and mailbox litigation holds.

- Data Loss Prevention reports allow you to view how Data Loss Prevention rules, and policies are being applied to message traffic.

- The Service Health Dashboard is available from the Microsoft 365 Admin Center, allowing you to determine the status of the various elements of Microsoft 365, including fault history and planned maintenance.

- Users assigned the global administrator role have access to all administrative features.

- Users assigned the billing administrator role are able to make purchases, manage subscriptions, manage support tickets, and monitor service health.

- Users assigned the Helpdesk administrator (password administrator) role are able to reset the passwords of most Office 365 user accounts (except those assigned the global admin, service admin, or billing roles).

- Users assigned the service administrator role are able to manage service requests and monitor service health.

- You can assign and remove licenses by editing an Office 365 user's properties.

- Deleting a user removes all licenses assigned to that user.

- Pilot users should provide a representative sample of your organization.

- You can use the SharePoint Migration Tool to migrate on-premises SharePoint document libraries, lists and regular file shares to SharePoint Online.

- The OneDrive client you to drag and drop files on a client computer and have those files sync either with OneDrive for Business or SharePoint Online.

- You can use the bulk import method to import a CSV file of user identities into Azure AD.

CHAPTER 2

Manage user identity and roles

A key aspect of deploying Microsoft 365 is ensuring that user identity is configured properly. When this is done, users are able to seamlessly access resources in the on-premises environment, as well as in the Microsoft 365 environment. If it is not done correctly, users have to juggle different accounts, depending on whether the accessible resources are hosted locally or in the cloud. In this chapter you will learn about designing an identity strategy, how to plan identity synchronization with Azure AD Connect, how to manage that synchronization, how to manage Azure AD identities, and how to manage Azure AD user roles.

Skills in this chapter:

- Design identity strategy
- Plan identity synchronization by using Azure AD Connect
- Manage identity synchronization by using Azure AD Connect
- Manage Azure AD identities
- Manage user roles

Skill 2.1: Design identity strategy

This skill deals with designing a strategy related to on-premises and cloud based identity. To master this skill, you'll need to understand how to determine your organization's requirements when it comes to synchronization, what an appropriate identity management solution is, and what type of authentication solution is appropriate for your environment.

> **This section covers the following topics:**
> - Evaluate requirements and solution for synchronization
> - Evaluate requirements and solution for identity management
> - Evaluate requirements and solution for authentication

Evaluate requirements and solution for synchronization

Synchronization is the process of replicating on-premises identities, such as users and groups, into the cloud. Synchronization is only necessary where an on-premises identity provider is present. In some synchronization models, every on-premises identity is replicated to the cloud. In other models, only a subset of the on-premises identities are replicated.

Another consideration in evaluating synchronization requirements is determining what information about a user's identity needs to be synchronized to the cloud. Depending on the model chosen, some, or all of the properties of those on-premises identities, can be replicated. For example, some organizations store sensitive private data about employees within Active Directory. Only replicating what is necessary is especially important given the increasing regulation of data involving personal information.

Should an organization choose, it is possible to perform a complete replication of every aspect of an Active Directory object to the cloud. For example, an organization can deploy a domain controller, SharePoint Farm, System Center, and Exchange Server in Azure IaaS VMs. You can have those VMs connected via VPN or an ExpressRoute connection to an on-premises Active Directory instance. In this scenario, the Azure IaaS VMs would essentially function as an expensive branch office site running in the Azure cloud.

When evaluating requirements and a solution for synchronization, consider the following questions:

- Which identities need to be replicated to the cloud?
- How often do those identities need to be replicated to the cloud?
- What properties of those identities need to be replicated to the cloud?

Which identities to replicate?

Deployment of Microsoft 365 gives organizations an ability to assess their existing identity needs. If an organization has been using Active Directory for a long time, it's likely that objects don't need to be replicated to the cloud, and probably don't need to be in the on-premises Active Directory instance. It's a good idea, prior to implementing any Microsoft 365 replication scheme, to do a thorough audit of all of the objects that are present within the on-premises directory, and to clean out those that are no longer required or necessary.

Another issue to address is whether every on-premises identity needs to be present in Azure Active Directory. Many organizations take a phased approach to the introduction of Microsoft 365, migrating small groups of users to the service rather than every user in the organization all at once. Users that are only present in the on-premises directory service won't need to have Microsoft 365 licenses assigned to them.

There are also special account types that are commonly present in an on-premises Active Directory instance that do not need to be replicated, or simply cannot be replicated , to Azure Active Directory. For example, there is no need to replicate service accounts or accounts that are used for specific administrative purposes for on-premises resources, such as the management of an on-premises SQL Server database server or other workload.

Another challenge to consider is that many on-premises environments are more complicated than a single Active Directory domain. Some organizations have multi-domain Active Directory forests and, as it is a recommended Microsoft secure administrative practice, an increasing number of large organizations have multi-forest deployments such as having an Enhanced Security Administrative Environment (ESAE) forest to store privileged accounts for the production forest.

User accounts are not the only identity that an organization may wish to replicate to the cloud. It may be necessary to replicate some groups to the cloud because these groups may be useful in mediating access to Microsoft 365 workloads. For example, if your organization already has a local security group that is used to collect together members of the accounting team, you may want that group also present as a method of mediating access to resources and workloads within Microsoft 365.

How often to replicate?

When evaluating requirements and a solution for synchronization, you need to answer several important questions. For example, how often do the properties of an on-premises identity change and how soon must those changes be present within Azure Active Directory?

You don't want a user who changes their password to have to wait 24 hours before that new password can be used against cloud identities. Similarly, if you deprovision a user account because a person's employment with the organization has been terminated, you'll want that action to be reflected in limiting access to Microsoft 365 workloads, rather than the user account having continued access for some time after their on-premises identity has been disabled.

While there can be bandwidth considerations around identity synchronization, the majority of such traffic is going to be the replication of changes, also known as "delta," rather than constant replications of the entire identity database. The amount of bandwidth consumed by delta identity synchronization traffic is often insignificant compared to the bandwidth consumed by other Microsoft 365 workloads and services.

Which properties to replicate?

Active Directory has been present at some organizations for almost two decades. One of the original selling points of Active Directory was that it could store far more information than just usernames and passwords. Because of this, many organizations use Active Directory to store a substantive amount of information about personnel, including information about telephone numbers, position within the organization, and which branch office the user may be located at.

When considering a synchronization solution, determine which on-premises Active Directory attribute information needs to be replicated to Azure Active Directory. For example, you may have an application running in Azure that needs access to the Job Title, Department, Company, and Manager attributes, as shown in Figure 2-1.

FIGURE 2-1 Which attributes to replicate

Evaluate requirements and solution for identity management

Evaluating the requirements and solution for identity management first involves determining what your organization's source of authority is. The source of authority is the directory service that functions as the primary location for the creation and management of user and group accounts. You can choose between having an on-premises Active Directory instance function as a source of authority, or you can have Azure Active Directory function as the source of authority.

Even though Azure Active Directory is present in a hybrid deployment, the source of authority will be the on-premises Azure AD Instance. Hybrid deployment accounts are used for authentication and authorization purposes with existing on-premises resources as well as Microsoft 365 workloads.

Source of authority is a very important concept when it comes to creating users and groups in an environment where Azure AD Connect is configured to synchronize an on-premises Active Directory with the Azure Active Directory instance that supports the Microsoft 365 tenancy. When you create a user or group in the on-premises Active Directory instance, the on-premises Active Directory instance retains authority over that object. Objects created within the on-premises Active Directory instance that are within the filtering scope of objects synchronized via Azure AD Connect will replicate to the Azure Active Directory instance that supports the Microsoft 365 tenancy.

Newly created on-premises user and group objects will only be present within the Azure Active Directory instance that supports the Microsoft 365 tenancy after synchronization has occurred. You can force synchronization to occur using the Azure AD Connect Synchronization Service Manager tool.

Evaluate requirements and solution for authentication

When evaluating authentication requirements, determine if your organization wants to still rely upon the traditional combination of username and password, or if you want to move toward more sophisticated and secure authentication techniques, such as multi-factor authentication. When making this determination, many organizations will decide that more secure technologies are appropriate for sensitive accounts, such as those used for administrative tasks, and that the traditional method of username and password will be sufficient for the majority of standard users.

Microsoft and Office 365 support a technology known as Modern Authentication. Modern Authentication provides a more secure authentication and authorization method than traditional authentication methods. Modern Authentication can be used with Microsoft 365 hybrid deployments that include Exchange Online and Teams. All Office and Microsoft 365 tenancies created after August 2017 that include Exchange Online have Modern Authentication enabled by default. Modern Authentication includes a combination of the following authentication and authorization methods, as well as secure access polices:

- **Authentication methods** Multi-factor authentication, Client Certificate-based authentication, and Active Directory Authentication Library (ADAL).
- **Authorization methods** Microsoft's implementation of OAuth (Open Authorization).
- **Conditional access policies** Mobile Application Management (MAM) and Azure Active Directory Conditional access.

MORE INFO **HYBRID MODERN AUTHENTICATION**

You can learn more about Hybrid Modern Authentication at the following address: *https://docs.microsoft.com/office365/enterprise/hybrid-modern-auth-overview.*

Meeting the Azure AD Connect installation requirements

Prior to installing Azure AD Connect, you should ensure that your environment, Azure AD Connect computer, and account used to configure Azure AD Connect meets the software, hardware, and privilege requirements. So, you need to ensure that your Active Directory environment is configured at the appropriate level, that the computer on which you will run Azure AD Connect has the appropriate software and hardware configuration, and that the account used to install Azure AD Connect has been added to the appropriate security groups.

MORE INFO **AZURE AD CONNECT PREREQUISITES**

You can learn more about Azure AD Connect prerequisites at the following address: *https://docs.microsoft.com/azure/active-directory/connect/active-directory-aadconnect-prerequisites.*

Azure AD and Office 365 requirements

Before you can install and configure Azure AD Connect, you need to ensure that you have configured an additional domain for Office 365. By default, an Azure AD tenant will allow 50,000 objects, however, when you add and verify an additional domain, this limit increases to 300,000 objects. If you require more than 300,000 objects in your Azure AD instance, you can open a support ticket with Microsoft. If you require more than 500,000 objects in your Azure AD instance, you'll need to acquire an Azure AD Premium or Enterprise Mobility and Security license.

On-premises Active Directory environment requirements

Azure AD Connect requires that the on-premises Active Directory environment be configured at the Windows Server 2003 forest functional level or higher. Forest functional level is dependent on the minimum domain functional level of any domain in a forest. For example, if you have five domains in a forest, with four of them running at the Windows Server 2012 R2 domain functional level, and one of them running at the Windows Server 2003 domain functional level, then Windows Server 2003 will be the maximum forest functional level. As Windows Server 2003 is no longer supported by Microsoft without a custom support agreement, your organization should have domain controllers at least running Windows Server 2008. Microsoft security best practice is to have domain controllers deployed with Microsoft's most recent version of the server operating system, so in theory you should have domain controllers running Windows Server 2016 or later. To support the Azure AD Connect password writeback functionality, you'll either need domain controllers running Windows Server 2008 R2 or Windows Server 2008 with all service packs applied as well as hotfix KB2386717.

You can check the forest functional level using the Active Directory Domains and Trusts console. To do this, perform the following steps:

1. Open the Active Directory Domains and Trusts console.

2. Select the Active Directory Domains and Trusts node.

3. On the Actions menu, click **Raise Forest Functional Level**.

4. The dialog box displays the current functional level and, if possible, provides you with the option of upgrading the forest functional level. Figure 2-2 shows the forest functional level configured at Windows Server 2012 R2, which is the highest possible forest functional level for an organization where all domain controllers are running the Windows Server 2012 R2 operating system. If all the domain controllers are running the Windows Server 2016 operating system, it is possible to raise the domain and forest functional level to Windows Server 2016.

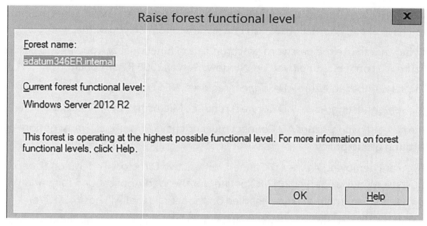

FIGURE 2-2 Forest functional level

You can also check the forest functional level by using the following Microsoft PowerShell command:

```
(Get-ADForest).ForestMode
```

Azure AD Connect Server requirements

Azure AD Connect is software that you install on a computer that manages the process of synchronizing objects between the on-premises Active Directory and the Azure Active Directory instance that supports the Microsoft 365 tenancy. You can install Azure AD Connect on computers running the following operating systems:

- Windows Server 2008 (x86 and x64)
- Windows Server 2008 R2 (x64)

- Windows Server 2012 (x64)
- Windows Server 2012 R2 (x64)
- Windows Server 2016 (x64)
- Windows Server 2019 (x64)

Azure AD Connect cannot be installed on Windows Server 2003. Given how Windows Server 2003 is no longer supported by Microsoft, and you are a diligent administrator, you will of course not have Windows Server 2003 in your environment.

Azure AD Connect has the following requirements:

- Must be installed on a Windows Server instance that has the GUI version of the operating system installed. You cannot install Azure AD connect on a computer running the Server Core operating system.
- You can deploy Azure AD Connect on a computer that is either a domain controller, a member server or, if you use the custom options, a standalone server.
- If installing on versions of Windows Server prior to Windows Server 2012, ensure that all service packs, updates, and relevant hotfixes are applied. As a diligent administrator, you have already done this so it isn't necessary to remind you of this.
- If you want to use the password synchronization functionality, you need to ensure that Azure AD connect is deployed on Windows Server 2008 R2 SP1 or later.
- The server hosting Azure AD Connect requires .NET Framework 4.5.1 or later.
- The server hosting Azure AD Connect requires Microsoft PowerShell 3.0 or later.
- The server hosting Azure AD Connect must not have PowerShell Transcription enabled through group policy.
- If you are deploying Azure AD Connect with Active Directory Federation Services, you must use Windows Server 2012 R2 or later for the Web Application Proxy, and Windows remote management must be enabled on the servers that will host AD FS roles.
- If global administrators will have multi factor authentication enabled (MFA), then the URL *https://secure.aadcdn.microsoftonline-p.com* must be configured as a trusted site.

Connectivity requirements

The computer with Azure AD Connect installed must be a member of a domain in the forest that you want to synchronize, and must have connectivity to a writable domain controller in each domain of the forest you wish to synchronize on the following ports:

- **DNS**   TCP/UDP Port 53
- **Kerberos**   TCP/UDP Port 88
- **RPC**   TCP Port 135
- **LDAP**   TCP/UDP Port 389
- **SSL**   TCP Port 443
- **SMB**   TCP 445

The computer with Azure AD Connect installed must be able to establish communication with the Microsoft Azure servers on the Internet over TCP port 443. The computer with Azure AD Connect installed can be located on an internal network as long as it can initiate communication on TCP port 443. The computer hosting Azure AD Connect does not need a publicly routable IP address. The computer hosting Azure AD Connect always initiates synchronization communication to Microsoft Azure. Microsoft Azure Active Directory does not initiate synchronization communication to the computer hosting Azure AD Connect on the on-premises network.

While you can install Azure AD Connect on a domain controller, Microsoft recommends that you deploy Azure AD Connect on a computer that does not host the domain controller role. If you are going to be replicating more than 50,000 objects, Microsoft recommends that you deploy SQL Server on a computer that is separate from the computer that will host Azure AD Connect. If you plan to host the SQL Server instance on a separate computer, ensure that communication is possible between the computer hosting Azure AD Connect and the computer hosting the SQL Instance on TCP port 1433.

If you are going to use a separate SQL Server instance, ensure that the account used to install and configure Azure AD Connect has "systems administrator" rights on the SQL instance, and that the service account used for Azure AD Connect has "public" permissions on the Azure AD Connect database.

Hardware requirements

The hardware requirements of the computer that hosts Azure AD Connect depend upon the number of objects in the Active Directory environment that you need to sync. The greater the number of objects that you need to sync, the steeper the hardware requirements. Table 2-1 provides a guide to the requirements, with all configurations requiring at least a 1.6 GHz processor.

TABLE 2-1 Azure AD Connect computer hardware requirements

Number of objects in Active Directory	Memory	Storage
Fewer than 10,000	4 GB	70 GB
10,000–50,000	4 GB	70 GB
50,000–100,000	16 GB	100 GB
100,000–300,000	32 GB	300 GB
300,000–600,000	32 GB	450 GB
More than 600,000	32 GB	500 GB

It's important to note that during the planning phase, a new Microsoft 365 tenancy has a limit of 50,000 objects. However, once the first domain is verified, this limit is increased to 300,000 objects. Organizations that need to store more than 300,000 objects in an Azure

Active Directory instance that supports an Microsoft 365 tenancy should contact Microsoft Support.

SQL Server requirements

When you deploy Azure AD connect, you have the option of having Azure AD Connect install a SQL Server Express instance, or you can choose to have Azure AD Connect leverage a full instance of SQL Server. SQL Server Express is limited to a maximum database size of 10 GB. In terms of Azure AD Connect, this means that Azure AD Connect is only able to manage 100,000 objects. This is likely to be adequate for all but the largest environments.

For environments that require Azure AD Connect to manage more than 100,000 objects, you'll need to have Azure AD Connect leverage a full instance of SQL Server. Azure AD Connect can use all versions of Microsoft SQL Server, from Microsoft SQL Server 2008 with the most recent service pack through to SQL Server 2017. It is important to note that SQL Azure is not supported as a database for Azure AD Connect. If deploying a full instance of SQL Server to support Azure AD Connect, ensure that the following prerequisites are met:

- **Use a case-insensitive SQL collation** Case insensitive collations have the _CI_ identifier included in their name. Case sensitive collations (those that use the _CS_ designation) are not supported for use with Azure AD Connect.

- **You can only use one sync engine per SQL instance** If you have an additional Azure AD Connect sync engine, or if you are using Microsoft Identity Manager in your environment, each sync engine requires its own separate SQL instance.

Installation account requirements

The accounts that you use to install and configure Azure AD Connect have the following requirements:

- The account used to configure Azure AD Connect must have the Administrator permission in the Microsoft 365 tenant. If you create a service account in Microsoft 365 to use in place of the account with tenant administrator permissions, ensure to configure the account with a password that does not expire.

- The account used to install and configure Azure AD Connect must have Enterprise Administrator permissions within the on-premises Active Directory forest if you will be using express installation settings. This account is only required during installation and configuration. Once Azure AD Connect is installed and configured, this account no longer needs Enterprise Administrator permissions. Best practice is to create a separate account for Azure AD Connect installation and configuration and to temporarily add this account to the Enterprise Admins group during the installation and configuration process. Once Azure AD Connect is installed and configured, this account can be removed from the Enterprise Admins group. You should not attempt to change the account used after Azure AD Connect is setup and configured, since Azure AD Connect always attempts to run using the original account.

■ The account used to install and configure Azure AD Connect must be a member of the local Administrators group on the computer on which Azure AD Connect is installed.

Installing Azure AD Connect

Installing Azure AD Connect with express settings is appropriate if your organization has a single Active Directory forest and you wish to use password synchronization for authentication. The Azure AD Connect express settings are appropriate for most organizations. To obtain Azure AD connect, download it from the following website: *https://www.microsoft.com/download/details.aspx?id=47594.*

To install Azure AD Connect with Express settings, perform the following steps:

1. Double click on the AzureADConnect.msi file that you've downloaded from the Microsoft download center and click **Run** on the security warning shown in Figure 2-3.

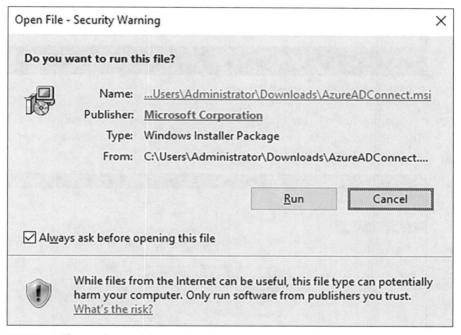

FIGURE 2-3 File security warning

2. Azure AD Connect will be installed on your computer. When the installation is complete, you will be presented with the splash screen. You must agree to the license terms and privacy notice as shown in Figure 2-4 and then click Continue.

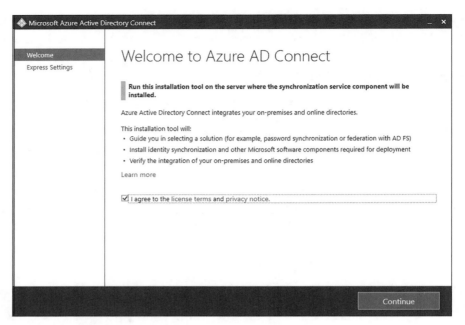

FIGURE 2-4 Welcome to Azure AD Connect

3. If your organization has an internal non-routable domain it will be necessary for you to use custom settings. Figure 2-5 shows the non-routable domain epistemicus.internal in use. To use custom settings, click Customize.

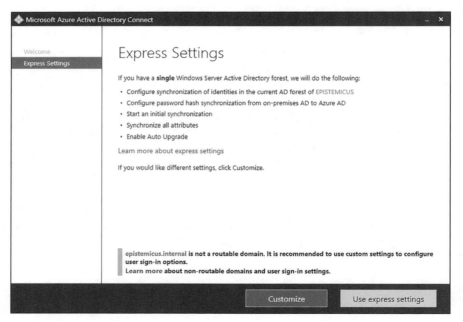

FIGURE 2-5 Express settings

4. On the Install Required Components page, shown in Figure 2-6, choose between the following options.

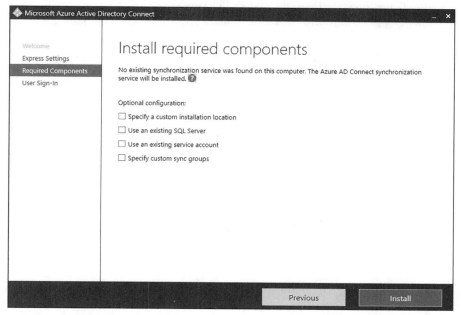

FIGURE 2-6 Install Required Components

- **Specify a custom installation location** Choose this option if you want to install Azure AD Connect in a separate location, such as on another volume.

- **Specify an existing SQL Server** Choose this option if you want to specify an alternate SQL server instance. By default, Azure AD Connect will install a SQL Server Express instance.

- **Use an existing service account** You can configure Azure AD Connect to use an existing service account. By default, Azure AD Connect will create a service account. You can configure Azure AD Connect to use a Group Managed Service account if you are installing Azure AD Connect on a computer running Windows Server 2012 or later. You'll need to use an existing service account if you are using Azure AD Connect with a remote SQL Server instance or if communication with Azure will occur through a proxy server that requires authentication.

- **Specify custom sync groups** When you deploy Azure AD Connect, it will create four local groups on the server that hosts the Azure AD Connect Instance. These groups are the Administrators group, Operators group, Password Reset group, and the Browse group. If you want to use your own set of groups, you can specify them here. These groups must be local to the host server and not a member of the domain.

5. Once you have specified which custom options you require, and you can select none if you want, but you have to perform a custom installation because you have a non-routable domain on-premises, click Install.

6. On the User sign-in page, shown in Figure 2-7, specify what type of sign on you want to allow. You can choose between the following options, the details of which were covered earlier in this chapter, with most organizations choosing password synchronization as this is the most straightforward:

    ■ Password Synchronization

    ■ Pass-through authentication

    ■ Federation with AD FS

    ■ Federation with PingFederate

    ■ Do not configure

    ■ Enable single sign-on

FIGURE 2-7 User sign-in options

7. On the Connect To Azure AD page, provide the credentials of a global admin account. Microsoft recommends you use an account in the default onmicrosoft.com domain associated with the Azure AD instance you will be connecting to. If you choose the Federation with AD FS option, ensure that you do not sign in using an account in a domain that you will enable for federation. Figure 2-8 shows sign-in with a password synchronization scenario.

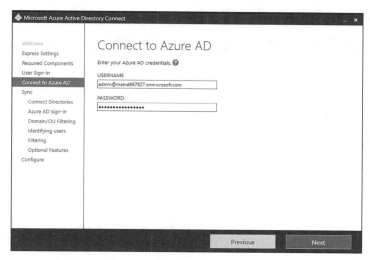

FIGURE 2-8 Connect to Azure AD

8. Once Azure AD Connect has connected to Azure AD, you will be able to specify the directory type to synchronize as well as the forest. Click Add Directory to add a specify forest. When you add a forest by clicking Add Directory, you will need to specify the credentials of an account that will perform periodic synchronization. Unless you are certain that you have applied the minimum necessary privileges to an account, you should provide Enterprise Administrator credentials and allow Azure AD Connect to create the account as shown in Figure 2-9. This will ensure that the account is only assigned the privileges necessary to perform synchronization tasks.

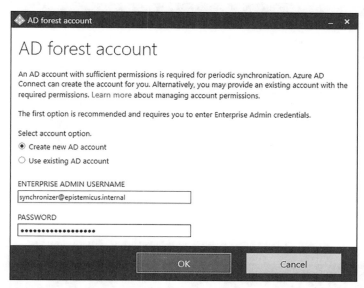

FIGURE 2-9 AD Forest Account

9. Once the credentials have been verified, as shown in Figure 2-10, click **Next**.

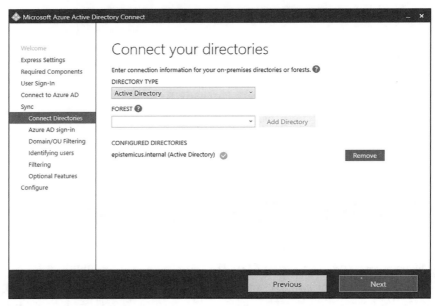

FIGURE 2-10 Connect Your Directories

10. On the Azure AD Sign-In configuration page, shown in Figure 2-11, review the UPN suffix and then inspect the on-premises attribute to use as the Azure AD username. You'll need to ensure that accounts use a routable Azure AD username.

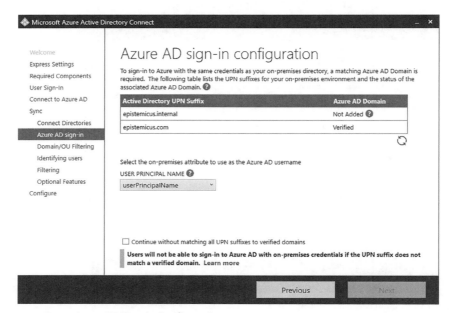

FIGURE 2-11 Azure AD Sign-In Configuration

11. On the Domain And OU Filtering page, shown in Figure 2-12, select whether you want to sync all objects, or just objects in specific domains and OUs.

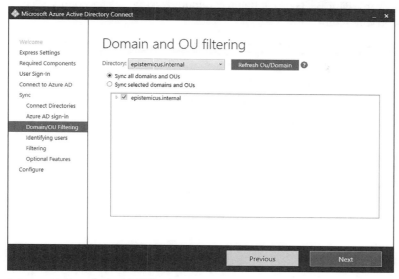

FIGURE 2-12 Domain And OU Filtering

12. On the Uniquely Identifying Users page, shown in Figure 2-13, specify how users are to be identified. By default users should only have one representation across all directories. In the event that users exist in multiple directories, you can have matches identified by a specific active directory attribute, with the default being the mail attribute.

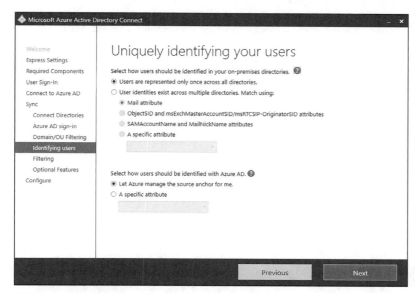

FIGURE 2-13 Uniquely Identifying Users

13. On the Filter Users And Devices page, specify whether you want to synchronize all users and devices, or only members of a specific group. Figure 2-14 shows members of the Microsoft 365-Pilot-Users group being configured so that their accounts will be synchronized with Azure.

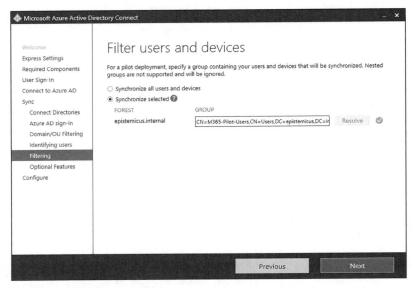

FIGURE 2-14 Filter Users And Devices

14. On the Optional Features page, shown in Figure 2-15, select any optional features that you want to configure. These features include the following.

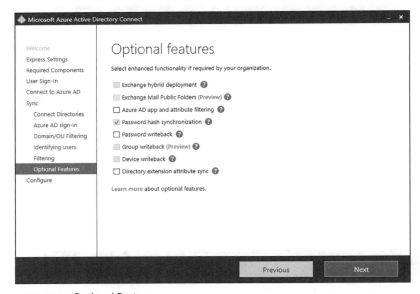

FIGURE 2-15 Optional Features

- Exchange hybrid deployment
- Exchange Mail Public Folders
- Azure AD app and attribute filtering
- Password synchronization
- Password writeback
- Group writeback
- Device writeback
- Directory extension attribute sync

15. On the Ready To Configure page, shown in Figure 2-16, you can choose to start synchronization or to enable staging mode, where synchronization will prepare to be run, but will not synchronize any data with Azure AD.

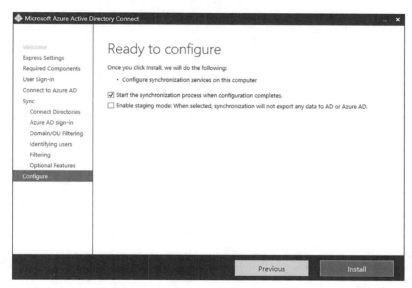

FIGURE 2-16 Ready To Configure

> **MORE INFO   AZURE AD CONNECT CUSTOM INSTALLATION**
>
> To install Azure AD Connect with the custom settings, consult the following article:
> *https://docs.microsoft.com/azure/active-directory/connect/active-directory-aadconnect-get-started-custom.*

Identifying synchronized attributes

Azure AD Connect synchronizes some, but not all, attributes from the on-premises Active Directory instance to Azure Active Directory instance that supports a Microsoft 365 tenancy.

143 separate attributes synchronize, depending on whether the object is a user account, a group account, or a mail enabled contact object. These attributes are as listed in Table 2-2.

TABLE 2-2 List of attributes synchronized by Azure AD Connect

accountEnabled	MsExchArchiveGUID	msExchTeamMailboxOwners
Assistant	MsExchArchiveName	msExchTeamMailboxSharePointLinkedBy
altRecipient	msExchArchiveStatus	msExchTeamMailboxSharePointUrl
authoring	msExchAssistantName	msExchUCVoiceMailSettings
C	msExchAuditAdmin	msExchUsageLocation
Cn	msExchAuditDelegate	msExchUserHoldPolicies
Co	msExchAuditDelegateAdmin	msOrg-IsOrganizational
company	msExchAuditOwner	msRTCSIP-ApplicationOptions
countryCode	MsExchBlockedSendersHash	msRTCSIP-DeploymentLocator
department	msExchBypassAudit	msRTCSIP-Line
description	MsExchBypassModerationFromDLMembersLink	msRTCSIP-OwnerUrn
displayName	MsExchBypassModerationLink	msRTCSIP-PrimaryUserAddress
dLMemRejectPerms	msExchCoManagedByLink	msRTCSIP-UserEnabled
dLMemSubmitPerms	msExchDelegateListLink	msRTCSIP-OptionFlags
ExtensionAttribute1	msExchELCExpirySuspensionEnd	objectGUID
ExtensionAttribute10	msExchELCExpirySuspensionStart	oOFReplyToOriginator
ExtensionAttribute11	msExchELCMailboxFlags	otherFacsimileTelephone
ExtensionAttribute12	MsExchEnableModeration	otherHomePhone
ExtensionAttribute13	msExchExtensionCustomAttribute1	otherIpPhone
ExtensionAttribute14	msExchExtensionCustomAttribute2	otherMobile
ExtensionAttribute15	msExchExtensionCustomAttribute3	otherPager
ExtensionAttribute2	msExchExtensionCustomAttribute4	otherTelephone
ExtensionAttribute3	msExchExtensionCustomAttribute5	pager
ExtensionAttribute4	MsExchGroupDepartRestriction	photo
ExtensionAttribute5	MsExchGroupJoinRestriction	physicalDeliveryOfficeName
ExtensionAttribute6	msExchHideFromAddressLists	postalCode
ExtensionAttribute7	MsExchImmutableID	postOfficeBox
ExtensionAttribute8	msExchLitigationHoldDate	PreferredLanguage
ExtensionAttribute9	msExchLitigationHoldOwner	proxyAddresses
Facsimiletelephone number	MsExchMailboxGuid	PublicDelegates

TABLE 2-2 *Continued*

givenName	msExchMailboxAuditEnable	pwdLastSet
GroupType	msExchMailboxAuditLogAgeLimit	reportToOriginator
hideDLMembership	MsExchModeratedByLink	ReportToOwner
homephone	MsExchModerationFlags	samAccountName
Info	MsExchRecipientDisplayType	sn
Initials	msExchRecipientTypeDetails	St
ipPhone	MsExchRemoteRecipientType	streetAddress
L	msExchRequireAuthToSendTo	targetAddress
legacyExchangeDN	MsExchResourceCapacity	TelephoneAssistant
Mail	MsExchResourceDisplay	telephoneNumber
mailnickname	MsExchResourceMetaData	thumbnailphoto
managedBy	MsExchResourceSearchProperties	title
Manager	msExchRetentionComment	unauthOrig
Member	msExchRetentionURL	url
middleName	MsExchSafeRecipientsHash	userAccountControl
Mobile	MsExchSafeSendersHash	userCertificate
msDS-HABSeniorityIndex	MsExchSenderHintTranslations	UserPrincipalName
msDS-PhoneticDisplayName	msExchTeamMailboxExpiration	userSMIMECertificate

> **MORE INFO** **ATTRIBUTES SYNCHRONIZED BY AZURE AD CONNECT**
>
> You can learn more about which attributes are synchronized by Azure AD Connect at *https://docs.microsoft.com/azure/active-directory/connect/active-directory-aadconnectsync-attributes-synchronized*.

EXAM TIP

Remember the Azure AD Connect prerequisites.

Skill 2.2: Plan identity synchronization by using Azure AD Connect

This skill section deals with planning the implementation of identity synchronization using Azure AD Connect as the synchronization solution. To master this skill, you'll need to understand some of the information you learned about in the previous skill as well as how to implement an appropriate Azure AD Connect sign-on option.

Azure Active Directory Connect

Azure AD Connect is designed to streamline the process of configuring connections between on-premises deployment and an Azure AD instance. The Azure Active Directory Connect tool is designed to make the process of configuring synchronization between an on-premises Active Directory deployment and Azure Active Directory as frictionless as possible.

Azure Active Directory Connect can automatically configure and install simple password synchronization or Federation / Single Sign-on, depending on your organizational needs. When you choose the Federation with AD FS option, Active Directory Federation Services is installed and configured, as well as a Web Application Proxy server to facilitate communication between the on-premises AD FS deployment and Microsoft Azure Active Directory.

The Azure Active Directory Connect tool supports the following optional features, as shown in Figure 2-17:

- **Exchange hybrid deployment**   This option is suitable for organizations that have an Office 365 deployment, where there are mailboxes hosted both on-premises and in the cloud.

- **Exchange mail public folders**   This feature allows organizations to synchronize mail-enabled public folder objects from an on-premises Active Directory environment to Microsoft 365.

- **Azure AD app and attribute filtering**   Selecting this option gives you the ability to be more selective about which attributes are synchronized between the on-premises environment and Azure AD.

- **Password synchronization**   Synchronizes a hash of the user's on-premises password Azure AD. When the user authenticates to Azure AD, the submitted password is hashed using the same process and if the hashes match, the user is authenticated. Each time the user updates their password on-premises, the updated password hash synchronizes to Azure AD.

- **Password writeback**   Password writeback allows users to change their passwords in the cloud and have the changed password written back to the on-premises Active Directory instance.

- **Group writeback**   Changes made to groups in Azure AD are written back to the on-premises AD instance.

- **Device writeback**   Information about devices registered by the user in Azure AD is written back to the on-premises AD instance.

- **Directory extension attribute sync** Allows you to extend Azure AD schema based on extensions made to your organization's on-premises Active Directory instance.

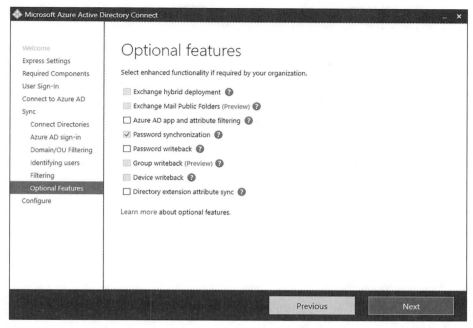

FIGURE 2-17 Azure Active DirectorF02xx17.

MORE INFO **AZURE ACTIVE DIRECTORY CONNECT**

You can learn more about Azure Active Directory Connect at *https://docs.microsoft.com/azure/active-directory/connect/active-directory-aadconnect*.

Cleaning up existing Active Directory objects

Before you deploy Azure AD Connect, it is prudent to ensure that your on-premises Active Directory environment is healthy. You should also have an excellent understanding of the current state of the Active Directory environment. This should include performing an audit to determine the following:

- Do any Active Directory objects use invalid characters?
- Do any Active Directory objects have incorrect Universal Principal Names (UPNs)?
- What are the current domain and forest functional levels?
- Are any schema extensions or custom attributes in use?

Prior to deploying Azure AD Connect, you should ensure that you have performed the following tasks.

- Remove any duplicate proxyAddress attributes.
- Remove any duplicate userPrincipalName attributes.
- Ensure that blank or invalid userPrincipalName attribute settings have been altered so that the setting contains only a valid UPN.
- Ensure that for user accounts that the sn and samAccountName attributes have been assigned values.
- Ensure that for group accounts, the member, alias, and displayName (for groups with a valid mail or proxyAddress attribute) are populated.
- Ensure that the following attributes do not contain invalid characters:
  - givenName
  - sn
  - samAccountName
  - givenName
  - displayName
  - mail
  - proxyAddress
  - mailNickName

UPNs that are used with Office 365 can only contain the following characters:

- Letters
- Numbers
- Periods
- Dashes
- Underscores

Rather than having to perform this operation manually, Microsoft provides some tools that allow you to automatically remediate problems that might exist with attributes prior to deploying Azure AD Connect.

IdFix

The IdFix tool, which you can download from Microsoft's website, allows you to scan an Active Directory instance to determine if any user accounts, group accounts, or contacts have problems that will cause them not to synchronize between the on-premises instance of Active Directory and the Microsoft 365 instance of Azure Active Directory. IdFix can also perform repairs on objects that would otherwise be unable to sync. IdFix runs with the security context of the currently signed on user. This means that if you want to use IdFix to repair objects in the forest that have problems, the security account you use to run IdFix must have permissions to modify those objects. The IdFix tool is shown in Figure 2-18, displaying an account detected with an incorrectly configured userPrincipalName.

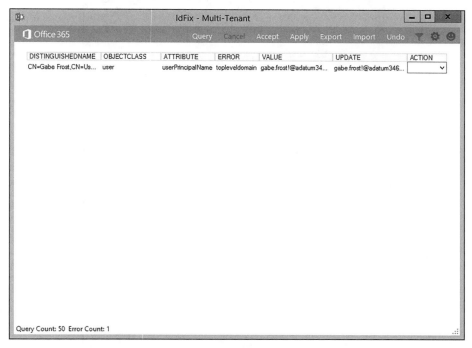

FIGURE 2-18 IdFix finds user with a problematic UPN

MORE INFO IDFIX

You can download IdFix at the following address: *https://www.microsoft.com/download/details.aspx?id=36832*.

ADModify.NET

ADmodify.NET is a tool that allows you to make changes to specific attributes for multiple objects. If you are using ADSIEdit or the Advanced mode of the Active Directory Users and Computers console, you are only able to modify the attribute of one object at a time. For example, Figure 2-19 shows ADModify.NET used to modify the format of the userPrincipal-Name attribute for a number of user accounts so that it conforms to a specific format.

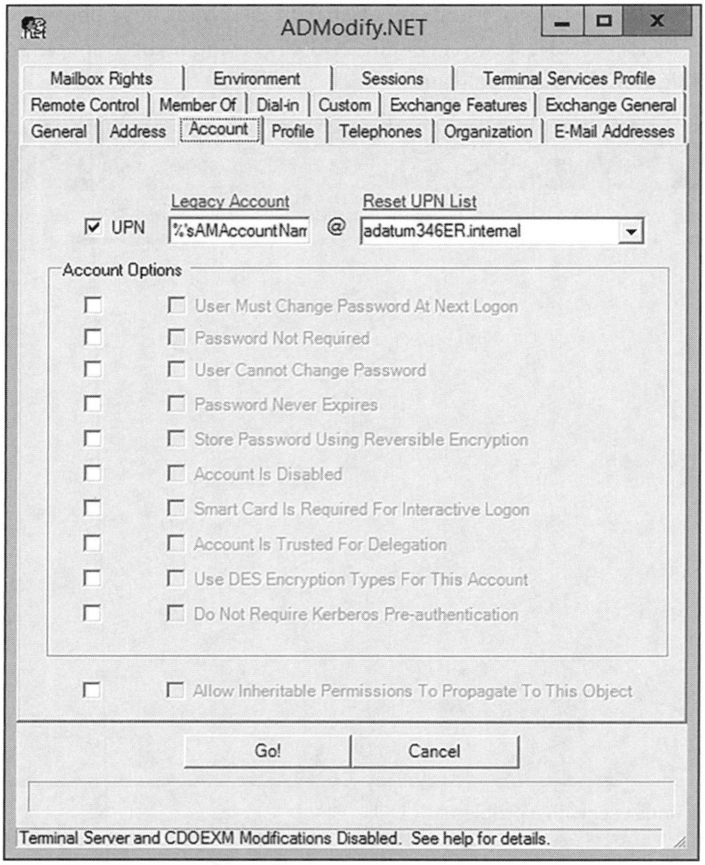

FIGURE 2-19 ADModify.NET

You can also use ADModify.NET to perform other system administration tasks, such as configuring a large number of accounts, so that the users have to change their password at next logon or to disable multiple accounts.

> **MORE INFO ADMODIFY.NET**
>
> You can learn more about ADModify.NET at: *https://archive.codeplex.com/?p=admodify.*

Using UPN suffixes and non-routable domains

Prior to performing synchronization between an on-premises Active Directory environment and an Azure Active Directory instance used to support a Microsoft 365 tenancy, you must ensure that all user account objects in the on-premises Active Directory environment are configured with a value for the UPN suffix that is able to function for both the on-premises environment and Microsoft 365.

This is not a problem when an organization's internal Active Directory domain suffix is a publicly routable domain. For example, a domain name, such as contoso.com or adatum.com that is resolvable by public DNS servers will suffice. Things become more complicated when the organization's internal Active Directory domain suffix is not publicly routable. For example, Figure 2-20 shows the adatum346ER.internal non-routable domain.

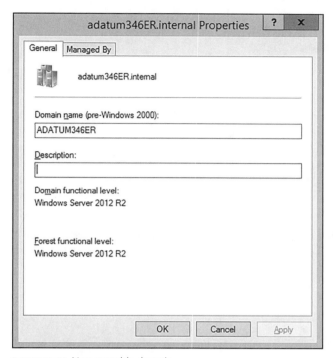

FIGURE 2-20 Non routable domain

If a domain is non-routable, the default routing domain, such as adatum346ER.onmicrosoft.com, should be used for the Microsoft 365 UPN suffix. This requires modifying the UPN suffix of accounts stored in the on-premises Active Directory instance. Modification of UPN after initial synchronization has occurred is not supported. So, you need to ensure that on-premises Active Directory UPNs are properly configured prior to performing initial synchronization using Azure AD Connect.

Perform the following steps to add a UPN suffix to the on-premises Active Directory in the event that the Active Directory domain uses a non-routable namespace:

1. Open the Active Directory Domains And Trust console and select **Active Directory Domains And Trusts**.

2. On the Action menu, click **Properties**.

3. On the UPN Suffixes tab, enter the UPN suffix to be used with Microsoft 365. Figure 2-21 shows the UPN suffix of epistemicus.com.

FIGURE 2-21 Routable domain

4. Once the UPN suffix has been added in Active Directory Domains And Trusts, you can assign the UPN suffix to user accounts. You can do this manually as shown in Figure 2-22 by using the Account tab of the user's properties dialog box in Active Directory Users And Computers.

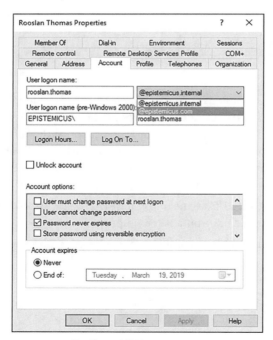

FIGURE 2-22 Configure UPN

5. You can use tools like ADModify.NET to reset the UPNs of multiple accounts as shown in Figure 2-23.

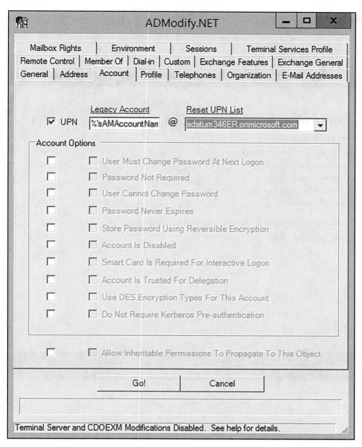

FIGURE 2-23 ADModify.NET

6. You can also use Microsoft PowerShell scripts to reset the UPNs of multiple user accounts. For example, the following script resets UPN suffixes of all user accounts in the epistemicus.internal domain to epistemicus.onmicrosoft.com.

```
Get-ADUser -Filter {UserPrincipalName -like "*@epistemicus.internal"} -SearchBase
"DC=epistemicus,DC=internal" |
ForEach-Object {
$UPN =
$_.UserPrincipalName.Replace("epistemicus.internal","epistemicus.onmicrosoft.com")
Set-ADUser $_ -UserPrincipalName $UPN
}
```

Azure AD Connect sign-on options

Azure AD Connect supports a variety of sign in options. You configure which one you want to use when setting up Azure AD Connect as shown in Figure 2-24. The default method, Password Synchronization, is appropriate for the majority of organizations who will use Azure AD Connect to synchronize identities to the cloud.

FIGURE 2-24 User sign-in

Password synchronization

Hashes of on-premises Active Directory user passwords synchronize to Azure AD, and changed passwords immediately synchronize to Azure AD. Actual passwords are never sent to Azure AD and are not stored in Azure AD. This allows for single sign-on for users of computers that are joined to an Active Directory domain that synchronizes to Azure AD. Password synchronization also allow you to enable password write-back for self service password reset functionality through Azure AD.

Pass-through authentication

When authenticating to Azure AD, the user's password is validated against an on-premises Active Directory domain controller. Passwords and password hashes are not present in Azure AD. Pass-through authentication allows for on-premises password policies to apply. Pass-through authentication requires that Azure AD Connect have an agent on a computer joined to the domain that hosts the Active Directory instance that contains the relevant user accounts. Pass-through authentication also allows single sign-on for users of domain joined machines.

With pass-through authentication, the user's password is validated against the on-premises Active Directory controller. The password doesn't need to be present in Azure AD in any form. This allows for on-premises policies, such as sign-in hour restrictions, to be evaluated during authentication to cloud services.

Pass-through authentication uses a simple agent on a Windows Server 2012 R2, Windows Server 2016, or Windows Server 2019 domain-joined machine in the on-premises environment. This agent listens for password validation requests. It doesn't require any inbound ports to be open to the Internet.

In addition, you can also enable single sign-on for users on domain-joined machines that are on the corporate network. With single sign-on, enabled users only need to enter a user-name to help them securely access cloud resources.

Active Directory Federation

This allows users to authenticate to Azure AD resources using on-premises credentials. It also requires the deployment of an Active Directory Federation Services infrastructure. This is the most complicated identity synchronization configuration for Microsoft 365 and is only likely to be implemented in environments with complicated identity configurations.

> **MORE INFO AZURE AD CONNECT SIGN-IN OPTIONS**
>
> You can learn more about sign-in options, consult the following article:
> *https://docs.microsoft.com/azure/active-directory/connect/active-directory-aadconnect-user-signin.*

> **EXAM TIP**
>
> Remember the difference between password synchronization and pass-through authentication.

Skill 2.3: Manage identity synchronization by using Azure AD Connect

This skill section deals with the process of managing identity synchronization with Azure AD Connect once it has been deployed. To master this skill you'll need to understand how to monitor Azure AD Connect health, manage Azure AD Connect synchronization, configure object filters, and configure password synchronization.

Monitor Azure AD Connect Health

Azure AD Connect Health is a tool available in the Azure Active Directory Admin Center, shown in Figure 2-25, that allows you to monitor the health of synchronization between your organization's on-premises directory and Azure Active Directory.

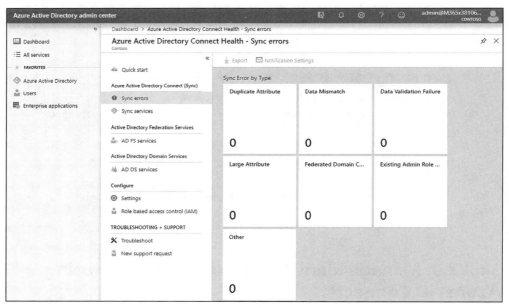

FIGURE 2-25 Azure AD Connect Health

You can use Azure AD Connect health to view information about:

- **Synchronization errors**   This will display errors including duplicate attributes, data mismatch, data validation failure, large attributes, Federated Domain Change, and Existing Admin Role Conflicts.

- **Synchronization services**   This handles information about which services are synchronizing with Azure Active Directory.

- **AD FS services**   Information about AD FS when Azure AD Connect is configured for federation. Includes information about errors and issues.
- **AD DS services**   Information about domains and forests connected to Azure Active Directory.

MORE INFO **AZURE AD CONNECT HEALTH**

You can learn more about Azure AD Connect Health at: *https://docs.microsoft.com/azure/ active-directory/hybrid/whatis-azure-ad-connect*.

Manage Azure AD Connect synchronization

You can manage synchronization using a variety of tools, including PowerShell cmdlets that are part of the ADSync PowerShell module. This module is automatically installed on a computer when you install Azure AD Connect.

To view the current configuration of the scheduler, you can run the Get-ADSyncScheduler cmdlet. The output of this cmdlet is shown in Figure 2-26.

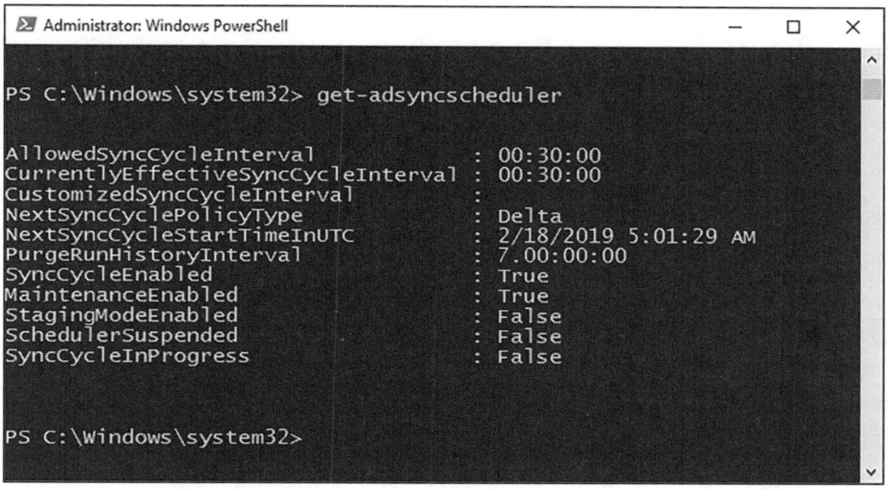

FIGURE 2-26 Get-ADSyncScheduler

The output of this cmdlet provides the following information:

- **AllowedSyncCyleInterval**   Minimum intervals between sync cycles supported by Microsoft. If you sync more often than this interval, your configuration will be deemed unsupported.
- **CurrentlyEffectiveSyncCycleInterval**   The schedule that currently applies.
- **CustomizedSyncCycleInterval**   Used when you have a custom schedule applied.

- **NextSyncCyclePolicyType** Specifies whether the next sync is a full synchronization or a delta synchronization.
- **NextSyncCycleStartTimeInUTC** The time when the next sync cycle will occur according to the schedule.
- **PurgeRunHistoryInterval** Specifies how long the logs should be kept.
- **SyncCycleEnabled** Specifies whether the scheduler is running an import, sync, or export process as part of its execution.
- **MaintenanceEnabled** Specifies if the maintenance process is enabled.
- **StatingModeEnaled** Lists whether the staging mode is enabled.
- **SyncCycleInProgress** Specifies whether synchronization is actually occurring.

You can use the Set-ADSyncScheduler cmdlet to configure the following settings that are displayed when you run the Get-ADSyncScheduler cmdlet:

- CustomizedSyncCycleInterval
- NextSyncCyclePolicyType
- PurgeRunHistoryInterval
- SyncCycleEnabled
- MaintenanceEnabled

> ***MORE INFO* MANAGING THE SCHEDULER**
>
> You can learn more about managing the Azure AD Connect scheduler at: *https://docs. microsoft.com/azure/active-directory/connect/active-directory-aadconnectsync-feature-scheduler.*

Forcing synchronization

By default, synchronization occurs between the on-premises directory and Azure every 30 minutes. In some cases you'll make a change to a user account or create a collection of user accounts and want to get those changes or new accounts up into the Azure Active Directory instance that supports the Office 365 tenancy as fast as possible. You can force synchronization by running the Azure AD Connect wizard again, or you can use the Synchronization Service Manager.

To perform a full synchronization using Synchronization Service Manager, perform the following steps:

1. Open the Synchronization Service Manager, either by clicking on **Synchronization Service** from the Start menu, or by running miisclient.exe located in the C:\Program Files\ Microsoft Azure AD Sync\UIShell folder.
2. Click the **Connectors** tab.
3. On the Connectors tab, click the name of your Active Directory domain service, as shown in Figure 2-27.

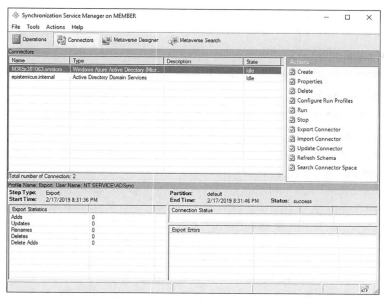

FIGURE 2-27 Synchronization Service Manager

4. On the Actions pane, click **Run**.

5. On the Run Management Agent dialog box, select **Full Synchronization**, as shown in Figure 2-28.

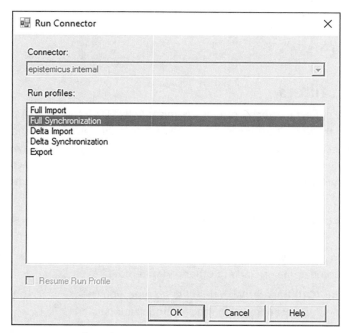

FIGURE 2-28 Full Synchronization

Rather than performing a Full Sync, you can trigger one of the following types of synchronization using the Synchronization Service Manager:

- **Full Synchronization**   Performs a full synchronization
- **Delta Import**   Imports changed schema and objects
- **Delta Synchronization**   Synchronizes only objects changed since the last sync
- **Export**   Writes data from the Azure instance to the on-premises instance
- **Full Import**   A full import and full sync is suitable for initiating the first full synchronization or the first full synchronization after you have changed the filtering parameters

You can also use the Synchronization Service Manager to configure extensive filtering options, though for tasks such as configuring OU based filtering, Microsoft recommends that you first attempt configuring filtering using the Azure AD Connect setup wizard and only rely on a tool such as Synchronization Service Manager if problems arise.

> **MORE INFO   SYNCHRONIZATION SERVICE MANAGER**
>
> You can learn more about Synchronization Service Manager at: *https://docs.microsoft.com/azure/active-directory/connect/active-directory-aadconnectsync-service-manager-ui.*

You can also force synchronization by using the Start-ADSyncCycle cmdlet. You can use this cmdlet to trigger either a delta or a full synchronization. To force a delta sync cycle, run the following command:

```
Start-ADSyncCycle -PolicyType Delta
```

To trigger a full sync cycle, run the command:

```
Start-ADSyncCycle -PolicyType Initial
```

Configure object filters

When you use Azure AD Connect to synchronize on-premises Active Directory to an Azure Active Directory instance, the default setting is to have all user accounts, group accounts, and mail-enabled contact objects synchronized up to the cloud. For some organizations, synchronizing everything is exactly what they want. Other organizations want to be more selective about which objects are synchronized from the on-premises Active Directory environment to the Azure Active Directory instance that supports the Office 365 tenancy.

With Azure AD Connect, you can choose to filter based on the following options as shown in Figure 2-29:

- **Domain based**   In a forest with multiple domains, you can configure filtering so that only objects from some domains, and not others, are filtered.
- **Organizational unit (OU) based**   With this filtering type, you choose which objects are filtered based on their location within specific organizational units.

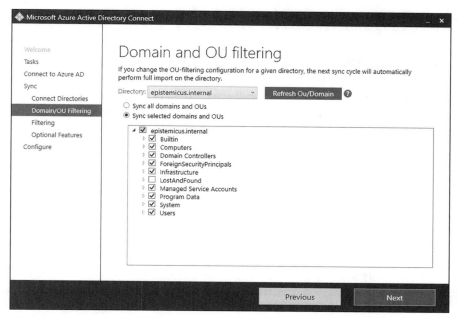

FIGURE 2-29 Domain and OU filtering

You can also configure filtering on the basis of group membership, as shown in Figure 2-30. You can configure separate group-based filters for each forest or domain synchronized using Azure AD Connect.

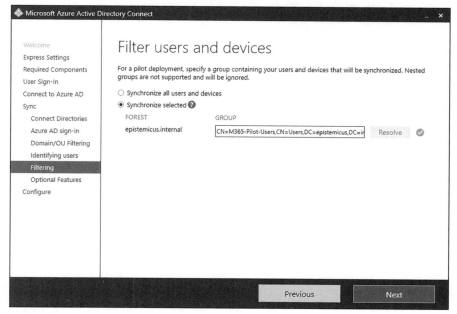

FIGURE 2-30 Filter Users And Devices

MORE INFO **CONFIGURE FILTERING**

You can learn more about Azure AD Sync filtering at: *https://docs.microsoft.com/azure/ active-directory/connect/active-directory-aadconnectsync-configure-filtering*.

While Azure AD Connect will address most organization's synchronization requirements, the most comprehensive tool that you can use to filter synchronization is the Synchronization Rules Editor, shown in Figure 2-31. You can use this tool to modify existing synchronization rules, but also to create new rules. Rather than configuring synchronization on a per-domain or per-OU basis, you can tailor rules for individual objects and specific Active Directory attributes.

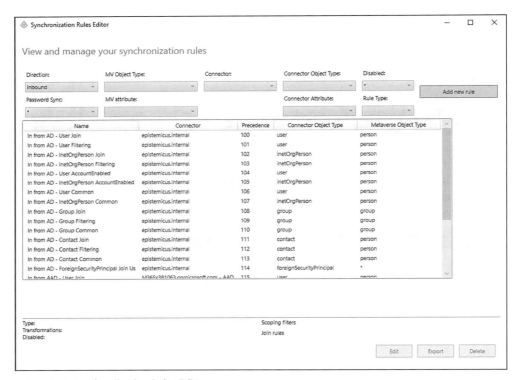

FIGURE 2-31 Synchronization Rules Editor

MORE INFO **SYNCHRONIZATION RULES EDITOR**

You can learn more about the Synchronization Rules Editor at: *https://docs.microsoft.com/ azure/active-directory/connect/active-directory-aadconnectsync-change-the-configuration*.

Configure password sync

Password Sync allows the synchronization of user account passwords from on-premises Active Directory to the Azure Active Directory instance that supports the Office 365 tenancy. The advantage of this is that users can sign on to Microsoft 365 using the same password that they use to sign in to computers on the on-premises environment. Password Sync does not provide single sign-on or federation.

When you enable Password Sync, the on-premises password complexity policies override password complexity policies configured for the Azure Active Directory instance that supports the Microsoft 365 tenancy. This means that any password that is valid for an on-premises user will be valid within Microsoft 365, even if it would not be normally.

Password expiration works in the following way: the password of the account of the cloud user object is set to never expire. Each time the user account password is changed in the on-premises Active Directory instance, this change replicates to the Azure Active Directory instance that supports the Microsoft 365 tenancy. This means that it is possible for a user account's password to expire on the on-premises Active Directory instance, but that user can still use the same password to sign on to Microsoft 365. The next time they sign on to the on-premises environment, they are forced to change their password and that change replicates up to the Azure Active Directory instance that supports the Microsoft 365 tenancy.

When Password Sync is enabled and you disable a user's account in the on-premises Active Directory instance, the user's account in the Azure Active Directory instance that supports the Microsoft 365 tenancy is disabled within a few minutes. If Password Sync is not enabled and you disable user account in the on-premises Active Directory instance, the user's account in the Azure Active Directory instance that supports the Microsoft 365 tenancy is not disabled until the next full synchronization.

> **MORE INFO PASSWORD SYNCHRONIZATION**
>
> You can learn more about password synchronization: *https://docs.microsoft.com/azure/active-directory/hybrid/how-to-connect-password-hash-synchronization.*

Implement multi-forest AD Connect scenarios

The Azure Active Directory Connect tool also supports synchronization from multiple on-premises Active Directory forests to a single Azure Active Directory instance. Multiple forest synchronization to a single Azure AD instance is supported only when a single Azure AD Connect server is in use. Microsoft does not support multiple Azure AD Connect servers synchronizing with a single Azure AD instance, whether there is one or multiple forests being synchronized.

By default, Azure AD Connect will assume that:

- A user has a single enabled account. Also, the forest where this account is located must host the directory that is used to authenticate the user. This assumption is used in both password sync and federation scenarios. On the basis of this assumption, the UserPrincipalName and sourceAnchor/immutableID are drawn from this forest.

- Each user has a single mailbox, and the forest that hosts that mailbox is the best source of attributes visible in the Exchange Global Address List (GAL). In the event that a user doesn't have an associated mailbox, any configured forest can function as the source for the attribute values.
- If a user account has a linked mailbox, there will be an account in an alternate forest used for the sign-in process.

The key to synchronizing user accounts from multiple forests is that only one user account from all synchronized forests should represent the user. This means that the synchronization engine should have a way to determine when accounts in separate forests represent the same user. You can configure how the Azure AD Connect sync engine identifies users on the Uniquely Identifying Your Users page, shown in Figure 2-32, using one of the following options.

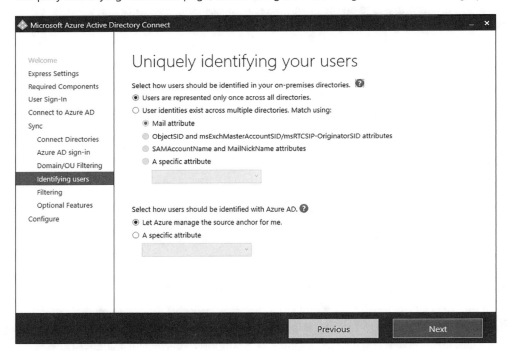

FIGURE 2-32 Uniquely identify users

- Match users using the mail attribute
- Match user using ObjectSID and msExchangeMasterAccountSID/msRTCIP-OrgiginatorSID attributes
- Match user using SAMAccountName and MailNickName attributes
- Specify a custom attribute upon which to match names

EXAM TIP

Remember what tools you can use to trigger synchronization.

Skill 2.4: Manage Azure AD identities

This skill deals with the management of identities within Azure Active Directory. This is of primary importance when Azure Active Directory functions as the source of authority. To master this skill you'll need to understand how to plan for the use of Azure AD identities, how to deploy self service password reset, manage access reviews, manage Azure AD groups, manage Azure AD passwords, manage product licenses, manage users, and perform bulk user management tasks.

This section covers the following topics :

- Plan Azure AD identities
- Implement and manage Azure AD self service password reset
- Manage access reviews
- Manage groups
- Manage passwords
- Manage product licenses
- Manage users
- Perform bulk user management

Plan Azure AD identities

In hybrid environments, you'll primarily perform the management of identities using on-premises management tools such as Active Directory Users and Computers. In environments where Azure AD forms the primary source of authority you can use the Microsoft 365 Admin Center to perform the management of user identities. You can also use the Azure Active Directory admin center as shown in Figure 2-33, or you can use Azure CLI or PowerShell.

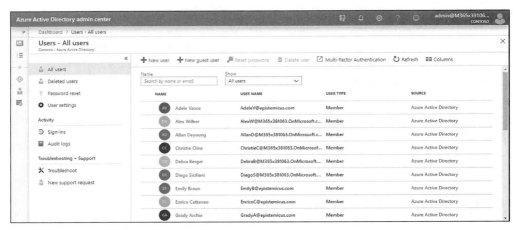

FIGURE 2-33 Azure Active Directory Admin Center

When planning the use of Azure identities, you'll need to consider the following questions:

- **What UPN will be used with the identity for logon to Microsoft 365 resources?** You can change the UPN suffix to any domain that is configured and authorized for use with the directory.

- **What authentication and authorization options will be required to access Microsoft 365 resources?** Will users need to regularly change their passwords? Will users be required to perform multi-factor authentication?

- **What roles will be assigned to users?** Will you need to assign Azure AD roles to specific users? What method will you use to perform this task?

- **Will Azure AD Groups be used?** What strategy will you use to manage collections of users into groups? Will your organization use a group naming convention?

You'll learn more about how to perform user management tasks later in this chapter.

Implement and manage Azure AD self service password reset

Something that is challenging to deploy in an on-premises environment, but which is relatively straightforward to deploy in an environment that uses Azure AD as a source of identity authority, is self service password reset. A self service password reset allows a user to reset their own password when they forget that password, rather than having to contact the service desk and have a member of the IT staff perform the task for them. To enable self service password reset, perform the following steps:

1. Open the Azure Active Directory portal at *https://aad.portal.azure.com* with an account that has tenant administrator permissions.

2. In the Azure Active Directory Admin Center, click the **Users** node. This will open the Users blade as shown in Figure 2-34.

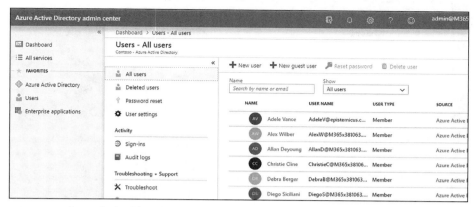

FIGURE 2-34 Azure Active Directory Admin Center

3. In the Users blade of the Azure Active Directory admin center, click **Password Reset**.

4. On the Password reset – Properties page, click **All**, as shown in Figure 2-35, to enable the self service password reset for all Microsoft 365 users.

FIGURE 2-35 Enable Self Service Password Reset

Once enabled, users will be prompted for additional information the next time that they sign in, which will be used to verify their identity if they use the self-service password reset tool. Users are able to reset their passwords by navigating to the website *https://passwordreset.microsoftonline.com*, shown in Figure 2-36, and completing the form.

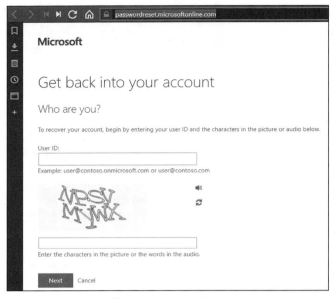

FIGURE 2-36 Enable Self-service Password Reset

> **MORE INFO SELF SERVICE PASSWORD RESET**
>
> You can learn more about configuring self service password at: *https://docs.microsoft.com/ office365/admin/add-users/let-users-reset-passwords*.

Manage access reviews

You can review a user's access to Microsoft 365 resources through the Azure Active Directory console. To perform this task, open up the user's properties page and select the sign-ins section of the User Management blade. Figure 2-37 shows the sign in activity of the administrator account used to manage a Microsoft 365 tenancy.

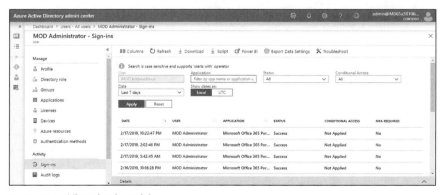

FIGURE 2-37 View sign in activity

The audit logs node will allow you to review the actions performed by accounts. Figure 2-38 shows that actions performed by the account used for Microsoft 365 tenancy administration are recorded for review.

FIGURE 2-38 Audit log

Manage groups

Groups allow you to collect users together and then assign them privileges and access to workloads or services. Rather than assign privileges and access to workloads or services directly to users, you can assign these rights to a group and then indirectly assign them to users by adding the user accounts to the appropriate group. Using groups in this way is a long standing administrative practice, because it allows you to determine a user's level of access and rights by looking at the user's group memberships, rather than checking each workload and service to determine if the user account has been assigned rights to that service.

You can use the Azure AD administrative console to manage groups. Azure AD supports two group types: Office 365 groups and Security groups. Figure 2-39 shows the selection of group type when creating the group. Office 365 groups are used for collaboration between users. These users can be inside our external to the organization. Each Office 365 group has an associated email address, shared workspace for conversations, shared location for files, calendar events, and a planner. Security groups are used to grant access to specific Microsoft 365 resources, such as SharePoint sites. Security groups can contain user accounts as well as device accounts. Device related groups are most often used with services such as Intune.

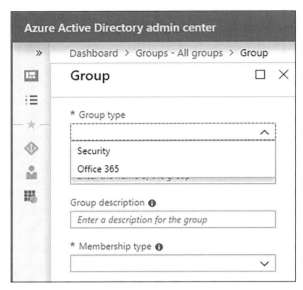

FIGURE 2-39 Create Azure AD Group

Group membership for both group types can be configured as assigned or dynamic. When the assigned option is selected, membership is managed manually. When the dynamic option is selected, group membership is determined based on the results of a query against user or device attributes. For example, you can have a user located in a specific department or city who may be managed by a specific person. Figure 2-40 shows an Office 365 group with dynamic membership, where users who have the department Marketing will automatically be assigned membership of the group.

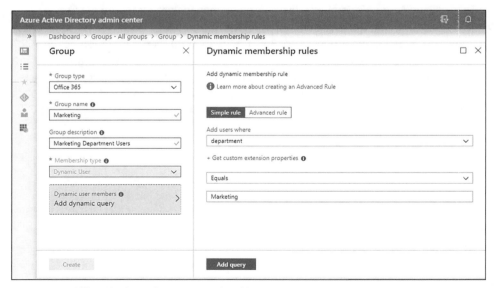

FIGURE 2-40 Office 365 dynamic group membership

Source of authority is important when it comes to making modifications to users and groups. Remember that modifications that occur in the on-premises Active Directory overwrite the current state of the objects within the Azure Active Directory instance that supports the Microsoft 365 tenancy. The only exception to this rule is with the assignment of licenses, which only occurs using the Microsoft 365 Admin Center or Microsoft PowerShell tools.

Modifications made to on-premises user and group objects will only be present within the Azure Active Directory instance that supports the Microsoft 365 tenancy after synchronization has occurred. By default, synchronization occurs every 30 minutes. You can force synchronization to occur using the Synchronization Service Manager tool or by using Microsoft PowerShell.

With deletion, the concept of source of authority again is very important. When you want to delete a user or group account created in the on-premises Active Directory instance, you should use tools, such as Active Directory Users and Computers, or Active Directory Administrative Center, to remove that user. When you delete the user or group using this method, the user will be deleted from the on-premises Active Directory instance and then, when synchronization occurs, will be deleted from the Azure Active Directory instance that supports the Microsoft 365 tenancy.

When you delete a user from Microsoft 365, their account remains in the Azure Active Directory Recycle Bin for 30 days. This means that you can recover the account online should it be necessary to do so. If you delete a user from your on-premises Active Directory environment, but have enabled the on-premises Active Directory Recycle Bin, recovering the user from the on-premises Active Directory Recycle Bin will recover the user account in Microsoft 365. If you don't have the Active Directory Recycle Bin enabled, you will need to create another account with a new GUID.

In some cases, synchronization doesn't work properly and objects that are deleted from the on-premises Active Directory instance don't delete from the Azure Active Directory instance that supports the Microsoft 365 tenancy. In this circumstance you can use the Remove-MsolUser, Remove-MsolGroup, or Remove-MsolContact Microsoft PowerShell cmdlets to manually remove the orphaned object.

You can use the following PowerShell commands from the AzureAD module to manage Azure AD Groups:

- **Get-AzureADGroup**   Provides information about Azure AD Groups.
- **New-AzureADGroup**   Creates a new Azure AD Group.
- **Set-AzureADGroup**   Configures the properties of an Azure AD Group.
- **Remove-AzureADGroup**   Removes an Azure AD Group.
- **Add-AzureADGroupMember**   Adds a user to an Azure AD Group.
- **Remove-AzureADGroupMember**   Removes a user from an Azure AD Group.
- **Add-AzureADGroupOwner**   Adds a user as an owner of an Azure AD Group. Gives the user limited group management privileges.
- **Remove-AzureADGroupOwner**   Removes a user as owner of an Azure AD Group.

Manage passwords

The only thing that people forget more often than where they have put their keys is what their password is. As someone who is supporting Microsoft 365, it's more likely than not that if you haven't enabled self service password reset, or even if you have, you're going to have to reset user passwords on a semi-regular basis.

To reset a Microsoft 365 user password, perform the following steps:

1. In the Microsoft 365 Admin Center, select the user whose password you want to reset in the list of Active users by selecting the checkbox next to the user's name.

2. On the User's properties page, click the **Reset Password** button shown in Figure 2-41.

FIGURE 2-41 Reset Password button

3. On the Reset Password page, shown in Figure 2-42, choose whether to have an automatically generated password, to create a password, or to select whether the password needs to be changed when the user next signs in.

FIGURE 2-42 Password reset

4. It will be necessary to provide either the automatically generated password or the administrator password to the user through a secure channel, such as in person or over the phone.

You can reset a user's password through PowerShell using the Set-MsolUserPassword cmdlet using the syntax:

```
Set-MsolUserPassword -UserPrincipalName <UPN> -NewPassword <NewPassword>-
ForceChangePassword $True
```

You can configure password expiration policy for all users by performing the following steps:

1. In the Microsoft 365 Admin Center, select **Security & Privacy** under Settings, as shown in Figure 2-43.

FIGURE 2-43 Security and privacy

2. Next to Password Policy, click **Edit**.

3. In the Password Policy page, shown in Figure 2-44, you can choose to have passwords never expire, or you can configure passwords to expire after a specific number of days. You can also configure the number of days before a user will be informed that their password will expire.

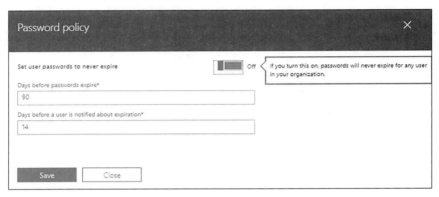

FIGURE 244 Password Policy

MORE INFO **RESET USER PASSWORDS**

You can learn more about resetting Microsoft 365 user passwords at: *https://docs.microsoft.com/office365/admin/add-users/reset-passwords*.

Manage product licenses

Users require licenses to use Microsoft 365 services and products. To assign a license to a user, perform the following steps:

1. In the Microsoft 365 console, select the Active Users node under Users as shown in Figure 2-45.

FIGURE 2-45 Active Users

2. Select the checkbox next to the user to which you wish to assign a license. This will bring up the user's properties page, as shown in Figure 2-46.

FIGURE 2-46 User properties page

3. On the user's properties page, click **Edit** next to Product Licenses. You will be provided with a location drop down and the ability to assign licenses for Enterprise Mobility and Security, Office 365 Enterprise, and Windows 10 Enterprise, as shown in Figure 2-47.

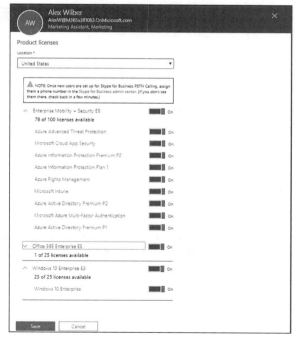

FIGURE 2-47 Product licenses page

4. Click Save to assign the licenses to the user.

It's important to remember that user accounts created in Microsoft 365 by the synchronization process will not automatically be assigned Microsoft 365 licenses. This means when you are creating new user accounts in the on-premises environment after you've initially configured Azure AD Connect, you'll also need to use Microsoft 365 Admin Center, or PowerShell, to provision those accounts with Microsoft 365 licenses.

One of the simplest methods to assign licenses to a large number of accounts is by using PowerShell. To accomplish this task using Microsoft PowerShell, you need to first ensure that a usage location is set for each unlicensed user, and then to assign a license using the proper SKU identifier.

To determine which Microsoft 365 users have not been properly configured with a license, enact the following Microsoft PowerShell command:

```
Get-MsolUser –UnlicensedUsersOnly
```

To assign all unlicensed users to a specific location, use the following command, where <location> is the location to which you wish to assign the unlicensed users:

```
Get-MsolUser –UnlicensedUsersOnly | Set-MsolUser –UsageLocation <location>
```

You'll need to apply the account SKU ID to each account. The way you can do this is first by assigning SKU information to a variable with the following command:

```
$Sku=Get-MsolAccountSku
```

Once you have this information, you can use the following command to apply the appropriate account SKU ID to correctly license each account.

```
Get-MsolUser –UnlicensedUsersOnly | Set-MsolUser –AddLicenses $Sku.AccountSkuID
```

> **MORE INFO ASSIGN LICENSES TO USERS**
>
> You can learn more about assigning licenses to users at: *https://docs.microsoft.com/office365/admin/subscriptions-and-billing/assign-licenses-to-users*.

Manage users

You can use the Microsoft 365 Admin Center, the Azure AD Admin Center, or Azure PowerShell to manage Azure AD User accounts. The Azure AD Admin Center gives you a greater set of options for managing the properties of user accounts than the Microsoft 365 Admin Center, because you can edit extended user properties as shown in Figure 2-48.

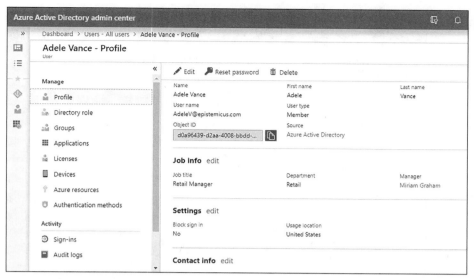

FIGURE 2-48 User properties page

To create a new Azure AD User, perform the following steps:

1. In the Azure AD console, select **Users – All Users** and then click **New User**.

2. In the New User blade, shown in Figure 2-49, provide the following information:

   - **Name** The user's actual name.
   - **User Name** The user's sign-in name in UPN format.
   - **Profile** The user's first name, last name, job title and department.
   - **Properties** This specifies the source of authority for the user. By default if you are creating the user using the Azure AD Admin Center or the Microsoft 365 Admin Center, this will be Azure Active Directory.
   - **Groups** This defines which groups the user should be a member of.
   - **Directory role** Choose whether the account has User, Global Administrator, or a Limited Administrator role.
   - **Password** This as the automatically generated password. With a **Show Password** option you can transmit the password to the user through a secure channel.

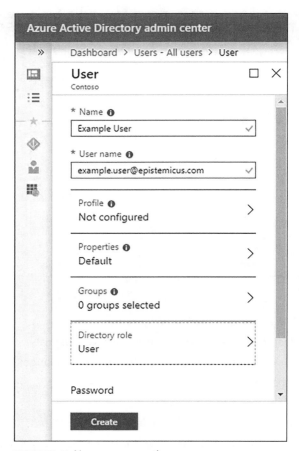

FIGURE 2-49 New user properties page

You can also use the Azure AD Admin Center to perform the following user admin tasks:

- Update profile information
- Assign Directory Roles
- Manage group membership
- Manage licenses
- Manage devices
- Manage access to Azure resources
- Manage authentication methods

MORE INFO **CREATING AZURE AD USERS**

You can learn more about Azure AD PowerShell cmdlets for managing users at: *https://docs. microsoft.com/powershell/azure/active-directory/new-user-sample.*

Perform bulk user management

The best tool for performing bulk user management is the Azure AD related PowerShell commands. You can use the following commands, some of which are shown in Figure 2-50, to script bulk user management tasks:

- **New-AzureADUser** Create a new Azure AD user.
- **Get-AzureADUser** Retrieve information about one or more Azure AD users.
- **Set-AzureADUser** Configure the properties of an Azure AD user.
- **Remove-AzureADUser** Remove an Azure AD user account.
- **Get-AzureADUserMembership** View group membership for a specific Azure AD user.
- **Set-AzureADUserPassword** Manage Azure AD user passwords.

```
PS C:\Windows\system32> get-command -noun AzureADUs*

CommandType    Name                                    Version    Source
-----------    ----                                    -------    ------
Cmdlet         Get-AzureADUser                         2.0.2.4    AzureAD
Cmdlet         Get-AzureADUserAppRoleAssignment        2.0.2.4    AzureAD
Cmdlet         Get-AzureADUserCreatedObject            2.0.2.4    AzureAD
Cmdlet         Get-AzureADUserDirectReport             2.0.2.4    AzureAD
Cmdlet         Get-AzureADUserExtension                2.0.2.4    AzureAD
Cmdlet         Get-AzureADUserLicenseDetail            2.0.2.4    AzureAD
Cmdlet         Get-AzureADUserManager                  2.0.2.4    AzureAD
Cmdlet         Get-AzureADUserMembership               2.0.2.4    AzureAD
Cmdlet         Get-AzureADUserOAuth2PermissionGrant    2.0.2.4    AzureAD
Cmdlet         Get-AzureADUserOwnedDevice              2.0.2.4    AzureAD
Cmdlet         Get-AzureADUserOwnedObject              2.0.2.4    AzureAD
Cmdlet         Get-AzureADUserRegisteredDevice         2.0.2.4    AzureAD
Cmdlet         Get-AzureADUserThumbnailPhoto           2.0.2.4    AzureAD
Cmdlet         New-AzureADUser                         2.0.2.4    AzureAD
Cmdlet         New-AzureADUserAppRoleAssignment        2.0.2.4    AzureAD
Cmdlet         Remove-AzureADUser                      2.0.2.4    AzureAD
Cmdlet         Remove-AzureADUserAppRoleAssignment     2.0.2.4    AzureAD
Cmdlet         Remove-AzureADUserExtension             2.0.2.4    AzureAD
Cmdlet         Remove-AzureADUserManager               2.0.2.4    AzureAD
Cmdlet         Revoke-AzureADUserAllRefreshToken       2.0.2.4    AzureAD
Cmdlet         Set-AzureADUser                         2.0.2.4    AzureAD
Cmdlet         Set-AzureADUserExtension                2.0.2.4    AzureAD
Cmdlet         Set-AzureADUserLicense                  2.0.2.4    AzureAD
Cmdlet         Set-AzureADUserManager                  2.0.2.4    AzureAD
Cmdlet         Set-AzureADUserPassword                 2.0.2.4    AzureAD
Cmdlet         Set-AzureADUserThumbnailPhoto           2.0.2.4    AzureAD
```

FIGURE 2-50 User related PowerShell cmdlets

MORE INFO USER MANAGEMENT POWERSHELL CMDLETS

You can learn more about Azure AD PowerShell cmdlets for managing users at: *https://docs. microsoft.com/powershell/module/azuread/?view=azureadps-2.0#users*.

EXAM TIP

Remember which PowerShell cmdlets you use to add and remove users from groups.

Skill 2.5: Manage user roles

This skill section deals with managing user roles within Azure Active Directory. To master this skill you'll need to understand how to plan Azure AD Roles, allocate roles, configure administrative accounts, configure Azure AD RBAC, delegate admin rights, manage administrator roles, and plan security and compliance roles.

This section covers the following topics :

- Plan user roles
- Allocate roles in workloads
- Configure administrative accounts
- Configure RBAC within Azure AD
- Delegate admin rights
- Manage admin roles
- Manage role allocations by using Azure AD
- Plan security and compliance roles for Microsoft 365

Plan user roles

Rather than assign all users who need to perform administrative tasks membership of the Global Administrators role, an organization's approach to planning and assignment of user roles should follow the principle of least privilege. This principle dictates that you should assign the minimum necessary privileges to an account that are required for the user associated with that account to perform tasks. When planning user roles, determine precisely what tasks the user needs to perform and then assign then the role that allows them to perform only those tasks. For example, if a support desk technician needs to be able to reset passwords, assign that technician the Password Administrator role rather than a more privileged role such as Security Administrator or Global Administrator.

Allocate roles in workloads

Several Azure AD Roles, such as Exchange Administrator, Intune Administrator, and SharePoint Administrator are specific to certain Microsoft 365 workloads. These roles often provide complete administrative rights for those workloads, but provide no administrative permissions beyond those workloads. In organizations where staff are responsible for one or more Microsoft 365 workloads, but not responsible for tasks such as user management or other workloads, ensure that you follow the principle of least privilege and only assign roles at the workload level.

Manage admin roles

Azure Active Directory includes a large number of roles that provide a variety of permissions to different aspects of Azure AD and Microsoft 365 workloads. These roles, and the permissions that they grant, are listed in Table 2-3

TABLE 2-3 Azure AD Roles

Role	Description
Application Administrator	Can administer enterprise applications, application registrations, and application proxy settings
Application Developer	Can create application registrations.
Authentication Administrator	Can view current authentication method settings. Can set or reset non-password credentials. Can force MFA on next sign on.
Billing Administrator	Can purchase and manage subscriptions. Can manage support tickets and monitor service health.
Cloud Application Administrator	Can manage all aspects of enterprise applications and registrations, but cannot manage application proxy.
Cloud Device Administrator	Can enable, disable, and remove devices in Azure AD. Can view Windows 10 BitLocker Drive Encryption Keys through the Azure portal.
Compliance Administrator	Manage features in the Microsoft 365 compliance center, Microsoft 365 Admin Center, Azure, and Microsoft 365 Security and Compliance Center.
Conditional Access Administrator	Administrative rights over Azure AD conditional access configuration.
Customer Lockbox access approver	Manages customer lockbox requests. Can also enable and disable the customer lockbox feature.
Device Administrators	Users assigned this role will become local administrators on all computers running Windows 10 that are joined to Azure AD.
Directory Readers	Role for applications that do not support consent framework. Should not be assigned to users.
Directory Synchronization Accounts	Assigned to the Azure AD Connect service and not used for user accounts.
Directory Writers	A legacy role assigned to applications that do not support the consent framework. Should only be assigned to applications and not user accounts.
Dynamics 365 Administrator / CRM Administrator	Administrative access to Dynamics 365 Online.
Exchange Administrator	Administrative access to Exchange Online.
Global Administrator / Company Administrator	Administrative access to all Azure AD features. This includes administrative access to services that use Azure AD Identities including Microsoft 365 security center, Microsoft 365 compliance center, Exchange Online, SharePoint Online, and Skype for Business Online. The account used to sign up for the tenancy becomes the global administrator. Global administrators can reset the passwords of any user, including other global administrators
Guest Inviter	Can manage Azure AD B2B guest user invitations.

TABLE 2-3. *Continued*

Role	Description
Information Protection Administrator	Has the ability to manage all aspects of Azure Information Protection including configuring labels, managing protection templates, and activating protection.
Intune Administrator	Has full administrative rights to Microsoft Intune.
License Administrator	Can manage license assignments on users and groups. Cannot purchase or manage subscriptions.
Message Center Reader	Can monitor notification and Microsoft advisories in the Microsoft 365 Message Center.
Password Administrator / Helpdesk Administrator	Able to perform the following tasks for all users except those that have administrative roles: ■ Change passwords ■ Invalidate refresh tokens ■ Manage service requests ■ Monitor service health
Power BI Administrator	Has administrator permissions over Power BI.
Privileged Role Administrator	Can manage all aspects of Azure AD Privileged Identity Management. Can manage role assignments in Azure AD.
Reports Reader	Can view reporting data in the Microsoft 365 reports dashboard.
Security Administrator	Has administrator level access to manage security features in the Microsoft 365 security center, Azure AD Identity Protection, Azure Information Protection, and Microsoft 365 Security and Compliance Center.
Security Reader	Has read-only access to security Microsoft 365 related security features.
Service Support Administrator	Can open and view support requests with Microsoft for Microsoft 365 related services.
SharePoint Administrator	Has global administrator permissions for SharePoint Online workloads.
Skype for Business / Lync Administrator	Has global administrator permissions for Skype for Business workloads.
Teams Administrator	Can administer all elements of Microsoft Teams.
Teams Communications Administrator	Can manage Teams workloads related to voice & telephony including telephone number assignment, voice and meeting policies.
Teams Communications Support Engineer	Can troubleshoot communication issues within Teams & Skype for Business. Can view details of call records for all participants in a conversation.
Teams Communications Support Specialist	Can troubleshoot communication issues within Teams & Skype for Business. Can only view user details in the call for a specific user.
User Account Administrator	Can create and manage user accounts. Can create and manage groups. Can manage user views, support tickets and monitor service health.

> *MORE INFO* **AZURE AD ADMINISTRATOR ROLES**
>
> You can learn more about Azure AD Administrator roles at: *https://docs.microsoft.com/azure/active-directory/users-groups-roles/directory-assign-admin-roles*.

Configure RBAC within Azure AD

Azure RBAC (Role Based Access Control) allows you to configure fine-grained access control to Azure resources, such as virtual machines and storage accounts. When you configure RBAC, you assign a role and a scope, with the scope being the resource you wish to have managed. Azure RBAC includes more than 70 roles. A full listing of the details of all 70 are beyond the scope of this text, but there are four fundamental roles that those responsible for managing Microsoft 365 should be aware of, which can be assigned to specific Azure subscriptions, resource groups, or resources. These roles are:

- **Owner**   Users that hold this role have full access to all resources within the scope of the assignment and are able to delegate access to others.
- **Contributor**   Users that hold this role can create and manage resources within the scope of the assignment, but cannot grant access to others.
- **Reader**   Users that hold this role are able to view resources within the scope of the assignment, but can't perform other tasks and cannot grant access to others.
- **User Access Administrator**   Can manage user access to Azure resources within the scope of the assignment.

> **MORE INFO   AZURE RBAC**
>
> You can learn more about Azure RBAC at: *docs.microsoft.com/azure/role-based-access-control/rbac-and-directory-admin-roles*.

Delegate admin rights

To view which users are assigned a specific role, perform the following steps:

1. In the Azure AD Admin Center, select **Roles and Administrators**, as shown in Figure 2-51.

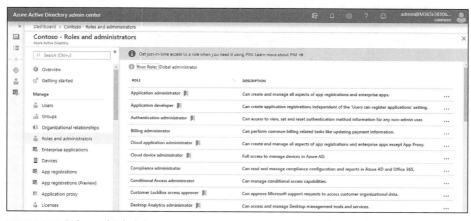

FIGURE 2-51 Roles and Administrators

2. Click on the role that you wish to learn the membership of. Figure 2-52 shows members of the Password Administrators role.

FIGURE 2-52 Members of the Password Administrators role

You can use the following Azure PowerShell cmdlets to view roles and role membership:

- **Get-AzureADDirectoryRole**   View a list of Azure AD Directory roles.
- **Get-AzureADDirectoryRoleMember**   View the users assigned membership in an Azure AD Directory role

> **MORE INFO DELEGATING ADMIN RIGHTS**
>
> You can learn more about delegating admin rights at: *https://docs.microsoft.com/azure/active-directory/users-groups-roles/roles-concept-delegation*.

Manage role allocations by using Azure AD

To assign a user to a specific role within Azure AD, perform the following steps:

1. In the Azure AD Admin Center, select **Roles And Administrators**.
2. Select the role to which you wish to add a user. This will open the role's properties page.
3. In the Role properties page, click **Add Member**. Figure 2-53 shows adding the user Adele Vance to the Security Administrator role.

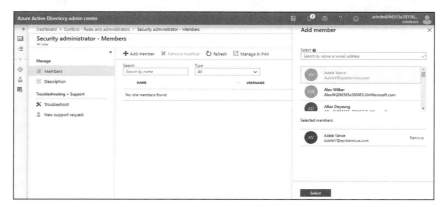

FIGURE 2-53 Members of the Password Administrators role

You can use the following Azure PowerShell cmdlets to manage role membership:

- **Add-AzureADDirectoryRoleMember** Add a user to an Azure AD Directory role.
- **Remove-AzureADDirectoryRoleMember** Remove a user from an Azure AD Directory role.

> **MORE INFO VIEW AND ASSIGN AZURE AD ADMINISTRATOR ROLES**
>
> You can learn more about viewing and assigning administrator roles at: *https://docs.micro-soft.com/azure/active-directory/users-groups-roles/directory-manage-roles-portal*.

Configure administrative accounts

Azure AD Privileged Identity Management (PIM) allows you to make role assignment tempo-rary and contingent on approval, rather than permanent, as is the case with manually adding a member to the role. PIM requires Azure AD P2 and must be enabled before you can configure it. To configure an Azure AD administrative role for use with PIM, perform the following steps:

1. In the Azure AD Admin Center, select **Roles And Administrators**.
2. Select the role to which you wish to add a user. This will open the role's properties page.
3. In the Role properties page, click **Manage In PIM**. The role will open and any members assigned permanently to the role will be listed with the status of permanent as shown in Figure 2-54.

FIGURE 2-54 Members of the Password Administrators role

4. Select the user that you wish to convert from permanent to eligible. An eligible user can request access to the role, but will not have its associated rights and privileges until that access is granted. On the user's properties page, click **Make Eligible**.

You can edit the conditions under which an eligible user can be granted by performing the following steps:

1. In the Privileged Identity Management blade, click **Azure AD Roles**.
2. Under Manage, shown in Figure 2-55, click **Settings**.

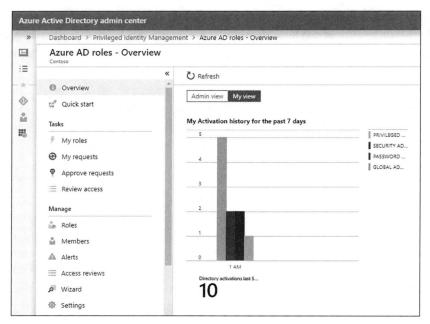

FIGURE 2-55 Manage PIM

3. Click **Roles** and then select the role that you wish to configure. Figure 2-56 shows the PIM settings for the Security Administrator role where role activation can occur for an hour at most, but where MFA and approval are not required.

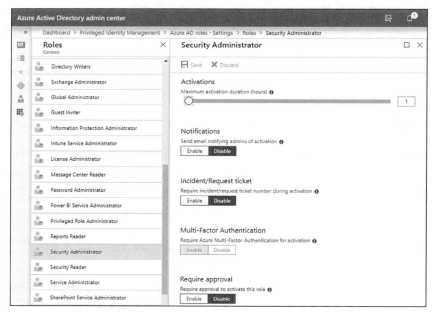

FIGURE 2-56 Manage PIM

Users can activate roles that they are eligible for from the Privileged Identity Management area of the Azure AD Administrative console. Administrators with the appropriate permissions can also use the Privileged Identity Management area of the Azure AD Administrative console to approve requests that require approval and review role activations.

> **MORE INFO** **PRIVILEGED IDENTITY MANAGEMENT**
>
> You can learn more about topic at: *https://docs.microsoft.com/azure/active-directory/ privileged-identity-management/pim-configure*.

Plan security and compliance roles for Microsoft 365

The Microsoft 365 Security and Compliance center includes default role groups that are appropriate for the most commonly performed security and compliance tasks. To assign users permission to perform these tasks, add them to the appropriate role group in the Microsoft 365 Security and Compliance Center. These Microsoft 365 security and compliance role groups are listed in Table 2-4.

TABLE 2-4 Security and compliance role groups

Role Group	Description
Compliance Administrator	Can manage device management settings, data loss prevention settings, and data preservation reports.
eDiscovery Manager	Can perform searches and place holds on SharePoint Online sites, OneDrive for Business locations and Exchange Online mailboxes. Can create and manage eDiscovery cases.
Organization Management	Can control permissions for accessing Security & Compliance Center. Can also manage settings for data loss prevention, device management, reports, and preservation.
Records Management	Manage and dispose of record content.
Reviewer	View the list of eDiscovery cases in the Security and Compliance center. Unable to create or manage eDiscovery cases.
Security Administrator	All the permissions of the Security Reader role, plus administrative permissions for Azure Information Protection, Identity Protection Center, Privileged Identity Management, the ability to monitor Office 365 Service Health, and Microsoft 365 Security and Compliance Center.
Security Reader	Provides read-only access to security features of the Identity Protection Center, Privileged Identity Management, Microsoft 365 service health, and Microsoft 365 Security and Compliance Center.
Service Assurance User	Provides reports and documentation that explain Microsoft's security practices for customer data stored in Microsoft 365.
Supervisory Review	Able to create and manage policies that mediate which communications are subject to review.

EXAM TIP

Remember the functionality of the different security and compliance roles that can be assigned to users.

Thought experiment

In this thought experiment, demonstrate your skills and knowledge of the topics covered in this chapter. You can find answers to this thought experiment in the next section.

You are in the process of consulting for Adatum about their planned synchronization solution that will allow them to replicate user account, group account, and mail enabled contacts from their on-premises Active Directory environment to an Azure Active Directory instance that supports an Office 365 tenancy. The Adatum environment consists of three forests with 21 separate domains. A preliminary assessment using the IdFix tool has found that it is necessary to make bulk changes to certain attributes used with user accounts before synchronization between the on-premises environment and Azure Active Directory can commence. Prior to full scale deployment of synchronization, it will also be necessary to have robust recovery procedures in the event that one or more accounts is deleted. Finally, all accounts at Adatum are in geography-based OUs. Attributes, such as the Department attribute, denote the departments that the users are associated with.

With this in mind, answer the following questions:

1. How many instances of Azure AD Connect are necessary to sync the Adatum environment to a single Azure AD instance?

2. What tool, besides Microsoft PowerShell, could be used to bulk modify the attributes of selected user accounts at Adatum?

3. How can you ensure that members of the Research department don't have their accounts synchronized to the Azure Active Directory instance that supports the Office 365 tenancy?

4. What feature can you enable on the on-premises Active Directory instance that will allow you to recover an accidentally deleted account without having to recreate it with a new GUID?

5. How long are objects deleted from the Azure Active Directory instance used to support Office 365 recoverable?

Thought experiment answers

This section contains the solution to the thought experiment. Each answer explains why the answer choice is correct.

1. You only need a single instance of Azure AD Connect to synchronize from three separate Active Directory forests.

2. ADModify.NET can be used to bulk modify the attributes of selected user accounts at Adatum.

3. You can configure Azure AD Connect to only replicate specific OUs. You could also use tools such as the Synchronization Rules editor if more complicated synchronization rules are necessary.

4. Enabling Active Directory Recycle Bin allows you to recover an accidentally deleted account without having to recreate it with a new GUID.

5. Objects are recoverable from the Azure Active Directory Recycle Bin for 30 days.

Chapter summary

- When determining an appropriate identity strategy, figure out which identities need to be replicated to the cloud, how often that replication should occur, and which aspects of those identities must be replicated.

- A hybrid approach is necessary when the on-premises Active Directory instance is still in operation.

- Azure AD Connect can be installed on a local member server and will allow synchronization of identities and password hashes to Azure AD.

- Prior to deploying Azure AD Connect, the on-premises directory should be cleaned up to remove any current settings that may block successful synchronization. Tools such as the IdFix tool and ADModify.NET can be used to perform this task.

- If your on-premises directory uses a non-routable domain, you will need to update on-premises accounts with a UPN suffix that is routable and configured to work with Microsoft 365. This will usually be a registered domain name associated with the tenancy.

- Password synchronization with Azure AD Connect synchronizes hashes of passwords from the on-premises environment to Azure AD. It can be configured for password write back if self-service reset is enabled.

- Pass-through authentication has the user's password validated against an on-premises AD instance. This requires an agent be installed on an on-premises domain controller.

- Active Directory Federation is appropriate for environments with more sophisticated identity requirements than those catered to by Azure AD Connect password synchronization or pass-through authentication.

- The health of Azure AD Connect can be monitored through the Azure Active Directory Admin Center console.

- Synchronization can be forced using the Synchronization Service Manager or through PowerShell.

- Azure AD identities can be managed through the Azure Active Directory admin center, the Microsoft 365 Admin Center, or Azure PowerShell.

- Self-service password resets allow users to reset their passwords after answering questions related to their identity.

- Azure AD supports two types of group, Office 365 groups and security groups. Office 365 groups have access to additional O365 resources such as shared mailbox and calendar. Membership can be directly assigned or dynamically configured through a query of Azure AD attributes.

- Users must be assigned licenses to use Microsoft 365 resources. This task can be performed through the Microsoft 365 Admin Center or Azure AD Admin Center.

- You can delegate administrative privileges by assigning roles. You should follow the principle of least privilege and only assign users the minimum necessary administrative permissions required to perform their duties.

CHAPTER 3

Manage access and authentication

Identity is becoming more and more important as a security control plane given how more services are moving to the cloud. This means that rather than worrying about firewall configuration, or which services are running on a server when managing your organization's security posture, you should increasingly be concerned about your organization's security practices around identities. This includes ensuring that Microsoft 365 credentials are being used in a secure manner, that risky sign in activity is detected and remediated, that multi-factor authentication is configured where appropriate, and that relationships can be established with partner organization's identity providers where appropriate. In this chapter you'll learn how to view auditing data and security reports related to identity, how to configure multi-factor authentication, how to configure access to applications for users, and how to integrate those applications into Azure Active Directory. You'll also learn what steps you can take to enable people within your organization to share content with people outside the organization, with partner organizations or lone individuals.

Skills covered in this chapter:

- Manage authentication
- Implement Multi-Factor Authentication (MFA)
- Configure application access
- Implement access for external users of Microsoft 365 workloads

Skill 3.1: Manage authentication

This skill section deals with managing authentication for Microsoft 365 and Office 365 workloads. To master this skill, you'll need to understand the process of designing an authentication method, configuring, managing and implementing authentication, and then monitoring authentication.

This section covers the following topics :

- Design authentication method
- Configure authentication
- Implement authentication method
- Manage authentication
- Monitor authentication

Design authentication method

When designing an authentication method for Microsoft 365, you need to make several decisions around basic and modern authentication, before getting into details about whether or not you wish to implement multi-factor authentication. The difference between the two are as follows:

- **Basic authentication** When a client performs basic authentication, it transmits base64 encoded credentials from the client to the server. These credentials are protected from interception within a Transport Layer Security (TLS) encrypted session. TLS is the successor protocol to Secure Sockets Layer (SSL). Basic authentication is also termed proxy authentication when the client sends credentials to an Office 365 related service in Microsoft 365, and the service proxies those credentials to an identity provider on behalf of the client. Depending on the organization's configuration, the identity provider can be Azure Active Directory or an on-premises Active Directory instance, if passed through Active Directory Federation Services is configured.

- **Modern authentication** Instead of just username- and password-based authentication, modern authentication supports technologies such as multi-factor authentication, smart card authentication, certificate based authentication, and SAML-based third party identity providers.

Legacy authentication, used by Office 2013 client apps by default, supports both basic authentication as well as the Microsoft Online Sign-In assistant. Office 2013 passed from mainstream support in October 2018. The Microsoft Online Sign-In Assistant is special software that allows authentication to a variety of Microsoft Online services without requiring the end user to regularly reenter their credentials. Office 2013 client apps can be configured to support modern authentication through editing the registry keys listed in Table 3-1 and shown in Figure 3-1.

TABLE 3-1 Modern Authentication Registry Keys

Registry Key	Type	Value
HKCU\SOFTWARE\Microsoft\Office\15.0\Common\Identity\EnableADAL	REG_DWORD	1
HKCU\SOFTWARE\Microsoft\Office\15.0\Common\Identity\Version	REG_DWORD	1

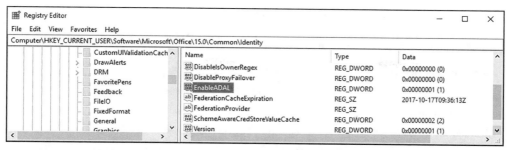

FIGURE 3-1 Office 2013 registry keys to allow use of modern authentication

Office 2016 and later client apps support modern authentication by default. While it's possible to configure Office 2016 and later client apps so that modern authentication is disabled and only basic authentication is used, this is not recommended because it will substantially decrease security.

> **MORE INFO UNDERSTANDING MODERN AUTHENTICATION FOR OFFICE CLIENT APPS**
>
> You can learn more about basic and modern authentication and how it impacts the Office client apps at: *https://docs.microsoft.com/office365/enterprise/modern-auth-for-office-2013-and-2016*.

Another important aspect around designing authentication is deciding which authentication methods will be supported if you want to support self-service password reset or Azure Multi-Factor authentication as shown in Figure 3-2.

FIGURE 3-2 Multiple methods of verifying identity during authentication

Table 3.2 lists the authentication methods and where they can be used.

TABLE 3.2 Authentication methods and usage

Authentication method	Where it can be used
Password	Multi Factor Authentication and Self-service Password Reset
Security questions	Self-service Password Reset only
Email address	Self-service Password Reset only
Microsoft Authenticator App	Multi Factor Authentication and Self-service Password Reset
OATH Hardware Token	Multi Factor Authentication and Self-service Password Reset
SMS	Multi Factor Authentication and Self-service Password Reset
Voice Call	Multi Factor Authentication and Self-service Password Reset
App passwords	Multi Factor Authentication in some cases

These authentication methods have the following properties:

- **Password** The password assigned to an Azure AD account is an authentication method. While you can perform password-less authentication, you cannot disable the password as an authentication method.

- **Security Questions** These are only available to Azure AD Self-Service Password Reset and can only be used with accounts that have not been assigned administrative roles. Questions are stored on the user object within Azure AD and cannot be read or modified by an administrator. They should be used in conjunction with another method. Azure AD includes the following predefined questions and it is possible to create custom questions:

- In what city did you meet your first spouse/partner?
- In what city did your parents meet?
- In what city does your nearest sibling live?
- In what city was your father born?
- In what city was your first job?
- In what city was your mother born?
- What city were you in on New Year's 2000?
- What is the last name of your favorite teacher in high school?
- What is the name of a college you applied to but didn't attend?
- What is the name of the place in which you held your first wedding reception?
- What is your father's middle name?
- What is your favorite food?
- What is your maternal grandmother's first and last name?
- What is your mother's middle name?
- What is your oldest sibling's birthday month and year? (e.g. November 1985)

- What is your oldest sibling's middle name?
- What is your paternal grandfather's first and last name?
- What is your youngest sibling's middle name?
- What school did you attend for sixth grade?
- What was the first and last name of your childhood best friend?
- What was the first and last name of your first significant other?
- What was the last name of your favorite grade school teacher?
- What was the make and model of your first car or motorcycle?
- What was the name of the first school you attended?
- What was the name of the hospital in which you were born?
- What was the name of the street of your first childhood home?
- What was the name of your childhood hero?
- What was the name of your favorite stuffed animal?
- What was the name of your first pet?
- What was your childhood nickname?
- What was your favorite sport in high school?
- What was your first job?
- What were the last four digits of your childhood telephone number?
- When you were young, what did you want to be when you grew up?
- Who is the most famous person you have ever met?
- **Email address**   This is only used for Azure AD self-service password resets and should be separate from the user's Microsoft 365 Exchange Online email address.
- **Microsoft authenticator app**   Is available for Android and iOS. Either involves the user being notified through the mobile app and being asked to select the same number on the mobile app as is displayed on the logon prompt, or involves the user entering a set of periodically changing numbers displayed on the mobile app.
- **OATH hardware tokens**   Azure AD supports the use of OATH-TOTP SHA-1 tokens of both the 30 and 60 second variety. Secret keys can have a maximum of 128 characters. Once a token is acquired, it must be uploaded in comma separated format including UPN, serial number, secret key, time interval, manufacturer and model.
- **Mobile Phone**   Can be used either to send a code through text message that must be entered into a dialog box to complete authentication, or where a phone call is made to the user who then needs to provide a personal authentication PIN. Phone numbers must include country code.
- **App Passwords**   A number of non-browser apps do not support multi-factor authentication. An app password allows these users to continue to authenticate using these

apps when multi-factor authentication is not supported. An app password can be generated for each app, allowing each app password to be individually revoked.

MORE INFO **WHAT ARE AUTHENTICATION METHODS**

You can learn more about what authentication methods are supported by Microsoft 365 and Azure AD at: *https://docs.microsoft.com/azure/active-directory/authentication/concept-authentication-methods.*

Configure authentication

Modern authentication is enabled by default for SharePoint Online, Exchange Online, and other Office 365 services available through Microsoft 365. You can verify that modern authentication is enabled by running the following PowerShell command when connected to your organization's Microsoft 365 tenancy:

```
Get-OrganizationConfig | Format-Table Name,OAuth* -Auto
```

Although not recommended, you can disable modern authentication by running the following PowerShell command when connected to your organization's Microsoft 365 tenancy:

```
Set-OrganizationConfig -OAuth2ClientProfileEnabled $false
```

To re-enable modern authentication, run the following command when connected to your organization's Microsoft 365 tenancy:

```
Set-OrganizationConfig -OAuth2ClientProfileEnabled $true
```

MORE INFO **ENABLE MODERN AUTHENTICATION IN EXCHANGE ONLINE**

You can learn more about enabling modern authentication in Exchange Online at: *https://docs.microsoft.com/exchange/clients-and-mobile-in-exchange-online/enable-or-disable-modern-authentication-in-exchange-online.*

Another aspect of configuring authentication is configuring a password policy. Password policies determine how often a user must update their password. By default, Microsoft 365 user passwords are configured to never expire as shown in Figure 3-3. Password policies for Microsoft 365 are configured in the Microsoft 365 admin center.

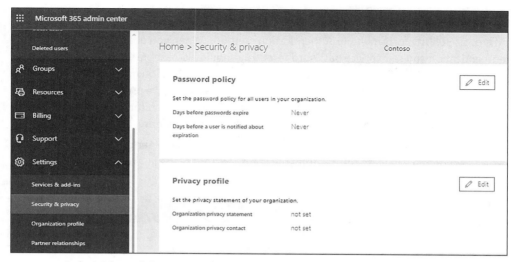

FIGURE 3-3 Default Microsoft 365 Password Policy

Users that have been assigned the Global Admin role are able to modify the password policy. Once you have configured passwords to expire, you can configure the number of days before passwords expire and the number of days before a user is notified that their password will expire. Figure 3-4 shows a maximum password age of 90 days and how a user will be notified 14 days before expiration occurs. You can configure a maximum password age of up to 730 days.

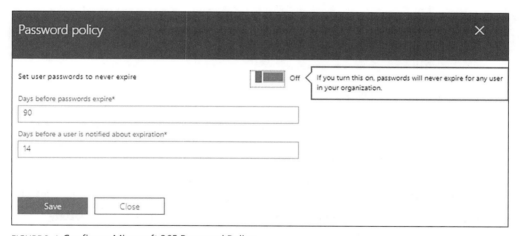

FIGURE 3-4 Configure Microsoft 365 Password Policy

MORE INFO PASSWORD EXPIRATION POLICIES

You can learn more about password expiration policies at: *https://docs.microsoft.com/office365/admin/manage/set-password-expiration-policy?view=o365-worldwide.*

Implement authentication method

Microsoft 365 supports multiple authentication methods. When you enable multi-factor authentication and self-service password reset, you should also enable multiple authentication methods. This allows the user to fall back to a different authentication method in the event that their chosen authentication method is not available. For example, if a user cannot get access to their mailbox, and needs to perform self-service password reset, you can allow them to answer a number of security questions as a method of validating their identity.

You configure the authentication methods that users can use to perform self-service password reset on the Password reset – Authentication Methods blade in Azure Active Directory Admin Center, as shown in Figure 3-5.

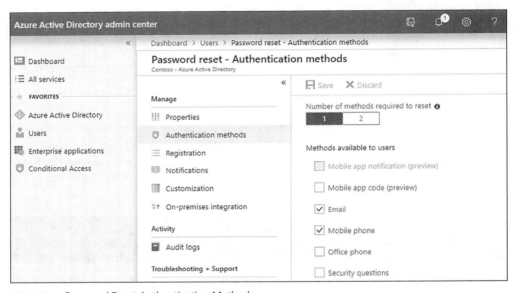

FIGURE 3-5 Password Reset Authentication Methods

Unless there is a good reason otherwise, you should enable as many authentication methods for self-service password reset as possible, and then require two methods to perform reset. This gives a user a maximum amount of flexibility while still ensuring a high level of security.

> ***MORE INFO*** **AUTHENTICATION METHODS**
>
> You can learn more about authentication methods at: *https://docs.microsoft.com/azure/ active-directory/authentication/concept-authentication-methods.*

Manage authentication

There are several technologies that you can use to manage authentication in a Microsoft 365 environment. These include enabling Azure AD Smart Lockout, Azure AD Password Protection,

Self-service Password Reset, Password-less phone sign in, and enabling certificate-based Azure AD authentication.

Azure AD Smart Lockout

Smart Lockout is a technology that allows you to lock out attackers who are trying to brute force user passwords. Based on machine learning, smart lockout is able to discern when sign-ins are coming from authentic users and treat those sign-ins differently to those that appear to come from attackers or other unknown sources. Smart Lockout locks out an account for 60 seconds after 10 failed sign-in attempts have occurred. If there are subsequent failed sign-in attempts after this 60 seconds has expired, the lock out period duration increases. Smart Lockout only tracks when different passwords are used, which is the pattern during a brute force attack, so if a user enters the same incorrect password 10 times, that will only count as one bad password towards the 10 that trigger account lockout.

Azure AD Smart Lockout is enabled by default on Microsoft 365 Azure AD tenancies. You can configure a custom smart lockout threshold in the Authentication Methods section of the Azure AD console as shown in Figure 3-6.

FIGURE 3-6 Custom Smart Lockout Policy

> **MORE INFO AZURE AD SMART LOCKOUT**
>
> You can learn more about Azure AD smart lockout at: *https://docs.microsoft.com/azure/active-directory/authentication/howto-password-smart-lockout.*

Azure AD Banned Passwords

Another aspect of managing authentication is implementing a custom Banned Password list as shown in Figure 3-7. Any password that is on the banned list cannot be used by a user in your organization. There are multiple lists of commonly used passwords that you can download from the Internet for free that you can add to the Azure AD Banned Password list. This allows you to block users from using commonly used passwords. There are also longer lists of all passwords that have been exposed in data breaches, which you could import if you wanted to ensure that users were blocked from using any password that had been made public through a data breach. You can only implement a custom banned password list if your organization has an Azure AD P1 or P2 license. Common character substitution within banned passwords is enabled by default.

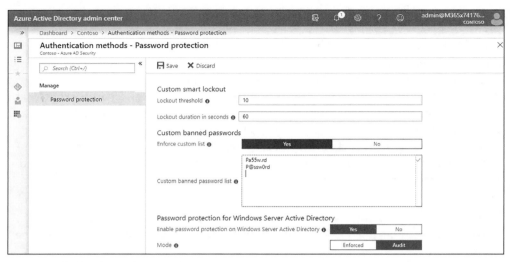

FIGURE 3-7 Custom banned passwords

> *MORE INFO* **AZURE AD BANNED PASSWORDS**
>
> You can learn more about Azure AD Banned Passwords Password at: *https://docs.microsoft. com/azure/active-directory/authentication/concept-password-ban-bad.*

Self-service Password Reset

Self-service Password Reset allows users to perform other forms of authentication in the event that they forget their accounts Azure AD password. As you can see in Figure 3-8, you can configure Self-service Password Reset so that users must sign up for the service when they first authenticate, and then periodically renew their information, with the default renewal period being every 180 days.

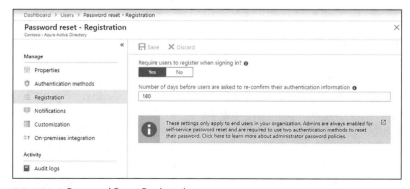

FIGURE 3-8 Password Reset Registration

As you learned earlier in this chapter, you can require users to provide multiple forms of authentication when performing A Self-service Password Reset. When a user signs up for Self-service Password Reset, they configure these alternate methods of authentication. These can include:

- Mobile App notification
- Mobile app code
- Email
- Mobile phone
- Office phone
- Security questions

> **MORE INFO** **CONFIGURE SELF-SERVICE PASSWORD RESET**
>
> You can learn more about configuring self-service password reset at: *https://docs.microsoft.com/azure/active-directory/authentication/quickstart-sspr.*

Password-Less phone sign-in

When password-Less phone sign-in is enabled, users are able to sign into an Azure AD account and then access Microsoft 365 resources using the Microsoft Authenticator app on their mobile device. When Password-Less phone sign-in is enabled, users do not have to provide a user-name and password, and instead key-based authentication enables the user to authenticate with the authenticator app using a biometric or PIN.

To enable Password-Less phone sign-in, users must have the latest version of the Microsoft Authenticator installed on their devices. Those devices should be running iOS 8.0 or greater, or Android 6.0 or greater. Users will also need to be enrolled for Multi-Factor authentication. When these conditions have been met, an authenticator sign-in policy needs to be configured. You can do this when a PowerShell connection is established to the Microsoft 365 tenancy by issuing the following command:

```
New-AzureADPolicy -Type AuthenticatorAppSignInPolicy -Definition '{"Authenticat
orAppSignInPolicy":{"Enabled":true}}' -isOrganizationDefault $true -DisplayName
AuthenticatorAppSignIn
```

To enable phone sign-in on the app, choose the drop down arrow next to the account name on the app and select Enable Phone Sign-On. If an icon with a key appears next to the Microsoft 365 account name, this means that phone sign-in for the account has successfully been configured.

A drawback of using Phone Sign-On is that due to the way that device registration functions with Azure AD, a device can only be registered against a single tenant. This means that if a user has multiple Microsoft 365 accounts, only one of those accounts can be enabled for Phone Sign-In.

Certificate based Azure AD authentication

Certificate based authentication allows you to eliminate the need for a username and password combination when authenticating against Exchange Online and other Microsoft 365 services. Certificate based authentication is supported on Windows, Android, and iOS devices, and has the following requirements:

- Is only supported for Federated environments for browser applications or where native clients use modern authentication through the Active Directory Authentication Library (ADAL). Exchange Active Sync (EAS) for Exchange Online (EXO) is exempt from the federation requirement and can be used with both federated and managed accounts.

- The organization's root certificate authority (CA) and any intermediate CAs must be integrated with Azure AD.

- Each organizational CA must publish a Certificate Revocation List (CRL) in a location that is accessible to the Internet.

- The Windows, Android, or iOS device must have access to an organizational CA that is configured to issue client certificates.

- The Windows, Android, or iOS device must have a valid certificate installed.

- Exchange ActiveSync clients require that the client certificate have the user's routable email address included in the Subject Alternative Name field.

To add an organizational CA that is trusted by Azure Active Directory, you need to ensure that the CA is configured with a CRL publication location that is accessible on the Internet and to then export the CA certificate. Once you have the CA certificate exported, which will include the internet accessible location where the CRL is published, use the New-AzureADTrustedCertificateAuthority PowerShell cmdlet to add the organizational CA's certificate to Azure Active Directory. You can view a list of trusted CAs for your organization's Azure AD instance using the Get-AzureADTrustedCertificateAuthority cmdlet.

Monitor authentication

There are several methods through which you can monitor authentication for your organization's Microsoft 365 tenancy. Azure AD's reporting architecture includes the following elements:

- **Sign-ins** Provides you with information about user sign in activity and the utilization of managed applications.
- **Audit logs** Allows you to view information about changes that have occurred within Azure Active Directory, such as adding or removing user accounts.
- **Risky sign-ins** Provides you with data about sign-in activity that has been flagged by Microsoft's security mechanisms as suspicious.
- **Users flagged for risk** Provides you with a list of users that Microsoft's security mechanisms suggest might have compromised accounts.

Users who have been assigned the Global Administrator, Security Administrator, Security Reader, or Report Reader Azure AD roles are able to view data in Azure AD reports. Users without membership in these roles are also able to view audit activities related to their account.

Each event recorded in the audit logs provides the following data:

- Data and time of the event
- Service that logged the event
- Name and category of the event logged
- Activity status (success or failure)
- Target of the action (which user, group, etc.)
- Which security principal initiated the action

Figure 3-9 shows the details of an event from the Azure AD Audit Log.

FIGURE 3-9 Azure AD Audit Log event

You can filter audit logs using the following fields:

- Service
- Category
- Activity
- Status
- Target
- Initiated by (Actor)
- Date Range

> **MORE INFO AUDIT ACTIVITY REPORTS**
>
> You can learn more about audit activity reports at: *https://docs.microsoft.com/azure/active-directory/reports-monitoring/concept-audit-logs*.

Sign-in logs

The sign-in logs provide information about user and managed application authentication activity. Figure 3-10 shows the basic sign-in report.

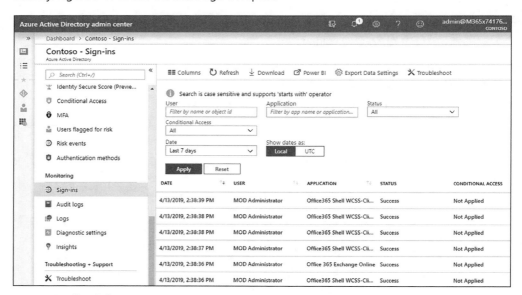

FIGURE 3-10 Sign-in log

The sign-in report allows you to answer the following questions:

- What patterns are present in a user's sign-in activities?
- How many users associated with the Microsoft 365 tenancy have signed in over the last week?

- How many sign-ins have been successful and how many have failed?

The sign-ins log provides the following information by default:

- Sign-in date
- User account
- Application the user has authenticated against
- Sign-in status (success or failure)
- Risk detection status
- Multi-factor authentication status

The Sign-in log can be filtered by the following fields as shown in Figure 3-11:

- User
- Application
- Sign-in status
- Conditional Access
- Date

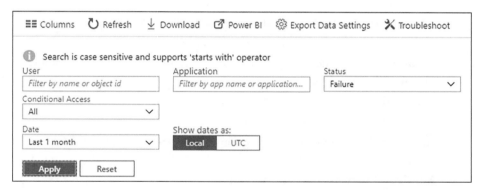

FIGURE 3-11 Filter Sign-in log

MORE INFO **SIGN-IN ACTIVITY REPORTS**

You can learn more about sign-in activity reports at: *https://docs.microsoft.com/azure/active-directory/reports-monitoring/concept-sign-ins*.

Risky sign-ins

A risky sign-in is one that Microsoft's security mechanisms have flagged as suspicious. Microsoft processes millions of sign-ins every day through services such as Azure AD, XBox Live, and Outlook.com. Telemetry is used from these sign-ins to determine the characteristics of what constitutes a normal sign-in and which sign-ins are suspicious and should be flagged for further investigation. The risky sign-ins report is shown in Figure 3-12.

FIGURE 3-12 Risky sign-ins

While the Risky Sign-ins report is available for all editions of Azure AD, the amount of detail you get through the report varies between the Free, Basic, P1, and P2 editions. The Free and Basic editions will provide you with a list of Risky Sign-ins and will provide you with events that include the following details:

- **User** This is the user the risky sign-in is associated with.
- **IP** The IP address that the sign-in occurred from.
- **Location** The location that Microsoft's security intelligence data indicates is associated with the IP address.
- **Sign-in time** When the sign-in occurred.
- **Status** The status of the sign-in.

When viewing the events in the Risky Sign-ins report, you can provide the following feedback on each event:

- **Resolve** This marks the event as resolved.
- **Mark as false positive** Marks the event as something that should not be classified as a Risky Sign-in.
- **Ignore** Marks the risk factors as ones that should be ignored in future.
- **Reactivate** Reactivates a risky sign-in that was previously assigned another status.

In addition to the information provided in the reports available at the Basic and Free Azure AD editions, organizations that are licensed at the Azure AD P1 and P2 level will get more information about the risk event type that triggered the inclusion of the entry in the report, the ability to create a user risk remediation policy, a detailed timeline on the risk event, and a list of other users for which the same risk event type has been detected.

Risk events

Azure AD detects the following types of suspicious activities and assigns them to the following risk event categories:

- **Users with leaked credentials**   Microsoft examines credential data breaches for username and password pairs associated with Azure AD tenancies. When a username and password pair associated with an Azure AD tenancy is found, these credentials are checked and if there is a match, a leaked credentials risk event is generated.

- **Sign-ins from anonymous IP addresses**   Microsoft security researchers have identified which IP addresses are used by anonymous proxy services. While it's not unusual for some users to route their traffic through anonymous VPN services, it's also a technique used by attackers attempting to compromise an account.

- **Impossible travel to atypical locations**   This risk event is generated when a user signs in from locations that are so geographically disparate that travel between those locations is impossible in the period between sign-in times. For example, a user signs in from Sydney Australia and then two hours later signs in from Copenhagen, Denmark.

- **Sign-ins from infected devices**   This risk category is assigned when a user signs on from an address that Microsoft security researchers have flagged as regularly communicating with a bot server.

- **Sign-ins from unfamiliar locations**   This risk event is generated when a user sign-in is from locations that are unusual for the user given past sign-in activity. For example, if a user is constantly signing in from locations around Melbourne, Australia and then signs on from Stockholm in Sweden, this risk event will be generated.

- **Sign-ins from IP addresses with suspicious activity**   This risk category is assigned when a user signs-in from an IP address or IP address range for which there are a substantial number of failed sign-in attempts across multiple accounts in a short period of time. The machine learning algorithm that assigns this category is attempting to detect credential guessing brute force attacks before they are successful. Sign-ins of this category are shown in Figure 3-13.

FIGURE 3-13 Risky Sign-ins

Once a risk category is assigned, a risk level is also calculated. The severity of the risk level allows you to understand the degree of confidence Microsoft has that the identity may have been compromised and how seriously you should take the alert. The severity levels are as follows:

- **High**   There is high severity and high confidence in the diagnosis. An identity related to an event that is assigned this severity level is almost certainly compromised. User accounts involved should be remediated immediately.

- **Medium**   Involves either high severity and lower confidence or lower severity and high confidence. Microsoft recommends that identities related to an event assigned this severity should be proactively remediated even if there isn't certainty that the account has been compromised.

- **Low**   Involves low severity and low confidence. This is an indicator that Microsoft has flagged activity involving the activity to be suspicious. An example of this may be a sign-in from an unfamiliar location in the same region of the world. For example, a user who has, up until now, only signed on from Sydney and Melbourne in Australia may instead sign on from Auckland in New Zealand.

> **MORE INFO** **RISK EVENTS**
>
> You can learn more about risk events at: *https://docs.microsoft.com/azure/active-directory/reports-monitoring/concept-risk-events*.

Users Flagged For Risk

The Users Flagged For Risk report, which is accessible under the Security section of the Azure Active Directory console, as shown in Figure 3-14, provides a list of users that have risk events associated with their accounts. Depending on the edition of Azure AD that has been licensed, you'll either get a simple list of users that are flagged for risk, or at the P1 or P2 levels, get detailed information about underlying risk events and why each specific user was flagged.

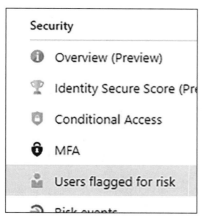

FIGURE 3-14 Users flagged for risk

MORE INFO **USERS FLAGGED FOR RISK**

You can learn more about users flagged for risk at: *https://docs.microsoft.com/azure/active-directory/reports-monitoring/concept-user-at-risk*.

Self-service password reset activity

You can view the self-service password reset audit log on the Password Reset – Audit Logs page of the Azure AD admin center, as shown in Figure 3-15. These logs will provide you with information about which user initiated the reset, the method used, as well as when the self-service password reset process was initiated.

FIGURE 3-15 Risky sign-ins

You can use the dialog boxes and drop downs on this page to generate reports that allow you to determine the following information:

- How many users have registered for self-service password reset?
- Which users have registered for self-service password reset
- What information are users providing when registering for self-service password reset?
- How many users reset their passwords using self-service password reset in the prior 7 days?
- What methods are being used for authentication when performing self-service password reset?
- Is there any suspicious activity occurring during the self-service password reset process?
- Which authentication methods are generating the most problems during the self-service password reset process?

> **MORE INFO** **SELF-SERVICE PASSWORD RESET REPORTS**
>
> You can learn more about self-service password reset monitoring at: *https://docs.microsoft.com/azure/active-directory/authentication/howto-sspr-reporting*.

EXAM TIP

Remember the different authentication options that can be configured for self-service password reset and the requirements for organizational CAs when implementing certificate based AD authentication.

Skill 3.2: Implement Multi-Factor Authentication

This skill section deals with implementing multi-factor authentication (MFA) in a Microsoft 365 environment. To master this skill, you'll need to understand the requirements for implementing multi-factor authentication, how to configure multi-factor authentication for applications and users, how to administer multi-factor authentication for users, and how to report on multi-factor authentication utilization.

> **This section covers the following topics :**
> - Design an MFA solution
> - Configure MFA for apps or users
> - Administer MFA users
> - Report MFA utilization

Design an MFA solution

When implementing MFA with Microsoft 365, you need to make decisions about which MFA capabilities will be included. MFA requires that more than one authentication method be used when signing in to a resource integrated with Microsoft 365. Usually this involves the user providing their username and password credentials, and then providing one of the following:

- **A code generated by an authenticator app** This can be the Microsoft Authenticator app or a third party authenticator app such as the Google authenticator app.

- **A response provided to the Microsoft authenticator app** When this method is used, Azure AD provides an on screen code to the user authenticating that must also be selected on an application that is registered with Azure AD.

- **A phone call to a number registered with Azure AD** The user needs to provide a pre-configured pin that they will be instructed to enter by the automated service that performs the phone call. Microsoft provides a default greeting during authentication phone calls, so you don't have to record one for your own organization.

- **An SMS message sent to a mobile phone number registered with Azure AD** The user provides the code sent in the message as a second factor during authentication.

When designing your solution, you'll need to have a way of ensuring that users have access to the appropriate MFA technology. This may require you to come up with a method of ensuring that all users in your organization already have the Microsoft Authenticator app installed on their mobile devices before you enable MFA on their accounts.

> **MORE INFO PLAN FOR MULTI-FACTOR AUTHENTICATION**
>
> You can learn more about designing a multi-factor authentication solution for Office 365 deployments at: *https://docs.microsoft.com/office365/admin/security-and-compliance/ multi-factor-authentication-plan.*

Configure MFA for apps or users

MFA is not enabled by default on Microsoft 365 tenancies. Before you can configure accounts to use MFA, you'll need to enable MFA on the tenancy. To enable MFA on a Microsoft 365 Azure AD tenancy and configure MFA for specific users, perform the following steps:

1. In Azure Active Directory Admin Center, navigate to Users and then click **All Users**.

2. Click **More**, and then click **Multifactor Authentication**, as shown in Figure 3-16.

FIGURE 3-16 Set up Azure MFA

3. After selecting this option, MFA will be enabled for the tenancy and you'll be provided with a list of Users similar to that shown in Figure 3-17.

FIGURE 3-17 Set up users for Azure MFA

4. Select the users that you wish to set up for MFA, as shown in Figure 3-18, and then click Enable.

FIGURE 3-18 Set up users for Azure MFA

5. On the About Enabling Multi-Factor Auth dialog box, shown in Figure 3-19, click **Enable Multi-Factor Auth.**

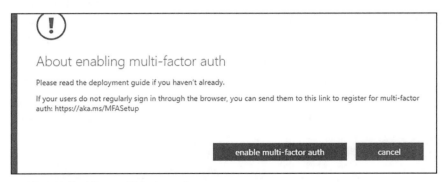

FIGURE 3-19 Enabling multi-factor auth

6. The next time that users sign on, they will be prompted to enroll in multi-factor authentication. You will be presented with a dialog box similar to that shown in Figure 3-20, asking them to provide additional information.

FIGURE 3-20 More information required

7. And then, choose between providing a mobile phone number, an office phone number, or configure a mobile app as shown in Figure 3-21.

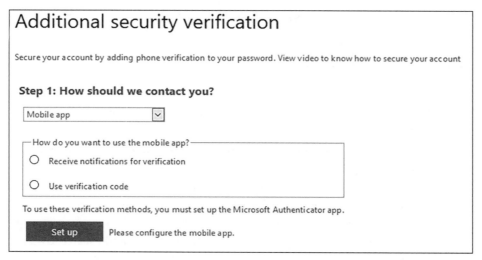

FIGURE 3-21 Contact preferences

8. When you specify one of these options, you are presented with a QR code. Within the app you can add a new account by scanning the QR code.

9. Once you have configured the application, you will be required to confirm that configuration has completed successfully by approving a sign-in through the app as shown in Figure 3-22.

FIGURE 3-22 Verify on the app

10. Once this is done, you'll be prompted to provide additional security information in the form of a phone number as shown in Figure 3-23.

Additional security verification

Secure your account by adding phone verification to your password. View video to know how to secure your account

Step 3: In case you lose access to the mobile app

Select your country or region ∨	

FIGURE 3-23 Verify on the app

You can configure the following multi-factor authentication service settings as shown in Figure 3-24.

- **App passwords** Allow or disallow users from using app passwords for non-browser apps that do not support multi-factor authentication.
- **Trusted IP addresses** Configure a list of trusted IP addresses where MFA will be skipped when federation is configured between the on-premises environment and the Microsoft 365 Azure AD tenancy.
- **Verification Options** Specify which verification options are available to users., including phone call, text message, app based verification, or hardware token.

- **Remember Multi-Factor Authentication** Decide whether to allow users to have MFA authentication remembered for a specific period of time on a device so that MFA does not need to be performed each time the user signs on. The default is 14 days.

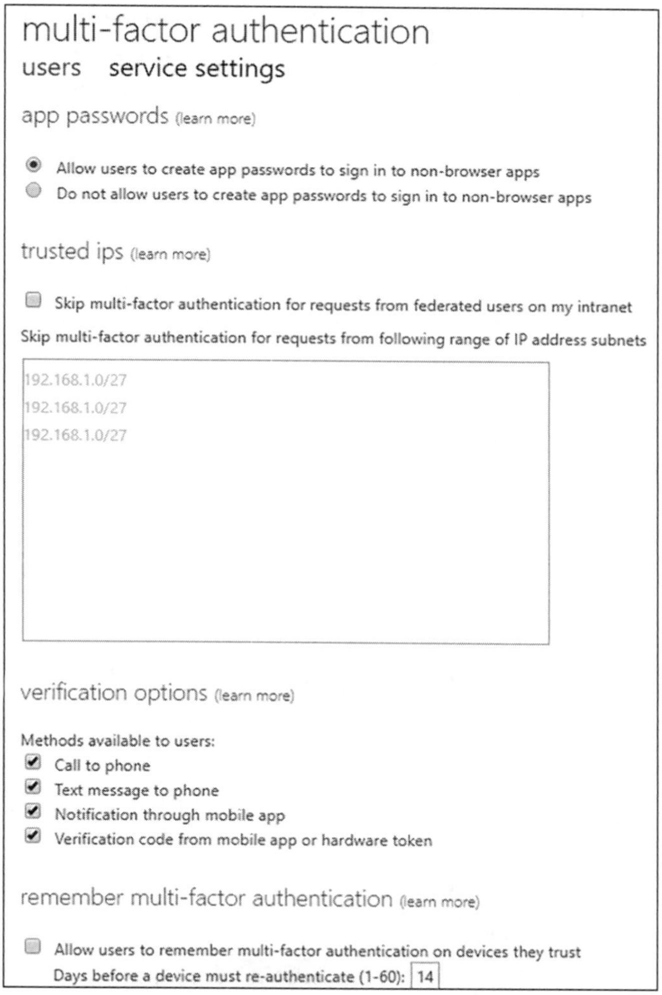

multi-factor authentication
users   service settings

app passwords (learn more)

- ⦿ Allow users to create app passwords to sign in to non-browser apps
- ○ Do not allow users to create app passwords to sign in to non-browser apps

trusted ips (learn more)

- ☐ Skip multi-factor authentication for requests from federated users on my intranet

Skip multi-factor authentication for requests from following range of IP address subnets

```
192.168.1.0/27
192.168.1.0/27
192.168.1.0/27
```

verification options (learn more)

Methods available to users:
- ☑ Call to phone
- ☑ Text message to phone
- ☑ Notification through mobile app
- ☑ Verification code from mobile app or hardware token

remember multi-factor authentication (learn more)

- ☐ Allow users to remember multi-factor authentication on devices they trust
  Days before a device must re-authenticate (1-60): 14

FIGURE 3-24 MFA service settings.

MORE INFO SET UP MULTI-FACTOR AUTHENTICATION

You can learn more about setting up multi-factor authentication at: *https://docs.microsoft. com/office365/admin/security-and-compliance/set-up-multi-factor-authentication.*

Administer MFA users

Once MFA is configured for users, there may be certain times when you want to force users to provide updated contact methods, you may wish to revoke all app passwords, or you may want to restore-MFA on all remembered devices. You can do this by performing the following steps:

1. With an account that has been assigned the Global Admin role, open the Azure AD Admin Center, and select the Users node as shown in Figure 3-25. Select the user to manage MFA.

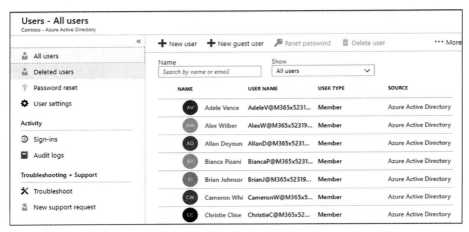

FIGURE 3-25 Select the user to manage MFA

2. On the user's properties page, select **Authentication Methods.**

3. On the Authentication Methods page, shown in Figure 3-26, select which action to perform.

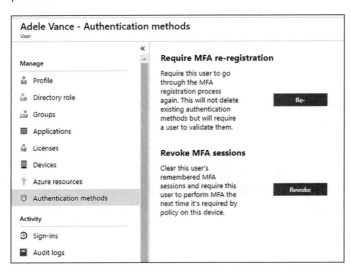

FIGURE 3-26 Authentication methods

If you want to perform a bulk reset for multiple users, perform the following steps:

1. From the All User's page, shown in Figure 3-27 click **Multi-Factor Authentication**

FIGURE 3-27 List of users

2. On the Multi-factor Authentication users page, shown in Figure 3-28, select the users for which you wish to reset MFA settings and click Manage user settings.

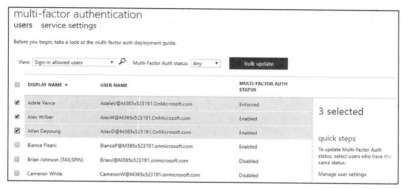

FIGURE 3-28 List of users

3. On the Manage User Settings page, shown in Figure 3-29, select which tasks you want to perform, such as requiring users to provide contact methods again, delete all existing app passwords, and restore MFA on remembered devices. After the selection, click **Save**.

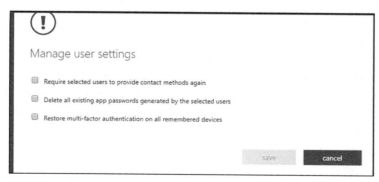

FIGURE 3-29 Managing user settings

Account Lockout

Account Lockout settings for MFA, shown in Figure 3-30, allow you to configure the conditions under which MFA lockout will occur. On this page you can configure the number of MFA denials that will trigger the account lockout process, how long before the account lockout counter is reset, and the number of minutes until the account will be unblocked. For example, if the account lockout counter is reset after 10 minutes, and the number of MFA denials to trigger account lockout is set to five, five denials in 10 minutes will trigger lockout, but five denials over a course of 30 minutes would not as the account lockout counter would reset during that period.

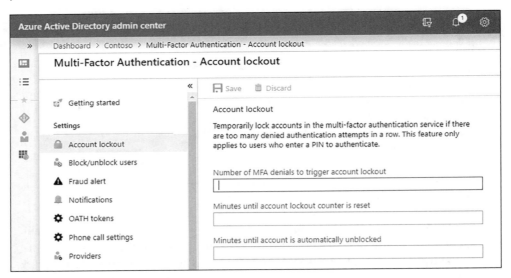

FIGURE 3-30 Account lockout settings

Block/Unblock Users

The blocked user setting, shown in Figure 3-31, allows you to block specific users of an on-premises MFA server from being able to receive MFA request. Any requests sent to a user on the list of blocked users will automatically be denied. Users on the blocked users list remain blocked for 90 days, after which they are removed from the blocked users list. To unblock a blocked user, click **Unblock**.

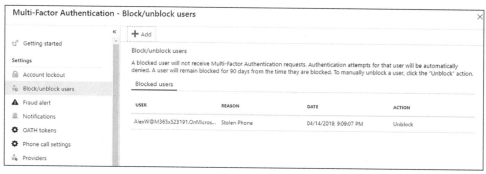

FIGURE 3-31 Blocked users list

Fraud Alert

Fraud Alert settings, shown in Figure 3-32, allow you to configure whether users are able to report fraudulent verification requests. A fraudulent verification request might occur when an attacker has access to a user's password, but does not have access to an alternative MFA method. A user becomes aware of this by receiving an MFA prompt, either through their app, an SMS, or a phone call when they haven't attempted to authenticate against a Microsoft 365 workload. When a user reports fraud, you can choose an option to have their account automatically blocked for 90 days, which indicates that the password is likely to be compromised.

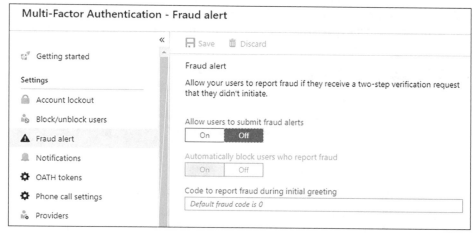

FIGURE 3-32 Fraud alert

OATH tokens

The OATH tokens page, shown in Figure 3-33, allows you to upload a specially formatted CSV file that contains the details and keys of the OATH tokens that you wish to use for multi-factor authentication. The specially formatted CSV file should include a header row that is formatted as:

```
''pn, serial number, secret key, time interval, manufacturer, mode''
```

Each file is associated with a specific user. If a user has multiple OATH tokens, these should be included in the file associated with their account.

FIGURE 3-33 OATH tokens

Phone call settings

Phone call settings allow you to configure the caller ID number that is displayed when the user is contacted for MFA authentication. This number must be a United States number. You can also use the phone call settings page, shown in Figure 3-34, to configure custom voice messages. The voice messages must be in .wav or .mp3 format, no larger than 5 MBs, and should be shorter than 20 seconds.

FIGURE 3-34 Phone call settings

> **MORE INFO MANAGING MFA SETTINGS**
>
> You can learn more about managing MFA settings at: *https://docs.microsoft.com/azure/active-directory/authentication/howto-mfa-mfasettings.*

Report MFA utilization

Azure MFA provides a number of reports that you can use to understand how MFA is being used in your organization. These reports include:

- **Blocked user history**   Provides a history of requests to block or unblock users.

- Usage and Fraud Alerts   Provides information on a history of fraud alerts submitted by users. Also provides information on overall MFA usage.

- **Usage for on-premises components**   Provides information of utilization of MFA through the Network Policy Server extension, Active Directory Federation Services, and on-premises MFA server.

- **Bypassed User History**   Provides information on requests to bypass MFA by a specific user.

- **Server Status**   Provides status data of MFA servers associated with your organization's Microsoft 365 tenancy.

> **MORE INFO** **AZURE MULTI-FACTOR AUTHENTICATION REPORTS**
>
> You can learn more about Azure multi-factor authentication reports at: *https://docs. microsoft.com/azure/active-directory/authentication/howto-mfa-reporting*.

EXAM TIP

Remember the steps that you can take to automatically lock out users who incorrectly answer MFA prompts.

Skill 3.3: Configure application access

When an application is registered with Azure AD, users are able to single sign-on to access that application in the same manner that they single sign-on once, and access Microsoft 365 workloads such as Exchange Online and SharePoint Online. Application registration allows users to access Software as a Service applications from third party vendors, applications deployed in your organization's on-premises environment, and line of business applications. When an application is registered with Azure AD, you can secure access to that application by implementing multi-factor authentication and conditional access policies.

> **This section covers the following topics:**
> - Configure application registration in Azure AD
> - Configure Azure AD application proxy
> - Publish enterprise apps in Azure AD

Configure application registration in Azure AD

You can register an application with Azure AD from the enterprise application gallery. You can then register an application that you are developing, configure an on-premises application, or add a third-party application that is not present in the gallery, as shown in Figure 3-35. Registering an application allows users who have accounts in your organization's Azure AD tenancy to be able to sign-in and use that application with their Microsoft 365 credentials, rather than having to use a separate set of credentials registered with the application.

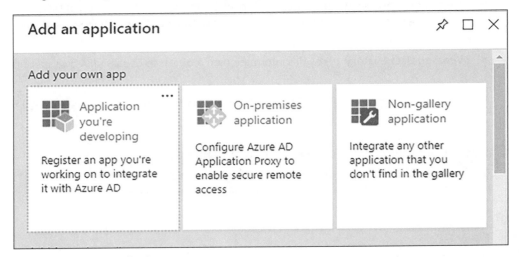

FIGURE 3-35 Add an application

> *MORE INFO* **APPLICATION MANAGEMENT WITH AZURE AD**
>
> You can learn more about application management with Azure AD at: *https://docs.microsoft.com/azure/active-directory/manage-apps/what-is-application-management*.

Planning application integration

Before beginning the process of integrating applications with Azure AD, you need to know what the authentication requirements are of each application. Azure AD supports signing certificates with applications that use WS-Federation, SAML 2.0, Open ID Connect Protocols and Password Single Sign-on.

You'll also need to think about how you might want to provide single sign-on access to applications hosted on your organization's internal network. You can do this by deploying Azure AD App Proxy. When you do this, a special connector is installed on a host on your internal network, allowing users both inside and outside the network to authenticate against and access the application.

> **MORE INFO** **PLANNING APPLICATION INTEGRATION**
>
> You can learn more about planning application integration at: *https://docs.microsoft.com/ azure/active-directory/manage-apps/plan-an-application-integration.*

Managing access to apps

How you assign access to applications depends on the edition of Azure AD that your organization has licensed. If your organization only has a free edition of Azure AD, you'll only be able to assign access to applications on a per-user basis. If your organization licenses a paid edition of Azure AD, then you'll be able to perform group based assignment. When you perform group based assignment, whether a user is able to access an application will depend on whether the user is a member of the group at the time they attempt to access the application.

The groups used to assign access to applications can be any form of Azure AD group, including attributed-based dynamic groups, on-premises Active Directory groups, or self-service managed groups. Nested group membership is not presently supported when it comes to assigning access to applications through Azure AD.

> **MORE INFO** **MANAGING ACCESS TO APPS**
>
> You can learn more about managing access to apps at: *https://docs.microsoft.com/azure/ active-directory/manage-apps/what-is-access-management.*

Assigning users access to an application

To assign a user or group access to an enterprise application, perform the following steps:

1. In the Azure AD Admin Center, select **Azure Active Directory** and under the Manage section, shown in Figure 3-36, click **Enterprise Applications**.

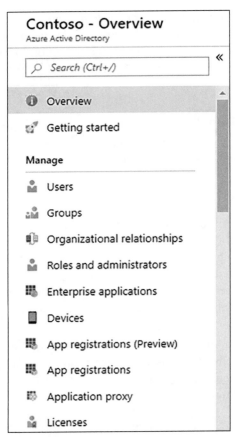

FIGURE 3-36 Azure AD Manage section

2. On the Enterprise Applications blade, ensure that **All Applications** is selected, as shown in Figure 3-37, and then select the application to enable user access.

FIGURE 3-37 All applications

3. Once the application opens, click **Users And Groups** from the application's navigation pane, shown in Figure 3-38.

FIGURE 3-38 Application overview

4. On the application's Users And Groups page, shown in Figure 3-39, click **Add User**. Note that you use the Add User button to also add a group assignment if Azure AD is licensed at the appropriate level.

FIGURE 3-39 Users and Groups

5. On the Add Assignment page, shown in Figure 3-40, search for the user or group that you wish to grant application access.

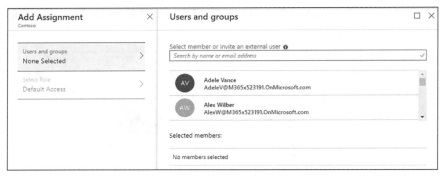

FIGURE 3-40 Add user and group assignment

6. When the user or group is selected, as shown in Figure 3-41, click **Select**.

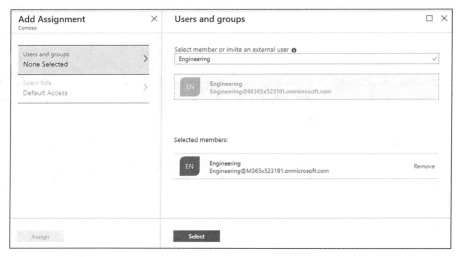

FIGURE 3-41 Select group assignment.

7. Once the user or group is selected, click Assign. Verify that the assignment has occurred by reviewing the newly updated list of users and groups as shown in Figure 3-42.

FIGURE 3-42 Enterprise application users and groups

Configure Azure AD application proxy

Azure AD application proxy allows users on the internet to access web applications that are hosted on your organization's secure internal network as well as in the cloud through an external URL or internal application portal. You can use Azure AD application proxy to allow single sign-on access to Teams, SharePoint, Remote Desktop and line of business applications.

Azure AD application proxy has the following benefits:

- Doesn't require applications to be updated to work with application proxy.
- On-premises applications can leverage Azure AD's authorization controls and security analytics. Features such as multi-factor authentication and conditional access policies can be applied to on-premises applications.
- Azure AD application proxy does not require inbound ports to be opened on your organization's perimeter firewall.
- Does not require the deployment of additional appliances on the on-premises internal or perimeter network.

The architecture of Azure AD Application Proxy has the Azure AD Application Proxy service running in the cloud with the Azure AD Application Proxy connector running on an on-premises server. In this configuration, Azure AD, the Azure AD Application Proxy Service, and the Azure AD Application Proxy Connector manage the secure transmission of a user's sign-on token from Azure AD to the web application the user wishes to access.

Azure AD Application Proxy supports single sign-on and works with the following applications:

- Web applications that use Integrated Windows Authentication for authentication
- Web applications that use header based or form based access
- Client apps integrated with Active Directory Authentication Library
- Applications hosted behind Remote Desktop Gateway

Azure AD Application Proxy functions in the following manner:

1. User accesses the application through a URL or an end user portal, which redirects the user to an Azure AD authentication page.
2. After the user successfully authenticates, Azure AD transmits a token to the user's device.
3. The device forwards the token to the Azure AD Application Proxy service.
4. The Azure AD Application Proxy service extracts the user principal name (UPN) and security principal name (SPN) from the token.

5. Azure AD Application Proxy service forwards the request to the Azure AD Application Proxy connector.

6. If single sign-on has been configured, the Azure AD Application Proxy Connector performs all additional authentication tasks on behalf of the user.

7. The Azure AD Application Proxy Connector forwards the request to the on-premises application.

8. The response from the application is routed through the Azure AD Application Proxy Connector and the Azure AD Application Proxy Service to the user.

> **MORE INFO** **ACCESS ON-PREMISES APPLICATIONS WITH AZURE AD APPLICATION PROXY**
>
> You can learn more about remote access to on-premises applications through Azure Active Directory Application Proxy at: *https://docs.microsoft.com/azure/active-directory/manage-apps/application-proxy.*

The Azure AD Application Proxy Connector is an agent that you install on an on-premises server running the Windows Server 2012 R2, Windows Server 2016, or Windows Server 2019 operating systems. Computers that host the Azure AD Application Proxy Connectors must be able to send outbound requests to the internet on TCP port 443 and also need to be able to communicate with the on-premises servers hosting the application that will be accessed by remote clients. As mentioned earlier, it is not necessary to open inbound ports to the Azure AD Application Proxy Connector for the service to function.

If your organization wants to support single sign-on (SSO) to applications that use Integrated Windows Authentication (IWA), the Azure AD Application Proxy Connector must be installed on a Windows Server computer that is domain joined or in a domain or forest that has a trust relationship with the computer that hosts the application. If SSO to applications that use IWA is not necessary, the Azure AD Application Proxy Connector can be installed on a computer that is not domain joined.

While it is possible to deploy only one Azure AD Application Proxy Connector on your organization's protected internal network, Microsoft recommends that you deploy multiple Azure AD Application Proxy Connectors to ensure that the service is redundant and remains available when the Azure AD Application Proxy Connector agent automatically updates.

Windows Server must have TLS 1.2 enabled before you install the Azure AD Application Proxy connector. You can ensure that TLS 1.2 is enabled by setting the following registry keys and restarting the server:

```
[HKEY_LOCAL_MACHINE\SYSTEM\CurrentControlSet\Control\SecurityProviders\SCHANNEL\
Protocols\TLS 1.2]

[HKEY_LOCAL_MACHINE\SYSTEM\CurrentControlSet\Control\SecurityProviders\
SCHANNEL\Protocols\TLS 1.2\Client] "DisabledByDefault"=dword:00000000
"Enabled"=dword:00000001
```

```
[HKEY_LOCAL_MACHINE\SYSTEM\CurrentControlSet\Control\SecurityProviders\
SCHANNEL\Protocols\TLS 1.2\Server] "DisabledByDefault"=dword:00000000
"Enabled"=dword:00000001

[HKEY_LOCAL_MACHINE\SOFTWARE\Microsoft\.NETFramework\v4.0.30319] "SchUseStrongCry
pto"=dword:00000001
```

The Azure AD Application Proxy Connectors are stateless and do not store any data on the host Windows Server computer. The Azure AD Application Proxy connectors regularly poll the Azure AD Application Proxy service to determine if updates are available. Updates to the Azure AD Application Proxy Connector are automatically downloaded and applied without requiring administrator intervention.

You can use connector groups to assign specific Azure AD Application Proxy Connectors to specific on-premises applications. You are able to group a number of Azure AD Application Proxy Connectors together and then assign each application that you want to make available to the group. Connector groups are especially useful when applications are hosted in different regions. For example, imagine you have one on-premises web application hosted in Sydney, Australia and another hosted in Copenhagen, Denmark. You could create one connector group for the Azure AD Application Proxy Connectors in the Denmark location and assign it to the application hosted in Denmark. You could then create another connector group for the Azure AD Application Proxy Connectors in the Australian location and assign it to the application hosted in Australia

> **MORE INFO** **AZURE AD APPLICATION PROXY CONNECTORS**
>
> You can learn more about Azure AD Application proxy connectors at: *https://docs.microsoft.com/azure/active-directory/manage-apps/application-proxy-connectors*.

> **MORE INFO** **WORKING WITH ON-PREMISES PROXY SERVERS**
>
> You can learn more about working with on-premises proxy servers at: *https://docs.microsoft.com/azure/active-directory/manage-apps/application-proxy-configure-connectors-with-proxy-servers*.

Publish enterprise apps in Azure AD

Azure includes a gallery that hosts thousands of applications that are configured for easy integration with Azure AD. To add an application from the gallery to the Azure AD tenant associated with your organization's Microsoft 365 tenancy, you need to sign into the Azure portal with an account that is assigned global admin privileges. The following procedure details how to add an enterprise application from the gallery.

1. In the Azure AD Admin Center, select Azure Active Directory and under the Manage section, shown in Figure 3-43, click Enterprise Applications.

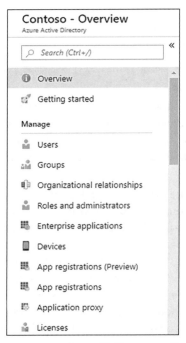

FIGURE 3-43 Azure AD Manage section

2. On the Enterprise Applications blade, ensure that **All Application**s is selected, as shown in Figure 3-44, and click **New Application**.

FIGURE 3-44 All applications

3. On the Add an application, shown in Figure 3-45, type the name of the application that you wish to add. You can also use this page to add an application you are developing, an on-premises application, or a non-gallery application.

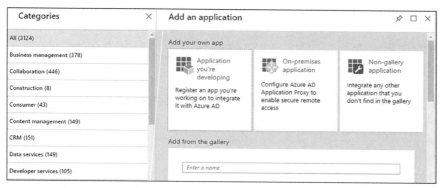

FIGURE 3-45 Add an application

4. In the search result pane, click the application that you want to add. If the application hasn't already been added to your Azure AD tenancy, you'll have the option to add it by clicking **Add**, as shown in Figure 3-46.

FIGURE 3-46 Adding GitHub

5. An application specific getting started page will then be displayed. Fill out the form on this page to configure the application for your organization.

> **MORE INFO ADD AN APPLICATION TO YOUR AZURE AD TENANCY**
>
> You can learn more about adding application to your Azure AD tenancy at: *https://docs. microsoft.com/azure/active-directory/manage-apps/add-application-portal*.

Remember what the requirements are for Azure AD application proxy connectors.

Skill 3.4: Implement access for external users of Microsoft 365 workloads

This objective deals with the creation of B2B and guest accounts, as well as methods of allowing external access to resources hosted in a Microsoft 365 tenancy. You perform these actions when you want to allow people in a partner organization, or external users such as temporary contractors, the ability to interact with resources hosted in Microsoft 365 services such as SharePoint Online. To master this objective you'll need to understand how to create B2B accounts, how to create guest accounts, and the factors that you will need to take into consideration when it comes to designing a solution to allow external users access to Microsoft 365 resources.

> **This section covers the following topics:**
> - Create B2B accounts
> - Create guest accounts
> - Design solutions for external access

Create B2B accounts

Business 2 Business (B2B) accounts are a special type of guest user account that resides within Azure Active Directory, and where you can assign privileges. B2B accounts are generally used when you want to allow one or more users from a partner organization to have access to resources hosted within your organization's Microsoft 365 tenancy. For example, if users in Contoso's partner organization, Tailwind Traders, need to interact with and publish content to a Contoso SharePoint Online site, one method of providing the necessary access is to create a set of B2B accounts.

B2B accounts have the following properties:

- They are stored in a separate Azure AD tenancy from your organization, but they are represented as a guest user in your organization's tenancy. The B2B user signs in using their organization's Azure AD account to access resources in your organization's tenancy.
- They are stored in your organization's on-premises Active Directory and then synced, using Azure AD Connect, and using the special UserType = Guest user type. This is different from the usual type of synchronization where user accounts are synced from an

on-premises directory, but the Azure AD accounts are traditional Azure AD accounts and are not assigned the UserType = Guest attribute.

Azure Active Directory accounts use the UserType attribute to display information about the account's relationship to the organization's tenancy. The two following values are supported.

- **Member** If the Member value is present, the user is considered to belong to the host organization. This is appropriate for full time employees, some types of contractors, or anyone else on the organizational payroll or within the organizational structure. Figure 3-47 shows a user account with the UserType attribute set to Member.

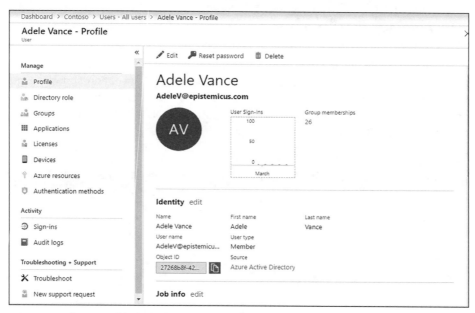

FIGURE 3-47 Account with the User Type attribute set to Member

- **Guest** The Guest attribute value for User Type indicates that the user is not directly associated with the organization. The guest user type applies to B2B and more generally guest accounts. It is used when the account is homed in another organization's directory or when the account is associated with another identity provider, such as a social network identity.

The UserType attribute does not determine how the user signs in, but is only an indication of the user's relationship to the organization that controls the Azure AD tenancy. It can also be used to implement policies that depend on the value of this attribute. It is the source attribute property that indicates how the user authenticates. This property can have the following values:

- **Invited user** A guest or B2B user that has been invited, but has yet to redeem their invitation

- **External Active Directory** This user's account resides in a directory managed by a partner organization. When the user authenticates, they do so against the partner organization's Azure AD instance.
- **Microsoft account** A guest account that authenticates using a Microsoft account, such as an Outlook.com or Hotmail.com account.
- **Windows Server Active Directory.** User is signed on from an on-premises instance of Active Directory that is managed by the same organization that controls the tenancy. This usually involves the deployment of Azure AD Connect. In the case of a B2B user though, the UserType attribute is set to Guest.
- **Azure Active Directory.** User is signed in using an Azure AD account that is managed by the organization. In the case of a B2B user, the UserType attribute is set to Guest.

When you create the first type of B2B account, an invitation is sent to the user that you wish to grant B2B access to. The process of creating and sending this invitation, shown in Figure 3-48, also creates an account within your organization's Azure AD directory. This account will not have any credentials associated with it. The reason for this is that authentication will be performed by the B2B user's identity provider.

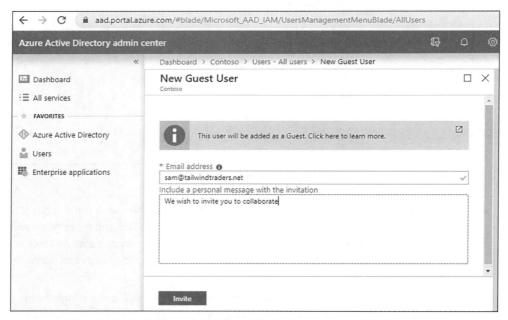

FIGURE 3-48 Creating a guest B2B user in the Azure AD admin center

Until the invitation is accepted, the source property of an invited B2B guest user account will be set to Invited User as shown in Figure 3-49. You can also resend the invitation in the event that the target user does not receive it.

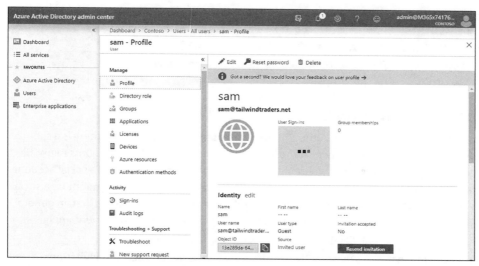

FIGURE 3-49 Source attribute set to Invited User

Once the invitation is accepted, the source attribute will be updated to External Azure Active Directory as shown in Figure 3-50. If the user's account is synchronized from an on-premises Active Directory instance, but the User Type is set to Guest, the Source property will be listed as Windows Server Active Directory.

FIGURE 3-50 Source attribute set to External Azure Active Directory

Create guest accounts

A B2B account is a guest account. Although the exam objectives suggest that there is a substantive difference between the two, at most the difference is that a guest accounts might be considered a type of B2B account where the account is a Microsoft account or a social account. For example, a guest account might have an @outlook.com email address, or might be a social media account such as a Facebook account. The difference between the two is that, in general, a B2B account implies a business to business relationship, whereas a guest account implies a business to individual relationship.

Guest account invitations use exactly the same process as the B2B account invitations outlined earlier. An invitation is sent, an account is created, the user accepts the invitation and then uses their account to access Microsoft 365 resources to which they have been granted permissions.

You can view a list of all users in an Azure AD instance that have guest accounts by setting the Show drop down in the All Users view to Guest Users Only, as shown in Figure 3-51.

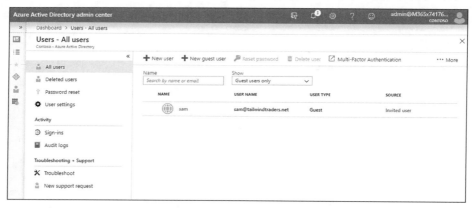

FIGURE 3-51 Viewing guest accounts

Guest Users are blocked from performing certain tasks, including enumerating users, groups and other Azure AD resources. You can remove the guest user default limitations by performing the following steps:

1. In the Azure Active Directory blade, under Manage, click **User Settings**.

2. In the User Settings blade, shown in Figure 3-52, click Manage **External Collaboration Settings**.

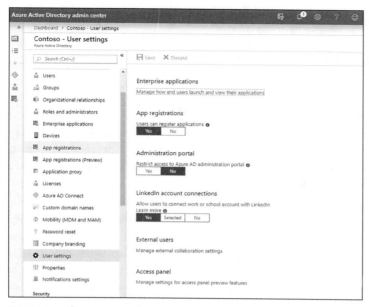

FIGURE 3-52 Guest user settings

3. On the External Collaboration Settings page, you can remove restrictions on guest users by selecting **No** under Guest Users Permissions Are Limited, as shown in Figure 3-53.

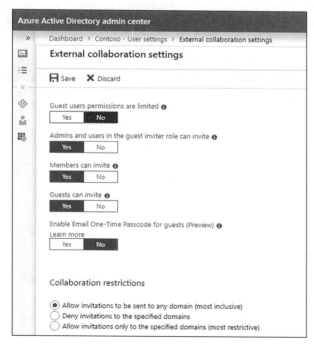

FIGURE 3-53 External collaboration settings

MORE INFO **ADDING GUEST USERS**

You can learn more about this topic at: *https://docs.microsoft.com/azure/active-directory/ b2b/b2b-quickstart-add-guest-users-portal.*

Design solutions for external access

When designing a solution to allow external access to Office 365 resources it is important to understand that Office 365 external sharing and Azure AD B2B collaboration are almost the same thing. Except for OneDrive and SharePoint Online, all external sharing uses the Azure AD B2B collaboration invitation APIs.

OneDrive and SharePoint Online have a separate invitation manager and have functionality that differs slightly from Office 365 external sharing and Azure AD B2B collaboration. This functionality differs from Azure AD B2B in several ways, primarily that OneDrive and SharePoint Online will only add a user to the Azure AD instance after the user has redeemed their invitation. Azure AD B2B adds the user to the directory during invitation creation. This means that you can perform actions, such as granting access to an Azure AD B2B guest user before they have accepted their invitation, because they will be present in the directory, something that is not possible with invitations sent through OneDrive and SharePoint online until the invitation has been accepted.

You manage external sharing for SharePoint online using the Sharing page of the SharePoint admin center. You can configure SharePoint so that only Azure AD B2C sharing is enabled by selecting the Allow Sharing only with external users that already exist in your organization's directory option, as shown in Figure 3-54.

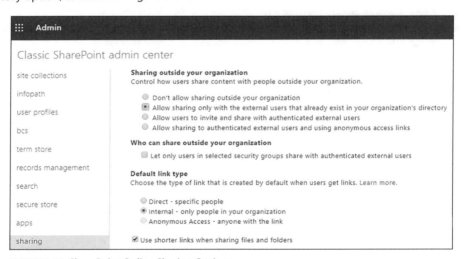

FIGURE 3-54 SharePoint Online Sharing Options

You can use the External Collaboration Settings, shown in Figure 3-55, which are accessible through the User Settings blade within Azure Active Directory, to configure the following collaboration settings:

- **Guest User Permissions are Limited**   Enabled by default, allows you to configure guest users so that they have the same permissions as standard users.

- **Admins and users in the guest inviter role can invite**   Users who hold the administrator and guest inviter roles can send invitations.

- **Members can invite**   Users that are not administrators and who have not been assigned the guest inviter roles can send invitations.

- **Guests can invite**   Users with Guest status can invite other users as B2B users or guests.

- **Enable Email One-Time Passcode for guests**   A one-time passcode for guests who do not have Azure AD or Microsoft account, and for which Google Federation has not been configured. Guests who use one-time passcodes remain authenticated for 24 hours.

- **Allow invitations to be sent to any domain**   The default setting. Allows guest and B2B invitations to be sent to any domain.

- **Deny invitations to specified domains**   Allows you to create a block list of domains to which guest and B2B invitations cannot be sent.

- **Allow invitations only to the specified domains**   Use this option to only allow guest and B2B invitations to specific domains. Invitations to domains not on the allowed list are blocked.

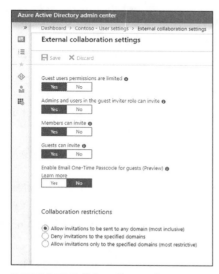

FIGURE 3-55 Collaboration settings

MORE INFO **ALLOW OR BLOCK B2B USERS FROM SPECIFIC ORGANIZATIONS**

You can learn more about allowing of blocking invitations from being sent to users from specific organizations at: *https://docs.microsoft.com/azure/active-directory/b2b/allow-deny-list*.

EXAM TIP

Remember that you can either configure an allow list of specific domains to which invitations can be sent, or you can configure a block list where you only block invitations to specific domains.

Thought experiment

In this thought experiment, demonstrate your skills and knowledge of the topics covered in this chapter. You can find answers to this thought experiment in the next section.

You are the Microsoft 365 administrator for Tailwind Traders. You are currently in the process of configuring authentication and authorization. You have access to a list of the 100 passwords most commonly seen in data breaches. You want to make sure that users in your organization do not use any of these passwords. When it comes to passwords, you also want to empower users to resolve the problem themselves when they forget their password. After several account compromise events in the past, you want to get an idea of which users are most likely to have compromised accounts. Similarly, if users receive 2FA notifications on their Microsoft Authenticator app, they should have a way of reporting this event so that your team can investigate.

Your final task in managing authentication and authorization involves an on-premises accounting application. You want users who are signed in to Microsoft 365 to be able to access this application using their Microsoft 365 credentials and without requiring them to reauthenticate.

With this information in mind, answer the following questions:

1. Which Azure AD authentication feature can you use to ensure that users do not use passwords that are on the list of 100 most commonly used passwords?

2. How can you ensure that users are able regain access to Microsoft 365 workloads if they forget their password without contacting the service desk?

3. Which report should you consult to determine if a user is likely to have a compromised account?

4. Which MFA feature should you enable so that users can report suspicious MFA notifications?

5. What do you need to deploy on-premises to allow access to the accounting app using Azure AD single sign on?

Thought experiment answers

This section contains the solution to the thought experiment. Each answer explains why the answer choice is correct.

1. Populate and enable the Azure AD custom banned passwords list with the passwords on the 100 most commonly used list.

2. You can ensure that users are able to regain access to Microsoft 365 workloads if they forget their password by ensuring that you configure Self-service Password Reset. The feature needs to be enabled, and the user or group should be included in the scope of the feature.

3. Consult the Users flagged for risk report to determine which users are likely to have compromised accounts.

4. You can enable the Fraud Alert option to allow users to notify you if they receive notifications for authorization on their Microsoft Authenticator app when they haven't attempted authentication.

5. Deploy the Azure AD Application Proxy connector on-premises to allow access to the on-premises accounting app using Azure AD single sign on.

Chapter summary

- Modern authentication supports technologies such as multi-factor authentication, smart card authentication, certificate based authentication, and SAML-based third party identity providers.

- Microsoft 365 supports a variety of authentication methods for SSPR and MFA including password, security questions, email address, Microsoft Authenticator App, OATH hardware token, SMS, voice call, and App Passwords.

- When configuring self-service password reset, enable multiple authentication methods and require 2 separate authentication methods to be used before allowing password reset.

- Smart-Lockout is a technology that allows you to lock out attackers who are trying to brute force user passwords.

- Any password that is on the Azure custom banned list cannot be used by a user in your organization.

- Certificate based authentication is supported for federated environments where an organizational CA is trusted by Azure AD and the CRL is published in an Internet accessible location.

- Azure AD's reporting architecture allows you to monitor sign-ins, risky sign-ins, users flagged for risk, and azure administrator activity.

- Multi-factor authentication methods include call to phone, text message to phone, notification through mobile app, or verification code from mobile app or hardware token.
- Applications must be registered with Azure AD before users can access them through Azure AD single sign-on.
- Azure AD Application Proxy allows users on the Internet to access web applications that are hosted on your organization's secure internal network, as well as in the cloud through an external URL or internal application portal.
- The Azure AD Application Proxy service runs in the cloud with the Azure AD Application Proxy connector running on an on-premises server.
- Computers that host the Azure AD Application Proxy Connectors must be able to send outbound requests to the internet on TCP ports 80 and 443 and also need to be able to communicate with the on-premises servers hosting the application that will be accessed by remote clients.
- Business 2 Business (B2B) accounts are a special type of guest user account that resides within Azure Active Directory and to which you can assign privileges.
- Authentication for guest accounts occurs through a trusted provider, after which the user gains access to resources they have been assigned permissions to within Azure AD.

CHAPTER 4

Plan Office 365 workloads and applications

Before they existed in the cloud, many Office 365 workloads were hosted on-premises in organizational datacenters. Some customers still have some Office 365 workload servers deployed on-premises, whilst other workloads are in the cloud, and some even exist in a hybrid state, with servers on-premises working in conjunction with servers in the cloud. Similarly, deployment of Office 365 applications has changed. Whereas you might have deployed previous versions of Office, such as Office 2007, from a CD-ROM drive or network share, today you're likely to deploy Office 365 applications either directly from Office 365 or through other automated tools. In this chapter you'll learn how to plan for Office 365 server workload deployments and to plan how to deploy the Office applications that interact with those server workloads.

Skills covered in this chapter:

- Plan for Office 365 workload deployment
- Plan Office 365 applications deployment

Skill 4.1: Plan for Office 365 workload deployment

This skill section deals with Office 365 workloads including Exchange, SharePoint, and Skype for Business. In this section, you'll learn how to identify the requirements that exist when you are running an on-premises and cloud deployment, how you configure connectivity and data flow for each workload, and the steps that you would take to migrate these workloads from an on-premises environment to the cloud.

> **This section covers the following topics:**
> - Identify hybrid requirements
> - Plan connectivity and data flow for each workload
> - Plan for Microsoft 365 workload connectivity
> - Plan migration strategy for workloads

Identify hybrid requirements

Hybrid deployments have some components located on-premises and other components located in the cloud. For example, with a hybrid Exchange deployment, you may host some mailboxes in your on-premises datacenter and other mailboxes in the Office 365 cloud. The three main Office 365 workloads, Exchange, SharePoint Server, and Skype for Business, all have their own separate hybrid requirements.

Hybrid Exchange

Before an organization that has an on-premises only Exchange deployment can shift to a hybrid deployment, it will need to meet certain prerequisites. The first requirement is that an organization needs to have Exchange 2007 or later on-premises. So, If your organization has Exchange 2003 deployed, you won't be able to deploy Exchange in a hybrid configuration.

The version of Exchange that you have deployed determines the type of hybrid deployment that is available (see Table 4-1).

TABLE 4-1 Hybrid deployment options

On-premises deployment	Hybrid deployment options
Exchange 2007	■ Exchange 2010-based hybrid deployment ■ Exchange 2013-based hybrid deployment
Exchange 2010	■ Exchange 2010-based hybrid deployment ■ Exchange 2013-based hybrid deployment ■ Exchange 2016-based hybrid deployment
Exchange 2013	■ Exchange 2013-based hybrid deployment ■ Exchange 2016-based hybrid deployment ■ Exchange 2019-based hybrid deployment
Exchange 2016	■ Exchange 2016-based hybrid deployment ■ Exchange 2019-based hybrid deployment
Exchange 2019	■ Exchange 2019-based hybrid deployment

When selecting a hybrid deployment option, you should choose the most modern version available for your organization. For example, if your organization has Exchange 2013 deployed, your preference should be to configure an Exchange 2019 based hybrid deployment.

Hybrid deployments require that the on-premises Exchange systems have the most recent cumulative update or update rollup deployed. Generally, the release prior to the most recent cumulative update or update rollup will also work, but older cumulative updates or update rollups will not be supported. Cumulative updates and update rollups are generally released on a quarterly basis.

You need to have specific roles deployed within the on-premises Exchange organization. Which roles are deployed depends on the hybrid deployment option you are choosing. These requirements are as follows:

- **Exchange 2010 hybrid deployment**   A minimum of one Exchange 2010 server with the Mailbox, Hub Transport, and Client Access server roles installed. You can also meet the prerequisite requirements by deploying these Exchange 2010 roles on separate servers. Autodiscover public DNS records for existing SMTP domains point at on-premises Client Access server.

- **Exchange 2013 hybrid deployment**   A minimum of one server with the Mailbox and Client Access roles installed. The prerequisites can also be met by deploying these roles on separate servers. Autodiscover public DNS records for existing SMTP domains point at on-premises Client Access server.

- **Exchange 2016 hybrid deployment**   A minimum of one server with the Mailbox server role installed. Autodiscover public DNS records for existing SMTP domains point at on-premises Mailbox server.

- **Exchange 2019 hybrid deployment**   A minimum of one server with the Mailbox server role installed. Autodiscover public DNS records for existing SMTP domains point at the on-premises Mailbox server.

Hybrid Exchange deployments have the following additional requirements:

- Azure AD Connect are configured to synchronize on-premises Active Directory with Azure Active Directory.

- Custom domains are registered with your organization's Azure AD tenancy.

- Connect the Office 365 organization to the Exchange Admin Center. You must do this prior to running the Hybrid Configuration Wizard.

- Install valid digital certificates purchased from a trusted CA on the IIS instance on Exchange servers configured in the hybrid deployment. The Exchange Web Services external URL and the Autodiscover endpoint specified in your organization's public DNS records must be listed in the Subject Alternative Name (SAN) section of these certificates.

- If your organization's Exchange deployment uses Edge Transport servers and you want to configure those servers for hybrid secure mail transport, you will need to ensure that EdgeSync is configured prior to running the Hybrid Configuration Wizard.

- If Unified Messaging enabled mailboxes are present in the on-premises Exchange deployment, and you want to migrate them to Office 365, the following conditions must be met prior to migrating these mailboxes:

  - You must have deployed Lync Server 2019, Lync Server 2013, or Skype for Business Server 2015 or later, and integrated it with your organization's on-premises telephony system. Alternatively, you have Skype for Business Online integrated with your organization's on-premises telephony system.

  - You have Unified Messaging mailbox policies created in Exchange Online that have names that reflect the Unified Messaging mailbox policies used with the on-premises deployment.

Hybrid SharePoint

Beyond the basics of having a functional on-premises Active Directory instance, and a configured Microsoft 365 tenancy, you will need to have a functional on-premises SharePoint Server farm. This SharePoint Server farm must be configured so that all services are running locally on the farm as farms that leverage federated services and are not supported in a hybrid configuration.

You will need to configure the SharePoint primary web application on the on-premises SharePoint farm to use a certificate from a trusted public third party CA for Transport Layer Security (TLS), also known as Secure Sockets Layer (SSL) communication. Microsoft recommends using the default SharePoint Security Token Services (STS) certificate when configuring hybrid workloads and it is not necessary to have a new certificate for this service issued by a public third party CA.

You will need to configure a reverse proxy device to support inbound connectivity for your hybrid SharePoint deployment if you want to support the following services:

- Inbound hybrid search
- Hybrid Business Connectivity Services
- Hybrid Duet Enterprise Online for Microsoft SharePoint and SAP

The certificate used for authentication and encryption between the reverse proxy device and SharePoint Online must be configured either as a wildcard certificate, or have an appropriate Subject Alternative Name. It must also be issued by a trusted public third party certification authority.

Hybrid Skype for Business

When configuring Skype for Business in a hybrid configuration with Skype for Business Online, you will need to ensure that the following steps are taken:

- Skype for Business Online must be enabled in the Microsoft 365 tenancy.
- On-premises servers must all run either Skype for Business Server 2019, Skype for Business Server 2015, or Lync Server 2013. A deployment that has a mixture of servers is

also supported, as long as that mixture is limited to two different versions of Skype for Business Server or Lync Server. You cannot configure a hybrid deployment if all three servers are present in the on-premises environment.

- You must federate the on-premises environment with Microsoft 365. While federation is more complicated than the default Azure AD Connect identity synchronization option, you can use Azure AD Connect to configure federation. Doing so will require the deployment of Active Directory Federation Services servers in your on-premises environment, although Azure AD Connect makes this process easier.

- You need to configure the on-premises environment to share SIP address space with Skype for Business Online. This will allow Skype for Business Online to host user accounts for the same set of SIP domains as the on-premises environment. It will also allow messages to be routed within the hybrid environment.

- You must enable the share SIP address space for Skype for Business Online. Configuring this shared address space is the second element in ensuring that messages can be routed between the on-premises and cloud environments.

Microsoft also recommends that you configure OAuth between Exchange on-premises and Skype for Business Online if you have both Exchange and Skype for Business in a hybrid configuration.

MORE INFO **SKYPE FOR BUSINESS HYBRID**

You can learn more about configuring Skype for Business Hybrid at: *https://docs.microsoft. com/skypeforbusiness/hybrid/configure-federation-with-skype-for-business-online.*

Plan for Microsoft 365 workload connectivity and data flow

Each Microsoft 365 workload has different requirements when it comes to network connectivity. These requirements generally involve ensuring that the appropriate DNS records are configured in publicly resolvable zones, but in some cases it involves the configuration allowing inbound traffic on an external firewall.

Exchange hybrid connectivity

The ports, protocols, and endpoints listed in Table 4-2 need to be configured to allow the appropriate connectivity in an Exchange hybrid deployment.

TABLE 4-2 Exchange hybrid ports, protocols, and endpoints

Protocol	Upper level protocol	Hybrid functionality	On-premises endpoint
TCP 25 (SMTP)	SMTP/TLS	Hybrid mail flow	■ Exchange 2016/2019 Mailbox/Edge ■ Exchange 2013 CAS/Edge ■ Exchange 2010 Hub/Edge
TCP 443 (HTTPS)	Autodiscover	Autodiscover	■ Exchange 2016/2019 Mailbox ■ Exchange 2010/2013 CAS
TCP 443 (HTTPS)	EWS	Free/busy, MailTips, Message Tracking	■ Exchange 2016/2019 Mailbox ■ Exchange 2010/2013 CAS
TCP 443	Autodiscover, EWS	When using OAuth	■ Exchange 2016/2019 Mailbox ■ Exchange 2010/2013 CAS

> **MORE INFO EXCHANGE HYBRID PORTS, PROTOCOLS, AND ENDPOINTS**
>
> You can learn more about Exchange hybrid ports, protocols, and endpoints at: *https://docs.microsoft.com/exchange/hybrid-deployment-prerequisites#hybrid-deployment-protocols-ports-and-endpoints.*

SharePoint Server hybrid connectivity

In a SharePoint Server hybrid configuration, you need to make sure the following networking requirements are met:

- Ensure that the publicly resolvable DNS record for the SharePoint primary site points at the external endpoint for the reverse proxy device, which publishes the primary site to the Internet.
- Ensure that the SharePoint primary site has a binding for a TLS certificate from a publicly trusted certificate authority.
- Choose an appropriate site collection strategy. Options include host-named site collection, path-based web application with alternate access mappings, or path-based web application without alternate access mapping.
- Configure split DNS so that internal clients connect to the internal IP address of the SharePoint primary site, and external clients connect to the external endpoint of the reverse proxy device.

> **MORE INFO SHAREPOINT SERVER HYBRID CONNECTIVITY**
>
> You can learn more about SharePoint Server Hybrid Connectivity at: *https://docs.microsoft.com/sharepoint/hybrid/configure-inbound-connectivity.*

Skype for Business hybrid connectivity

In a hybrid configuration, all Skype for Business external DNS records must point to on-premises servers. There are specific DNS resolution requirements for the following records:

- DNS SRV record for _sipfederationtls._tcp.<sipdomain.com> must resolve to the Access Edge external IP addresses. This record must be resolvable by Edge servers in the hybrid configuration.
- DNS A record or records for Edge Web Conferencing Service must resolve to the Web Conferencing Edge external IP addresses. This record or records must be able to be resolved by any user's computers on the organization's internal network.

Your organization's firewall needs to be configured to accept incoming traffic from Office 365 domain names:

- *.lync.com
- *.teams.microsoft.com
- *.broadcast.skype.com
- *.skypeforbusinesss.com
- *.sfbassets.com
- *.skype.com

> **MORE INFO SKYPE FOR BUSINESS HYBRID CONNECTIVITY**
>
> You can learn more about Skype for Business hybrid connectivity at: *https://docs.microsoft.com/skypeforbusiness/hybrid/configure-hybrid-connectivity.*

Plan migration strategy for workloads

The migration strategy that you choose will depend on the workload. Exchange mailboxes require a different approach to the strategy you'll use to move SharePoint connectivity or Skype for Business services.

Exchange migration strategy

How you migrate Exchange mailboxes from an on-premises deployment to Exchange Online will depend on the nature of your existing deployment. The approach you use with Exchange 2007 may be different to your approach if you have Exchange 2019, but will depend on the number of mailboxes that need to be moved. Table 4-3 lists the difference between the different methods you can use to migrate from an on-premises messaging environment to Exchange Online.

TABLE 4-3 Migration type comparison

On-premises messaging environment	Number of mailboxes	Will user accounts be managed on-premises	Migration method
Exchange 2007 to Exchange 2019	Less than 2,000	No	Cutover migration
Exchange 2007	Less than 2,000	No	Staged migration
Exchange 2007	More than 2,000	Yes	Staged migration or remote move migration in hybrid deployment
Exchange 2010, to Exchange 2019	More than 2,000	Yes	Remote move migration in hybrid deployment
Exchange 2010 or later with no ongoing directory synchronization	No maximum	No	Minimal Hybrid / Express Migration
Non-Exchange on-premises messaging system	No maximum	Yes	IMAP migration

> *MORE INFO* **CHOOSING A MIGRATION PATH**
>
> You can learn more about choosing a migration path at: *https://docs.microsoft.com/ exchange/mailbox-migration/decide-on-a-migration-path*.

IMAP MIGRATION

IMAP migrations use the IMAP protocol to move the contents of on-premises user mailboxes to Exchange Online. IMAP migrations are suitable where the on-premises mail server is not running Exchange Server, but is instead running an alternate mail server solution.

IMAP migration is supported for the following on-premises messaging solutions:

- Courier-IMAP
- Cyrus
- Dovecot
- UW-IMAP

IMAP migrations involve the following general steps:

1. A tenant administrator creates Office 365 user accounts and assigns them Exchange Online user licenses. This provisions the user accounts with Exchange Online mailboxes.

2. The tenant administrator creates a CSV file. This CSV file includes a row for each on-premises user who will be migrated to Exchange Online using IMAP. This CSV file needs to include the passwords used by each on-premises IMAP mailbox user. It is recommended that you reset user passwords for on-premises IMAP mailbox users to simplify this process.

3. The administrator creates and then triggers an IMAP migration batch. This can be done using the Migration dashboard, available from the Microsoft 365 console.

4. Once the migration batch is initiated, the following occurs:

   - Exchange Online creates a migration request for each user in the CSV file.

   - Each migration request includes the credentials for the user in the on-premises IMAP messaging system.

   - Messages from each user's IMAP mailbox are copied to the corresponding Exchange Online mailbox until all data is migrated.

5. Exchange Online provides a status email to the administrator informing them of the status of the migration. This email contains statistics about the number of mailboxes successfully migrated, how many could not be migrated, and any error reports.

6. Exchange Online and the IMAP messaging system are synchronized every 24 hours to move any new messages from the on-premises environment to Exchange Online.

7. Once all migration issues have been resolved, the administrator updates MX records to point to Exchange Online. Once mail is flowing to Exchange Online, the administrator deletes the migration batches.

> **MORE INFO IMAP MIGRATIONS TO EXCHANGE ONLINE**
>
> You can learn more about IMAP migrations at: *https://docs.microsoft.com/exchange/mailbox-migration/migrating-imap-mailboxes/migrating-imap-mailboxes*.

IMPORT SERVICE

Network upload allows you to import PST files into Office 365. This can be done either by directly uploading the files to Azure blob storage or by shipping hard drives to Microsoft and having them import data directly.

To import PST files, perform the following steps:

1. In the Data governance section of the Security & Compliance center, use the Import section to create a Shared Access Signature (SAS) key, also known as the SAS URL. This key provides the necessary permission and location to upload PST files to an Azure storage location.

2. Download and install the Azure AzCopy tool. Use AzCopy with the SAS URL to upload one or more PST files.

3. Once uploaded, review the list of PST files that have been successfully transferred to Office 365. You can do this with Azure Storage Explorer.

4. Create a mapping file that maps uploaded PST files to Office 365 mailboxes. This file must be in CSV format.

5. Create a PST import job from the Data governance section of the Security & Compliance center. You specify the mapping file when creating this job.

6. Run the job to import the data into the appropriate Office 365 mailboxes.

> **MORE INFO** **IMPORT SERVICE**
>
> You can learn more about the import service at: *https://docs.microsoft.com/office365/ securitycompliance/use-network-upload-to-import-pst-files*.

SharePoint Server migration strategy

While it's possible to directly upload one file at a time to a SharePoint online tenant, or install the OneDrive sync client and have that content automatically synchronize to either OneDrive or SharePoint online, most organizations that are migrating from an on-premises SharePoint Server deployment to SharePoint online will use the SharePoint Migration Tool.

The SharePoint Migration Tool (SPMT) allows for the migration of files from on-premises SharePoint Server document libraries to SharePoint Online. You can also use the SPMT to migrate existing file shares to SharePoint Online. To allow web parts to be migrated, 24 hours prior to performing a migration with the SPMT, you need to configure the following settings in the SharePoint Admin Center:

- Allow users to run custom script on personal sites
- Allow users to run customer script on self-service created sites

When running the tool, you have the option of specifying a migration either from a SharePoint on-premises deployment or from a file share. When migrating a SharePoint on-premises site, you'll need to specify the site location, the credentials to access that site, and the specific document library that you wish to migrate. If you are migrating an on-premises file share to SharePoint online, you'll need to specify the file share location, the URL of the SharePoint Online site that is the destination for the migrated files, and the document library within that site that will host the files.

After you perform a migration, you have the option of saving the migration job so that it can be run at a different time. This allows you to migrate any files that were modified or created after the last migration from the source location to the destination SharePoint online site.

> **MORE INFO** **SHAREPOINT MIGRATION TOOL**
>
> You can learn more about the SharePoint migration tool at: *https://docs.microsoft.com/ sharepointmigration/how-to-use-the-sharepoint-migration-tool*.

Skype for Business migration strategy

You can move users from an on-premises deployment to the cloud by either using the Skype for Business Admin Control panel or the Move-CsUser PowerShell cmdlet. Both tools are used in the on-premises environment. It's also possible to use these tools to move users from Skype for Business Online to an on-premises host when Skype for Business Online is in a hybrid configuration. You can move a user from Skype to Business Online directly to Teams only if Skype for Business Server 2019 or Skype for Business Server 2015 with cumulative update 8 or later is deployed in the on-premises environment.

When migrating users from an on-premises environment to the cloud, the user performing the migration must have the CSServerAdministrator role in the on-premises Skype for Business Server deployment and must be either the Microsoft 365 Global Administrator role or have both the Microsoft 365 Skype for Business Administrator and Microsoft 365 User Administrator roles.

> **MORE INFO SKYPE FOR BUSINESS MIGRATION**
>
> You can learn more about Skype for Business migration at: *https://docs.microsoft.com/ skypeforbusiness/hybrid/move-users-between-on-premises-and-cloud.*

EXAM TIP

Remember the different options for Exchange migration.

Skill 4.2: Plan Office 365 applications deployment

This objective deals with the deployment of Office 365 applications to client computers. In the past you might just bake Office 365 applications into a deployment image, however, with Office 365 applications you are more likely to leverage the online nature of the product and to use Office 365, rather than a local deployment share, as the installation source for the product. This is especially true for those Microsoft 365 organizations that have no on-premises infrastructure beyond client computers. To master this objective you'll need to understand how to manage Office 365 download, plan for Office 365 apps, including updates and connectivity, as well as plan for Office online and the deployment of Office 365 Pro plus.

> **This section covers the following topics:**
> - Manage Office 365 software downloads
> - Plan for Office 365 apps
> - Plan for Office 365 Pro plus apps updates
> - Plan for Office 365 Pro plus connectivity
> - Plan for Office online
> - Plan Office 365 Pro plus deployment

Manage Office 365 software downloads

Depending on the policies of your organization, you might want to allow users to install software directly from the Microsoft 365 portal, to restrict this ability entirely, or to allow users to install some applications but restrict them from installing others. Office 365 ProPlus is the version of Microsoft Office that is available to appropriately licensed users in a Microsoft 365 tenancy. Office 365 ProPlus includes the following software products:

- Access
- Excel
- InfoPath
- OneNote
- Outlook
- PowerPoint
- Publisher
- Word

Depending on the Microsoft 365 subscription associated with a tenancy, the Skype for Business, Project, and Visio, and other applications might also be available.

To configure which Office software users are able to install from the portal, perform the following steps:

1. When signed in to Microsoft 365 with a user account that has Administrator permissions, open the Microsoft 365 Admin Center, click **Software Download Settings** under Office Software as shown in Figure 4-1.

FIGURE 4-1 Manage User Software

2. To restrict users from deploying software from the Office 365 portal, switch the slider next to the listed software as shown in Figure 4-2.

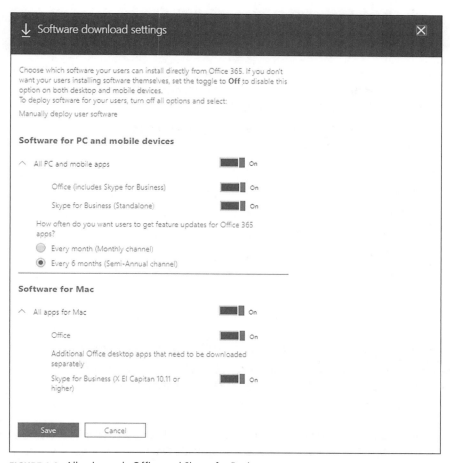

FIGURE 4-2 Allowing only Office and Skype for Business

The software that users will be able to install depends upon the type of Microsoft 365 subscription. Different Microsoft 365 subscriptions have different software options. It is also likely that software options will change over time.

While you can make Office 365 software available to users through the Microsoft 365 portal, this doesn't mean that users will automatically be able to successfully install this software. When allowing users to self-provision software from the Microsoft 365 portal, keep the following in mind:

- To successfully run Office 365, users will need an Office 365 license.
- For users to be able to install the software they downloaded from the Office 365 portal, they will need to have local administrator privileges on their computer. This means that self-provisioning of software through the Office 365 portal is a suitable strategy in Bring Your Own Device (BYOD) scenarios where the user is the owner of the computer and is responsible for its configuration. Self-provisioning of software is less of a concern for

most environments where each user is assigned a computer with a Standard Operating Environment (SOE), as users in these environments rarely have local administrator credentials.

- If you do not make Office software available to users, they will see a message that informs them that Office installations have been disabled when they navigate to the Software page in the Office 365 portal.

- Office 365 ProPlus is only run on the following operating systems:
  - Windows 7
  - Windows 8
  - Windows 8.1
  - Windows 10
  - Windows Server 2008 R2
  - Windows Server 2012
  - Windows Server 2012 R2
  - Windows Server 2016
  - Windows Server 2019

> **MORE INFO CONTROL WHICH SOFTWARE USERS CAN INSTALL FROM THE PORTAL**
>
> You can learn more about controlling the Office software users can install from the Office 365 portal at: *https://docs.microsoft.com/DeployOffice/manage-software-download-settings-office-365*.

By default, if a user installs Office 365 ProPlus from the Microsoft 365 portal, all programs included with Office 365 ProPlus (Access, Excel, InfoPath, OneNote, Outlook, PowerPoint, Publisher, and Word) will also install. Administrators can configure deployments so that only some, not all, of these programs will install. You can configure which programs are excluded from Office 365 ProPlus using the Office Deployment Tool. You will learn more about configuring the Office Deployment Tool later in this chapter.

> **MORE INFO EXCLUDE PROGRAMS FROM OFFICE 365 PROPLUS**
>
> You can learn more about excluding programs from Office 365 ProPlus at: *https://docs.microsoft.com/DeployOffice/configuration-options-for-the-office-2016-deployment-tool*.

Plan for Office 365 apps

Microsoft has made Word, Excel, Outlook, PowerPoint, and OneNote apps available for the iOS and Android mobile platforms. There are several ways that you can install these apps on these devices.

The first is to navigate to the Microsoft 365 portal using the mobile device on which you want to install each application. From here you can click Install Office as shown in Figure 4-3.

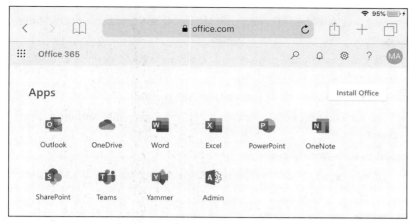

FIGURE 4-3 List of apps available for the iPad platform

Clicking **Get Office Apps** will open a page on Microsoft's website that will provide a link to the app's page in the appropriate vendor's app store. Figure 4-4 shows the Apple App Store page that opens when the Excel link on the Microsoft 365 portal is opened. The application can then be downloaded from the App Store and installed on the device.

FIGURE 4-4 Excel app in the Apple App Store

These applications can also be installed directly from each mobile device operating system vendor's app store. To use all the available features of each app, such as accessing documents in OneDrive for Business that are associated with your organization's Microsoft 365 subscription, it will be necessary to sign in to the app using your Microsoft 365 user account credentials. Premium features include:

- The ability to track changes, change page orientation, insert chart elements, and add WordArt and picture effects in the Word app.
- Use Pivot Tables, add and modify chart elements in the Excel app.
- Use Presenter View with speaker notes, perform audio and video edits, and use picture styles in the PowerPoint app.
- Technical support options from Microsoft.

Select the Sign In option of an app, shown in Figure 4-5, to connect the app to a Microsoft 365 subscription.

FIGURE 4-5 Sign In to Office 365

MORE INFO **OFFICE 365 AND MOBILE DEVICES**

You can learn more about deploying at: *https://support.office.com/article/Office-365-mobile-setup---Help-7dabb6cb-0046-40b6-81fe-767e0b1f014f?CorrelationId=93e770bc-f158-40da-8052-f27b45564eee.*

Plan for Office 365 Pro plus apps updates

Office 365 provides new features and updates to Office programs on a regular basis. Depending on your organization, you can choose between an update channel that provides new features as they become available, or you can choose an update channel that provides new features less frequently. The following Office 365 update channels are available:

- **Monthly channel** This channel provides users with the most recent features. Updates occur on a monthly basis.

- **Semi-annual channel** This channel provides users with new features on a less frequent basis. Updates occur in January and July.

- **Semi-annual channel (targeted)** Use this channel for pilot users and compatibility testers when you are using semi-annual channel. This allows these users to test updates and changes before they are released in the semi-annual channel. Updates to this channel occur in March and September.

You configure which update channel is used by editing the configuration.xml file for the Office Deployment Tool or by configuring the Update Channel group policy setting under Computer Configuration\Administrative Templates\Microsoft Office 2016 (Machine)\Updates when the Office 2016 group policy template files are installed. You can also configure release channel settings in the Microsoft 365 Admin Center through Software Download Settings as shown in Figure 4-6.

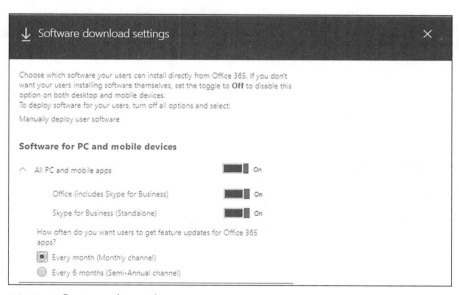

FIGURE 4-6 Feature update settings

Plan for Office 365 ProPlus connectivity

Network connectivity for Office 365 ProPlus depends on how you have determined you want to install updates. If you want to manage the update deployment from a location on your organization's internal network, then client computers will only need to be able to access the location on the network that hosts the updates. The majority of Office 365 ProPlus deployments are more likely to use the default option of obtaining updates from Microsoft over the Internet. To obtain Office 365 ProPlus updates over the Internet, client computers will require access to the Office Content Delivery Networks.

The Office Content Delivery Networks (CDNs) are used not only for the deployment of Office 365 ProPlus updates, but also improve the performance of SharePoint Online pages by hosting cached versions of static assets in locations more proximate to the organization's users. Access to the Office 365 CDNs is over the HTTP/2 protocol. This maximizes compression and improves download speeds when clients access content that the CDNs host. Office 365 CDNs are hosted with Akamai. To ensure the best performance and minimize latency, ensure that traffic from Office 365 ProPlus clients to the Office CDNs is not routed through proxies and instead can pass directly from the client to the Office CDN. Office 365 ProPlus also requires Internet connectivity for activation and reactivation.

Plan for Office online

Office Online allows you to access the basic functionality of a variety of Microsoft Office applications through a supported web browser. You can open Word Online, Excel Online, PowerPoint Online, and OneNote Online directly from the Microsoft 365 portal, as shown in Figure 4-7.

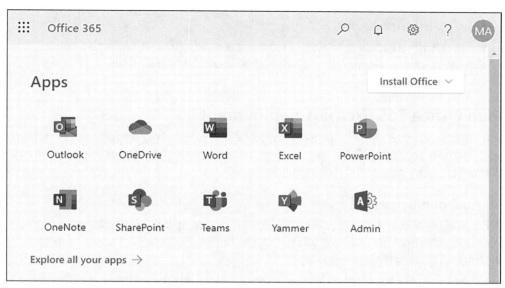

FIGURE 4-7 Office Online

People with Microsoft 365 User Accounts will be able to access documents stored in organizational locations such as OneDrive for Business and SharePoint Online. Documents will also be able to be opened directly from the Outlook Web App. Figure 4-8 shows the interface of the Word Online Office Web App.

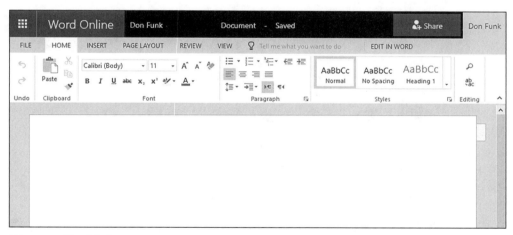

FIGURE 4-8 Word Online

MORE INFO OFFICE ONLINE

You can learn more about Office Online at: *https://support.office.com/article/Get-started-with-Office-Online-in-Office-365-5622c7c9-721d-4b3d-8cb9-a7276c2470e5*.

Plan Office 365 Pro plus deployment

You can use a number of methods to deploy Office 365 ProPlus on a computer. In this section you'll learn about manual deployments, centralized deployments, the Office Deployment Tool, the configuration.xml file, and click-to-run versus MSI.

Manual deployment

The typical method of deploying Office 365 ProPlus on a computer is for a user to access the installation files from the Microsoft 365 portal. You can install Office 365 ProPlus on a computer by performing the following steps:

1. Sign in to the computer with a user account that is a member of the local administrators group.

2. Open a web browser and sign in to the Office 365 portal at https://portal.office.com. You can click **Install Office** if you want to install using the default, or click **Other Installs** if you want to choose between the 32 bit and the 64 bit option.

3. If you want to install the 64-bit version of Office ProPlus, select the language and click **Advanced** as shown in Figure 4-9.

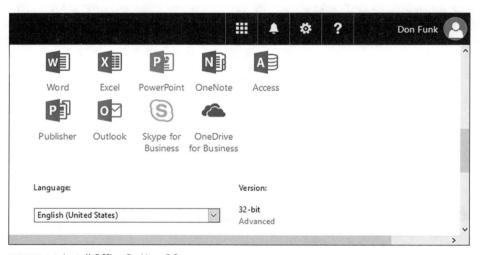

FIGURE 4-9 Install Office On Your PC

4. Once you click Advanced, you can select between the 32-bit and the 64-bit option. Once you've selected the appropriate option, click **Install**. This will begin the download of the Office 365 ProPlus installer Click-to-Run setup file.

5. Choose to Save or Run the installation file. It's often sensible to save the file and then run it as this simplifies the process of running the installer again should something interrupt the installation process.

6. Once the Click-to-Run installer has downloaded, double click on it to initiate installation. On the User Account Control dialog box, verify that the Program name is set to Microsoft Office, as shown in Figure 4-10, and then click Yes. The installation process will commence.

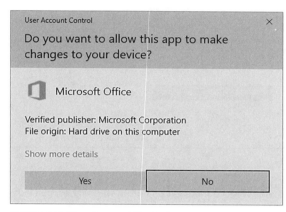

FIGURE 4-10 User Account Control

7. On the "You're all set!" page, shown in Figure 4-11, click **Close**.

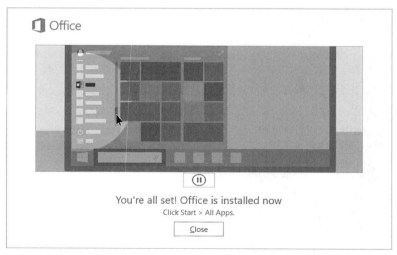

FIGURE 4-11 Office is installed

8. Open one of the Office ProPlus applications. The first time you run one you'll be presented with the "Office is almost ready" screen shown in Figure 4-12. Click Accept and start Word, or whichever Office ProPlus application you selected to run first.

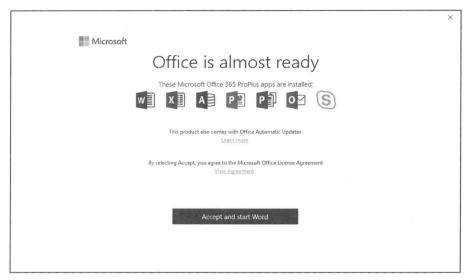

FIGURE 4-12 Office is almost ready

9. On the Word Recent page shown in Figure 4-13, click "Sign in to get the most out of Office."

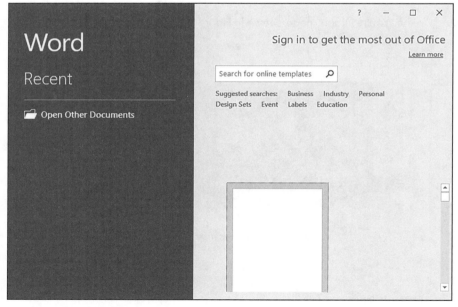

FIGURE 4-13 Word Recent page

10. On the Sign In page, shown in Figure 4-14, enter the email address of your Office 365 account and click **Next**.

FIGURE 4-14 Sign In

11. On the Work or school account page shown in Figure 4-15, enter the password and click **Sign In**.

FIGURE 4-15 Enter work or school account credentials

12. Once you have signed in, your account will be listed on the Recent page as shown in Figure 4-16 and documents stored in Office 365 will be available.

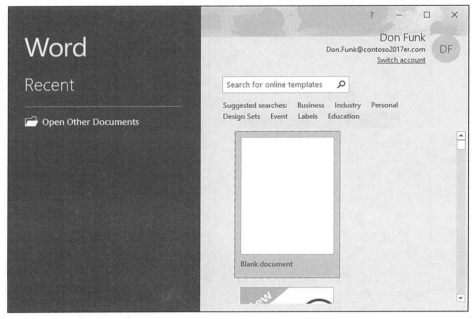

FIGURE 4-16 Signed in to Office 365

> ***MORE INFO*** **MANUALLY INSTALLING OFFICE 365 PROPLUS**
>
> You can learn more about installing Office 365 ProPlus at: *https://support.office.com/article/Download-and-install-Office-using-Office-365-for-business-on-your-PC-or-Mac-72977511-dfd1-4d8b-856f-405cfb76839c.*

Central deployment

With special preparation, Office 365 ProPlus can be downloaded to a local shared folder and then deployed centrally. To use this central deployment method, the IT department must use the Office Deployment Tool to download the Office 365 ProPlus software from Microsoft servers on the Internet. While it is possible to deploy Office 365 ProPlus centrally, successful installation of Office 365 ProPlus requires the ability for the software to activate against Microsoft Office 365 servers on the Internet. You can't use a volume licensing activation solution, such as a Key Management Services (KMS) server, to activate Office 365 ProPlus even when you are deploying it centrally.

Office Deployment Tool

The Office Deployment Tool allows IT departments to perform the following tasks:

- **Generate a Click-to-Run for Office 365 installation source** This allows administrators to create a local installation source for Office 365 rather than requiring that the files be downloaded for each client from the Internet.

- **Generate Click-to-Run for Office 365 clients** This allows administrators to configure how Office 365 ProPlus is installed. For example, blocking the installation of PowerPoint.

- **Creating an App-V package** Allows administrators to configure Office 365 ProPlus to work with application virtualization.

To install the Office Deployment Tool, perform the following steps:

1. On the computer on which you want to deploy the Office Deployment Tool, open a web browser and navigate to the following address: *https://www.microsoft.com/download/ details.aspx?id=49117*.

2. On the Office Deployment Tool For Click-To-Run webpage, shown in Figure 4-17, click **Download**.

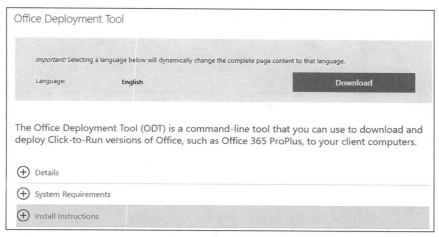

FIGURE 4-17 Office Deployment Tool For Click-To-Run

3. Save the installer file to a location on the computer. Figure 4-18 shows the file downloaded to the Downloads folder.

FIGURE 4-18 Office Deployment Tool setup file.

4. After the deployment tool has downloaded, double-click the self-extracting executable file to start the deployment tool setup.

5. On the User Account Control dialog box, click **Yes**.

6. On the Microsoft Software License Terms page, select the **Click Here To Accept The Microsoft Software License Terms** option and click **Continue**.

7. On the Browse For Folder page, select the folder in which to store the files associated with the tool. While these files can be extracted anywhere, you will need to interact with the tool frequently so you should create a folder in the root folder of a volume.

8. Four files will be extracted as shown in Figure 4-19.

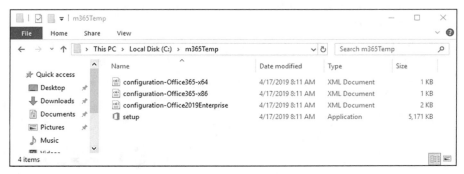

FIGURE 4-19 Deployment Tool folder

The Office Deployment Tool is a command line utility that provides administrators with three general options:

- The download mode allows administrators to download the Click-to-Run installation source for Office 365 ProPlus, as well as language pack files to a central on-premises location.

- The configure mode allows for the configuration and installation of Click-to-Run Office products and language packs.

- The packager mode allows for the creation of an App-V package from downloaded Click-to-Run installation files.

- The customize mode allows you to apply new application settings to computers that already have Office 365 ProPlus installed.

The Office Deployment Tool must be run from an elevated command prompt in the /configure and /packager modes. To run the Office Deployment tool in download mode against a configuration file stored in the c:\ClickToRun folder, use the syntax:

```
Setup.exe /download c:\ClickToRun\configuration.xml.
```

To run the Office Deployment Tool in configure mode, when the tool is hosted on the share \\SYD-Deploy\O365 and the configuration file is stored on the share \\SYD-Deploy\Configs, run the command:

```
\\SYD-Deploy\O365\Setup.exe /configure \\SYD-Deploy\Configs\Configuration.xml.
```

Configuration.xml

The deployment tool ships with three example Configuration.xml files: Configuration-Office365-x64.xml, Configuration-Office365-x86.xml and Configuration-Office2019Enterprise.xml. You use these Configuration.xml files to perform the following tasks:

- Add or remove Office products from an installation.
- Add or remove languages from the installation.
- Specify display options, such as whether the installation occurs silently.
- Configure logging options, such as how much information will be recorded in the log.
- Specify how software updates will work with Click-to-Run.

Figure 4-20 shows one of the example Configuration.xml files that is available with the Office Deployment Tool.

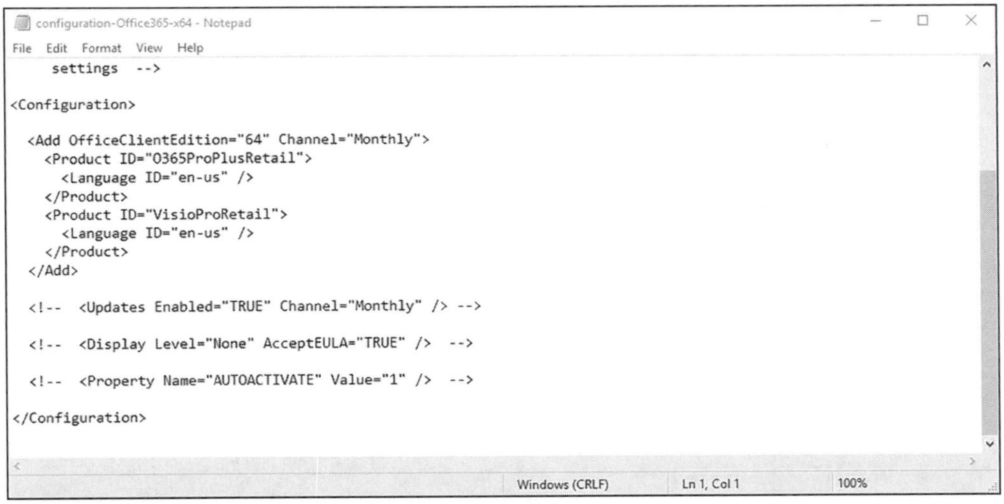

```
configuration-Office365-x64 - Notepad                          —    □    ×
File  Edit  Format  View  Help
    settings  -->

<Configuration>

  <Add OfficeClientEdition="64" Channel="Monthly">
    <Product ID="O365ProPlusRetail">
      <Language ID="en-us" />
    </Product>
    <Product ID="VisioProRetail">
      <Language ID="en-us" />
    </Product>
  </Add>

  <!-- <Updates Enabled="TRUE" Channel="Monthly" /> -->

  <!-- <Display Level="None" AcceptEULA="TRUE" /> -->

  <!-- <Property Name="AUTOACTIVATE" Value="1" /> -->

</Configuration>

                          Windows (CRLF)      Ln 1, Col 1      100%
```

FIGURE 4-20 The Office365 x65 Configuration.xml

Important attributes include:

- **SourcePath** When you run the tool in download mode, the SourcePath attribute determines the location where the Click-to-Run files will be stored. When you run the tool in configure mode, the SourcePath attribute determines the installation source.
- **OfficeClientEdition** This value is required and either must be set to 32 or 64. This determines whether the x86 or x64 version of Office applications are retrieved or installed.

- **Version**   If this element is not set, the most recent version of files will be either downloaded or installed. If a version is set, then that version of the files will either be downloaded or installed.
- **Display**   The display element allows you to specify what information the user sees during deployment. The options are:
  - **Level=None**   The user sees no UI, completion screen, error dialog boxes, or first run UI.
  - **Level=FULL**   The user sees the normal Click-to-Run user interface, application splash screen, and error dialog boxes.
  - **AcceptEULA=True**   The user does not see the Microsoft Software License Terms dialog box.
  - **AcceptEULA=False**   The user will see the Microsoft Software License Terms dialog box.
- **ExcludeApp**   You use this element to exclude applications from being installed. Valid values of this attribute are as follows:
  - Access
  - Excel
  - Groove (used for OneDrive for Business)
  - InfoPath
  - Lync (used for Skype for Business)
  - OneNote
  - OneDrive
  - Outlook
  - PowerPoint
  - Project
  - Publisher
  - SharePointDesigner
  - Visio
  - Word
- **Language ID**   This element allows you to specify which language packs are installed. For example, you have en-us for US English. You can have multiple Language ID elements, one for each language that you wish to install.
- **Logging**   This element allows you to disable logging, enable logging, and specify the path where the log file is to be written.
- **Product ID**   This element allows you to specify which products to install. The available options are:
  - **O365ProPlusRetail**   Office 365 ProPlus

- **VisioProRetail**   Visio Pro
- **ProjectProRetail**   Project Professional
- **SPDRetail**   SharePoint Designer

- **Remove**   If this element is set ALL=TRUE then all Click-to-Run products are removed.
- **Updates**   The updates element allows you to configure how updates are managed and includes the following options:
  - **Enabled**   When set to true, Click-to-Run update system will check for updates.
  - **UpdatePath**   If this element is not set, updates will be retrieved from Microsoft servers on the Internet. If the element is set to a network, local, or HTTP path, then updates will be sourced from the specified path.
  - **TargetVersion**   Allows you to have updates applied to a specific Office build version. If not specified, the most recent version is updated.
  - **Deadline**   Specifies the deadline by which updates must be applied. You can use Deadline with Target Version to force Office applications to be updated to a specific version by a specific date. The Deadline will only apply to a single set of updates. To ensure that Office applications are always up-to-date, it is necessary to revise the deadline when new updates are available.

> ***MORE INFO* CONFIGURATION.XML**
>
> You can learn more about the format of Configuration.xml at: *https://docs.microsoft.com/deployoffice/configuration-options-for-the-office-2016-deployment-tool*.

Click-to-Run vs. MSI

Click-to-Run and MSI are two different formats through which Office applications can be distributed to users. Click-to-Run offers the following features:

- **Streaming installation**   Streaming installation allows an application to be run before installation has completed. When the installation of an application is streamed, the first part of the application installed provides the minimum functionality necessary to get the application running. This allows the user to begin working with the application while installation completes.
- **Slipstreamed Servicing**   The Click-to-Run functionality of Office 365 ProPlus means that updates are included in the installation. Rather than installing Office in a traditional manner and then running a Windows Update check to locate and install any relevant updates, relevant updates are already included within the Click-to-Run installation files. Slipstreamed Servicing means that end users have the most secure and up-to-date version of the application immediately, rather than having to wait for the post-deployment update cycle to complete.
- **User-based licensing**   User-based licensing means that the Office 365 ProPlus license is associated with the Office 365 user account, not the computer that the user is signed

on to. Depending on the type of license associated with the user and the tenancy, the user is able to install Office 365 ProPlus on up to five different computers as well as tablets and phones. It is possible to remove licenses from computers that have had Office 365 ProPlus installed on them at an earlier point in time.

- **Retail activation**   Office 365 ProPlus is activated using retail rather than volume license methods. Activation occurs over the Internet. This means that the computer must connect to the Internet every 30 days, otherwise Office ProPlus will enter reduced functionality mode.

- **SKU-level application suites**   Unless an administrator configures an appropriate configuration file, Office 365 ProPlus installs all products in the suite. The products that are installed will depend on the specifics of the Office 365 subscription, but this usually means Access, Excel, InfoPath, OneNote, Outlook, PowerPoint, Publisher, and Word. The products that are installed will be installed to all users in the tenancy. It is not possible to choose to install the PowerPoint program to some users but not to others when all users are using the same Click-to-Run installation file and configuration file. It is possible to have separate sets of applications deployed to users, but this requires separate configuration files for each set of applications.

MSI files are a method through which applications are packaged. MSI files allow organizational IT departments to automate the deployment applications, such as Office, using tools such as Microsoft Intune and System Center Configuration Manager. MSI files are appropriate for organizations that have a managed desktop environment and are less suitable for the types of "Bring Your Own Device" scenarios in which Click-to-Run products, such as Office 365 ProPlus, are suitable. MSI files offer the following features:

- **Classic installation**   MSI files can be installed by double-clicking on the installer file, can be deployed using Group Policy, Microsoft Intune, System Center Configuration Manager, or third-party application deployment products. The application is not available to the user until the installation of the application is complete. This differs from the Click-to-Run method's streaming technology which allows a user to begin using an application with a reduced set of features before the installation of the application completes.

- **Layered servicing**   MSI files represent the application at the time that it was packaged as an MSI file. This means that after deployment it will be necessary for the IT department to apply any necessary software updates to the application. Depending on the age of the MSI file and the number of software updates that have been released since the application was first packaged, it can take quite some time for the application to be updated to the current patch level after the application is deployed. This substantially increases the amount of time between an application being deployed and the user being able to use the application to perform their job role. IT departments can update MSI files with the latest updates and patches, but this is a complex, usually manual, process which requires deploying the application to a reference computer, updating the application, and then performing a technique known as a capture that creates the new updated MSI file. With Click-to-Run technology, the application updates are slipstreamed into the application by Microsoft, meaning that the application is current with updates as soon as it is deployed.

- **Volume licensing**   The versions of Office that you can deploy from an MSI file, including Office 2016 and Office 2019, have editions that support volume licensing. Volume licensing gives you the option of using a volume license key. Volume licensing is not something that is automatically supported by the MSI format and depends on the properties of the deployed software. Volume licensing is only available to organizations that have volume licensing agreements with Microsoft.

- **Volume activation**   Like volume licensing, volume activation is not a property of an MSI file, but a feature that is supported by some versions of Office that use this packaging format. Volume activation allows large numbers of products to be activated, either through use of a special activation key used each time the installation is performed, or through technologies such as a Key Management Services (KMS) server on the organization's internal network. Volume activation is only available to organizations that have volume-licensing agreements.

- **Selective application installation**   Rather than deploying all products in the Office suite, the MSI-based deployment method makes it simple for organizations to deploy individual products in the suite. For example, it is possible to choose to deploy Word and Excel to some users, and PowerPoint to others.

- **Scenario limitations**   Unlike Click-to-Run Office 365 ProPlus, which uses retail activation, the volume-licensed versions of Office 2016 and Office 2019 can be used on Remote Desktop Services servers, can be deployed on Windows To Go USB devices, and can be deployed on networks that do not have Internet connectivity.

While there are differences between the Click-to-Run Office 365 ProPlus and MSI-based Office 2019, there are also certain similarities:

- Both can be configured through Group Policy.
- Both provide telemetry visible through the Telemetry Dashboard.
- Extensions designed for the Office 2019 version of a product will work with the Office 365 version of that product.

> *MORE INFO* **CLICK-TO-RUN VERSUS MSI**
>
> You can learn more about Click-to-Run versus MSI at: *http://blogs.technet.com/b/office_ resource_kit/archive/2013/03/05/the-new-office-garage-series-who-moved-my-msi.aspx.*

EXAM TIP

Remember the different elements used in the Configuration.xml files.

Thought experiment

In this thought experiment, demonstrate your skills and knowledge of the topics covered in this chapter. You can find answers to this thought experiment in the next section.

There are an increasing number of iPad and Android tablet users at Contoso who want to use these mobile devices to perform work tasks. Several of the users of Android tablets have already installed apps from the Google Play Store, but are unable to access documents stored in SharePoint online. Some of the iPad users have heard that Office apps are available, but don't know where to start when it comes to obtaining them. For your desktop computers, you are interested in centrally deploying Office 365 ProPlus using Click-to-Run files.

Don Funk is a user at Contoso. Don has just purchased a new consumer laptop for use at home and wants to set up Outlook and Skype for Business. Don signs in to his domain joined work computer using the contoso\don.funk user name. Don signs in to Office 365 using the don.funk@contoso.com user name. Single sign-on is configured with Office 365.

With this information in mind, answer the following questions:

1. What instruction should you give to iPad users about locating Office apps?
2. What instruction should you give to Android tablet users who have already installed apps from the Google Play Store?
3. Which tool should you use to obtain the Office 365 ProPlus Click-to-Run files from the Microsoft servers on the Internet?
4. Which file should you edit to retrieve a specific version of the Office 365 ProPlus Click-to-Run files?

Thought experiment answers

This section contains the solution to the thought experiment. Each answer explains why the answer choice is correct.

1. You should tell the iPad users to sign in to the Microsoft 365 portal. This will allow them to view the available Office 365-related apps for iPad. It will also provide them with direct links to those apps in the app store.
2. You should instruct them to sign in to their Microsoft 365 accounts in each app so that they can gain access to documents stored in enterprise locations.
3. You should use the Office Deployment Tool, also known as the Office Deployment Tool for Click-to-Run, to obtain the Office 365 ProPlus Click-to-Run files from the Internet.
4. You must edit the appropriate configuration.xml file to specify a specific version of the Office 365 ProPlus files.

Chapter summary

- Exchange hybrid deployment requires Exchange 2007 or later on-premises.

- The version of Exchange that you have deployed determines the type of hybrid deployment that is available. When selecting a hybrid deployment option, you should choose the most modern version available to your organization.

- The SharePoint primary web application on the on-premises SharePoint farm must use a certificate from a trusted public third party CA.

- A Skype for Business hybrid deployment requires federation.

- You use a remote move (also known as a batch) migration when you have an existing Exchange hybrid deployment.

- In a staged migration, you migrate mailboxes from your on-premises Exchange organization to Office 365 in groups, termed batches.

- In a cutover migration, all mailboxes in an on-premises Exchange deployment are migrated to Office 365 in a single migration batch.

- Network upload allows you to import PST files into Office 365.

- Most organizations that are migrating from an on-premises SharePoint Server deployment to SharePoint online will use the SharePoint Migration Tool.

- An activated copy of Office 365 ProPlus must be able to communicate with Microsoft servers on the Internet every 30 days. If this communication does not occur, Office 365 ProPlus will enter reduced functionality mode.

- The Office Deployment Tool is a command line utility used if you want to centralize the deployment of Office 365 Click-to-Run files from a location on your local area network.

- You can use the Office Deployment Tool to download the Office 365 Click-to-Run files and language pack files from Microsoft servers on the Internet.

- You use the Office Deployment Tool in download mode to retrieve files from the Microsoft servers on the internet.

- You use the Office Deployment Tool in configure mode to install Office 365 using an installation source on the local area network.

- The configuration.xml file is used with the Office Deployment Tool in both download and configure mode. In download mode it allows you to specify which files are downloaded. In configure mode it allows you to specify how Office Click-to-Run applications and language packs are installed and how updates are applied.

Index

Plug into learning at

MicrosoftPressStore.com

The Microsoft Press Store by Pearson offers:

- Free U.S. shipping

- Buy an eBook, get three formats – Includes PDF, EPUB, and MOBI to use with your computer, tablet, and mobile devices

- Print & eBook Best Value Packs

- eBook Deal of the Week – Save up to 50% on featured title

- Newsletter – Be the first to hear about new releases, announcements, special offers, and more

- Register your book – Find companion files, errata, and product updates, plus receive a special coupon* to save on your next purchase

 Pearson